Baedeker

Iceland

www.baedeker.com

Verlag Karl Baedeker

TOP ATTRACTIONS ✶ ✶

The list of sights is long, but where are Iceland's highlights to be found? How much time do you need in Reykjavík? Is a trip inland worthwhile? Does circumnavigating Iceland on the ring road guarantee that everything will be seen? In order to make planning easier, we have put together a list of must-sees!

1 ✶✶ Reykjavík
The country's best museums are located in the capital of Iceland. The nightlife of Reykjavík is legendary. ► page 231

2 ✶✶ Blue Lagoon
Pure relaxation on the Reykjanes Peninsula. A soak amid the lava is a must on any trip to Iceland. ► page 226

3 ✶✶ Þingvellir
The oldest parliament in the world convened here. Since 2004, Þingvellir has been a UNESCO World Heritage Site. ► page 306

4 ✶✶ Haukadalur
Iceland's best-known geothermal area. The Strokkur geyser erupts by the minute. ► page 167

5 ✶✶ Gullfoss
The »Golden Fall« is one of the most impressive waterfalls of the North Atlantic island. ► page 166

6 ✶✶ Hekla
An ever-changing landscape. With regular eruptions, the active volcano Hekla ensures that life is always interesting. ► page 173

14 Húsavík/
Whale watching

13 Jökulsárgljúfur
National Park

12 Dettifoss

16 West Fjords

17 Látrabjarg

15 Mývatn

©Baedeker

11 Askja

18 Snæfellsnes/
Snæfellsjökull

10 Kverkfjöll

4 Haukadalur

5 Gullfoss

1 Reykjavík 3 Þingvellir

8 Landmannalaugar

9 Vatnajökull/
Skaftafell National Park

2 Blue
Lagoon

6 Hekla

7 Þórsmörk

Haukadalur
Trust the Strokkur geyser to put on a good show

Reykjavík
The Hallgrímskirkja dominates the city

BAEDEKER'S BEST TIPS

Of all the Baedeker tips in this book, we have put together the most interesting here. Experience and enjoy the best of Iceland!

The outlaw Fjalla Eyvindur ...
... lived for years in a cave

Highlands tours...
... need to be well planned

Midnight sun
The northeast of Iceland is the closest you can get to the Arctic Circle. The »true« midnight sun is only seen on Grímsey

Icelandic horses
Hacks and trail rides are offered everywhere in Iceland. The most interesting ones take riders into the highlands

The Gullfoss in its winter robes
► page 172

Price categories

► **Hotels**
Budget: up to 9000 ISK
Mid-range: 9000 – 18 000 ISK
Luxury: over 18 000 ISK
per night, 2 people in a
double room

► **Restaurants**
Inexpensive: under 1500 ISK
for a main dish
Moderate: 1500 – 3000 ISK
Expensive: from 3000 ISK

Architectural gems in
Reykjavík: hot water tanks
don't come much more
beautiful than this
► page 256

TOURS

SIGHTS FROM A to Z

Background

CONCISE, EASY
TO READ AND
ACCESSIBLE AT A GLANCE:
EVERYTHING VISITORS NEED TO
KNOW ABOUT THE COUNTRY AND
ITS PEOPLE, ECONOMY AND POLITICS,
SOCIETY AND EVERYDAY LIFE

SHAPED BY ELEMENTAL FORCES

Fire-spewing volcanoes, eternal ice. Harsh winds sweep across un-forgiving landscapes, dark clouds promise rain. Here, nature is still nature in the raw sense of the word: pure, sometimes threatening, rarely soothing with colourful flowers or lush, green grass. Welcome to Iceland, to a country where the elemental forces of nature have created landscapes of breathtaking beauty!

Visitors arriving at Keflavík airport and heading for Reykjavík are confronted straightaway with Iceland's volcanic past as, up to the suburbs of the capital, the road leads through a barren lava field. Seeming bleak and hostile in gloomy weather, just a few rays of sun are enough to transform it into a fascinating fairytale landscape. How-

ever, this is only a taster of the many varied forms of volcanic phenomena awaiting visitors. Those arriving by ship in Seyðisfjörður, on the island's east coast, see Iceland's second face, characterized by ice but no less impressive. The colourful houses of Seyðisfjörður lie on a deeply-cut fjord, framed by steep hills with numerous layers of basalt and volcanic slag. While East Iceland cannot deny its volcanic origin either, the times when fire and lava shaped this landscape lie further back in the past. Here, the glaciers of the last Ice Age were the shaping forces of the landscape, carving deep gashes into the coastline and creating picture-book fjords.

Fiery peak
The Hekla volcano shows its true face

Slowly does it...

Whether arriving at Keflavík or Seyðisfjörður, be sure to leave enough time to explore – Iceland is not a country that can be 'done' in a hurry. If nothing else, the roads demand a leisurely pace, with the traveller forced to slow down by the dirt tracks and narrow strips of tarmac that wend their way around dozens of fjords like unravelling balls of wool. This is just as well, as the panoramas going by outside the car window are often breathtaking. Hardly any other country on earth is as varied as Iceland, which in geological terms is still young and constantly changing – sometimes even highly dramatic – with violent volcanic eruptions or glacier-bursts. But between these cataclysms, Iceland still offers spectacular displays of nature: in the

Ice Age
Islands of frozen water in the Jökulsárlon glacier lake at the foot of the Vatnajökull

A sight to fall for
Some impress with a roaring deluge, others, such as the Seljalandsfoss, by a veiled lightness: Iceland's waterfalls are waiting to be discovered.

As far as the eye can see
Iceland in its winter coat. Travelling to the far north is worth it in the cold months too

Solitude
Some 300,000 people live on a surface area larger than Portugal; Iceland certainly has its quiet places

Textures
Ice formations flow towards the sea on the Þjórsá river.

Energy
Pipelines crisscross the dark lava fields around the Krafla geothermal power plant at the Mývatn.

numerous high-temperature areas, when geysers aren't spouting jets of water high into the sky, there is a constant bubbling, steaming and hissing. Seething mud-pots and water holes, yellow and ochre-coloured steam fountains and sinter deposits form surreal lunar landscapes. Liparite mountains in flamboyant colours, dark ash cones, bizarre volcanoes, pseudo craters and, again and again, lava fields – some black, barren and menacing, others covered by thick green carpets of moss – characterize large parts of the island. Alongside the volcanoes, the glaciers are the main attraction, as the most imposing of them, Vatnajökull, is by itself larger than all the glaciers of the European mainland put together. From its mighty plateau, icy tongues move down the valley, forming abysses, caves and lagoons, with bizarrely eroded icebergs swimming on top.

Pleasant surprises

However, Iceland also has a pretty face that is unexpected in an island this far north. The narrow coastal strip and some valleys surprise with lush green meadows, where countless sheep graze. Or take the Mývatn, in reality a geologically restless area shaped by volcanoes, but which, with its islands, bays and headlands, seems like a green oasis. Although the summer sun, even in northern Iceland, still disappears for a few minutes below the horizon – the »real« midnight sun only shines on the small island of Grímsey – there are several weeks where it never really gets dark. For the locals this »light shower« is the long-awaited compensation for the long dark winter months. And for visitors from more southern regions, the light-filled Nordic summer nights work like a drug. In this period, day and night meld into one, and those who have enjoyed the stillness of the night and the often fantastic light ambiences of the midnight sun will never forget the experience.

Sparse vegetation
Iceland's flora keeps up the fight against all the odds

Facts

What are pseudo craters, solfataras and fumaroles? How does a geyser work? Are the Iceland glaciers shrinking too? What is so special about the Icelandic horse? Does Iceland have an army? Who settled this island in the North Atlantic? When did the country become independent?

Nature

Geology of a Young Island

Iceland is a very young island, which only emerged from the sea 20 million years ago. The island owes its existence to a **hot spot**, where magma rises continuously from the bowels of the earth; its centre is assumed to lie under the Vatnajökull, the largest glacier in Europe. Forming part of the Mid-Atlantic Ridge, Iceland is one of the few sections that peak out of the sea. The ridge runs from the southwest to the northeast across the island, a geologically highly active strip some 50km/31 miles wide, with numerous volcanoes, hot springs and high-temperature areas.

According to the theory of plate tectonics, the earth's surface consists of several plates, floating on the underlying liquid magma. On the plates' edges, the Earth's crust is particularly thin – and here in Iceland, two tectonic plates drift apart. Depending on the direction of the plates' movement, along the boundaries mountain ranges rise up, earthquakes or volcanic eruptions happen, or the earth's crust is restructured. Along the Mid-Atlantic Ridge, the North American and the Eurasian continental plates drift apart by about two centimetres each year, with rising magma constantly filling up the gap created. That Iceland is an island split in two can clearly be seen along the **Almannagjá Gorge at Þingvellir**, which scores the landscape for several kilometres. Steep, craggy walls of dark basalt, along with narrow gorges and trenches characterize this dramatic landscape. Geology doesn't get more vivid than here at the interface of two continental plates, where visitors can stand with one leg in Europe and the other in America.

Split island

Picture-perfect volcanoes

On Iceland, traces of volcanism are everywhere. Thirty still active volcanoes constantly change the island's surface as well as its geological make-up. How active the Icelandic volcanoes have been over the past 500 years is demonstrated by the fact that around a third of the lava worldwide was produced by volcanoes on Iceland. It comes as no surprise then that the island consists nearly exclusively of basalt rock, tuff (rock composed of volcanic ash) and lava.

Iceland features practically all the different types of volcano. The shape a volcano has depends on many factors, such as the amount and temperature of the lava or the number of eruptions. Generally, scientists distinguish between fissure volcanoes and central volca-

Types of volcano

← *The Strokkur erupts every few minutes*

Facts and Figures Island

©*Baedeker*

Topography
▶ In the North Atlantic, some 1,000km/ 620 miles west of the Norwegian coast, and some 300km/185 miles east of Greenland

Surface area
▶ 103,000 sq km/just under 39,800 sq miles, of which 23% covered in vegetation, 63% desert/barren land/ lava, 3% lakes, 11% glaciers. Claimed fishing zones: 758,000 sq km/293,000 sq miles

Geography
▶ Highest elevation: Hvannadalshnúkur (2,119m/6,952ft)
▶ Largest lake: Þingvallavan 83 sq km/32 sq miles
▶ Longest river: Þjórsá (230km/143 miles)
▶ Length of coastline: 4,970km/3,088 miles
▶ Largest glacier: Vatnajökull, with around 8,300 sq km/3,200 sq miles

Population
▶ 320,000 inhabitants
▶ Population density: 2.9/sq km (UK: 246, US: 31)
▶ Life expectancy: women 82.9, men 79.4 years (world record)

Religion
▶ 82% of the population belong to the Evangelical Lutheran state church

Language
▶ Icelandic, which retains many similarities with Old Norse

State
▶ Form of government: since 17 June 1944 Republic of Iceland (Lýðveldið Ísland)
▶ Administrative structure: 8 regions, 122 rural municipalities
▶ Prime minister: Geir Haarde
▶ President: Ólafur Ragnar Grímsson
▶ Parliament: Alþing with 63 deputies, elected for four years
▶ Capital: Reykjavík (118,000 inhabitants, Metropolitan Area approx. 195,000 inhabitants)

Economy
▶ GDP (2007 est.): 20 billion US$ (Great Britain: £1.4 trillion, US: US$14.3 trillion)
▶ Per-capita income (2007 est.): 38,000 US$ (Great Britain: £23,000, US: US$46,000)
▶ Unemployment rate: 3 %
▶ Employment structure: Agriculture/Fishing 8% Industry 23% Services 69%

noes. With fissure volcanoes, the lava extrudes along a cleft which can be kilometres long and can also result in smaller craters that may sometimes merge into one. During the eruption on the Westman Islands (the small archipelago south of Iceland) in 1973, such a cleft opened up; the **»fire canyon« of Eldgjá and the Laki volcanic fissure** also fall into this category. Alongside fissure volcanoes, Iceland also has many central volcanoes, divided into various subgroups. The most common are stratovolcanoes, also called composite volcanoes, which can be recognized by their high, perfectly formed, relatively steep cones. These volcanic cones usually only form over the course of several eruptions. Not all volcanoes in Iceland appear as such at first glance, as some lie hidden below glaciers. Examples of **stratovolcanoes** are Snæfellsjökull, Eyjafjallsjökull, Öræfajökull and the highest mountain in Iceland, Hvannadalshnúkur.

Shield volcanoes have very flat slopes, which is why they can sometimes be difficult to recognise as volcanoes. Formed by eruptions that brought up thin liquid lava but little ash, this otherwise fairly rare type is quite common in Iceland where some 20 shield volcanoes formed following the last Ice Age. **Skjaldbreiður at Þingvellir** is a typical shield volcano, and in fact gave this type of volcano its name. Also of volcanic origin are slag cones, ash cones, maars and table mountains. The latter emerged during the last Ice Age, when the volcanoes erupted under a carapace of ice. Good examples of this kind of table volcano are Bláfjall, Búrfell, Þórisjökull and one of the most beautiful mountains in Iceland, Herðubreið.

Shield volcanoes and table mountains

Impressive examples of so-called pseudo craters can be found at **Mývatn** and on a lava stream north of **Mýrdalsjökull**. Strictly speaking, pseudo craters are not volcanoes, as they have no vent through which the lava could extrude. They were formed by lava streams flowing over moist ground or flat lakes. Due to the heat, the water evaporated explosively, blasting away the lava lying above and leaving a crater that can easily be mistaken for a volcano.

Pseudo craters

Post-volcanic Phenomena

At many places in Iceland, columns of steam rise up, hot mud cauldrons simmer and bubble away, or warm springs and rivers force their way to the surface. All of these are signs of the post-volcanic activities that occur when molten magma cools down inside the earth, releasing gases and vapours. Penetrating upwards through cracks and fissures to the earth's surface, these create spectacular landscapes.

Solfataras count amongst the most beautiful and colourful manifestations of post-volcanism. Particularly impressive examples can be seen in high-temperature areas, such as the **Námafjall** near the

Solfataras

Bubbling mud pot in the high-temperature area of Námafjall

Mývatn. Solfataras occur when groundwater beneath the earth's surface heats up to the point of evaporating. The steam, mixed with the gases of the magma, emerges through cracks onto the surface. At the point of escape, with the steam mixture reaching temperatures of $100\,°C - 250\,°C$ ($212\,°F - 482\,°F$), sulphur is deposited around the vent, glowing in all shades of yellow and orange.

Fumaroles Fumaroles are also openings that allow gases to rise to the surface. As opposed to the solfataras, fumaroles are usually situated directly in or on a volcano crater. The extruding gases, mainly water vapour, are very hot and fortified with acids. When the gas rises up to the surface it cools down, at which point **iron or sulphur compounds** crystallize near the vent, colouring the surrounding lava yellow, orange or red.

Hot springs What is interesting looking at the distribution of hot springs is that they tend to occur in places where there hasn't been volcanic activity for a long time. They are particularly common in plains, valleys and fjords. Even if the volcanoes in those areas have long been extinguished, there is enough residual heat to warm the groundwater that penetrates the cracks. At depths of up to 2,000m/6,560ft, the water heats up through contact with the hot rocks and enters a circuit that may last for thousands of years, at the end of which it emerges onto the surface again. Hot springs are rich in minerals, containing com-

eruption of the Katla below the Mýrdalsjökull, which could lead to a similarly huge glacier run as during its last eruption in 1918. Since records began, the Katla has on average become active every 50 years, so that a new eruption is in fact already overdue.

Land without Forests: Iceland's Flora

Compared with Central Europe, the vegetation of Iceland is extremely sparse. Even compared to regions with a similar climate, the number of species is lower. Particularly conspicuous is the near-complete absence of forest. The vegetation consists mainly of mosses covering many lava fields, and meadows, mostly found in the plains and along the coast. Otherwise, dwarf shrubs, the stunted Arctic downy birch, heather and lingonberries flourish.

Plants fare better along warm springs and brooks, as shown by the often lush green vegetation. The landscape is given **spots of colour** by herbs such as Arctic thyme, cotton grass, cranesbill, angelica, yarrow, dandelion, marsh marigold, marsh violet and stemless bladder campion.

David against Goliath: the little plants won't be denied

Exploited nature

Before the long Ice Ages of the Tertiary Period, when a much milder climate reigned on the island in the North Atlantic, large stretches of land were covered in dense deciduous and mixed woodlands. There were oak, beech, bald cypress and elm, as well as the North American **sequoia**, as evidenced by brown coal deposits and fossilised leaves. Still, even after the last Ice Age and before settlement by humankind, Iceland must have looked completely different. The old texts report that the island was wooded from the mountains to the sea. Estimates say that at the time around half of the lowlands was covered in woods. However, the early settlers soon set about decimating the forest. Wood was needed for the construction of houses and ships, for heating and to smelt bog ore. Whatever young shoots remained were gobbled up by sheep, which the settlers had brought with them. Due to the harsh Arctic conditions, the delicate vegetation was never able to recover from this **exploitation**, and so the island's current appearance is also a product of 1,000 years of settlement history. Today, only a few old place names containing the word »forest« (Skógur, Mörk) remind visitors of the time before humans appeared on the island.

The Ice Age reduces plant variety

Not only did the last Ice Age decisively shape the landscape of Iceland, today's flora and fauna is also a result of this cold spell. With the ice many plant species disappeared, and due to the country's isolation, its harsh climate and volcanic activities, after the warming-up and melting of the ice sheet relatively few species managed to settle anew. Although there might be some **5,000 different species of plants and fungi** growing on Iceland today, only 440 are higher-order flowering plants, and of those some only came to Iceland with human help. Apart from a few endemic species, all Icelandic plants can also be encountered in Norway and the British Isles. The fact that the island still appears green in many places is due to the lava surfaces covered in moss, as basalt lava, full of nutrients, offers an ideal soil for dense carpets of moss and lichen. However, Rhyolitic and obsidian lava do not support vegetation.

Some Company for the Fox: Iceland's Wildlife

Visiting polar bears

The wildlife of Iceland cannot boast much variety of species either. Before the arrival of the first settlers, the **Arctic fox** was the only mammal on the island. The only creatures sharing its huge territory were those that reached the remote island more or less by chance, usually by air or sea. There would have been the occasional insects and birds, and perhaps the odd **polar bear** would drift by on an ice floe, but none ever decided to stay. Humans brought **sheep and horses** and, as stowaways probably, **mice and rats** too. In 1771, a few **reindeer** were introduced from Norway, in order to enrich the Icelanders' diet. The animals bred well, and today there are still around 3,000 of them living in the wild in the east and northeast, but without ever becoming a significant economic factor as in Lapland. A few mink managed to break out of fur farms and have since been decimating the bird population.

Icelandic horses

The first settlers also brought the first horses to Iceland. Due to the island's isolated position in the North Atlantic, these **original Icelandic horses** have hardly changed over the past 1,000 years. In order to preserve this unique breed, in 982 the Althing enacted a law prohibiting the import of animals. This import ban is still in place today, and even an Icelandic horse born and bred on the island that has been abroad is not allowed to return. As a result, Icelandic horses are the purest bred in the world. The animals are excellently adapted to the hard conditions, being small, muscular, sure-footed and with a lot of stamina, and having a dense fur that turns shaggy in winter. For many centuries, they were the only means of transportation on the difficult terrain of the island. Their distinctive characteristic, known as the fourth gait or the **tölt**, makes riding very comfortable. Unlike with the trot, the rider is not lifted from the saddle, as a horse doing the tölt always keeps one or two alternating legs on the ground. Icelandic horses that can do the tölt as well as walk, trot and gallop are called »**four-gaiters**«, while those that on top of this can also do the **skeið**, or »flying pace«, are known as »**five-gaiters**«.

The Icelandic horse: muscular, tireless, surefooted – and thoughtful?

»Darling, how was your day?« Puffins enjoy tender relationships

Organized chaos on the bird rocks

Unlike the land mammals, the bird population is numerous. Visitors might encounter snow grouse, gyr falcons, oystercatchers, golden plovers, snow buntings, redwings, godwits, Arctic terns and, at the Mývatn in particular, many different species of duck. One of the most impressive natural spectacles in Iceland is provided by the **bird rocks** on the coast, each year hosting millions of breeding sea birds. The rocks operate by a strict hierarchy where each species has its allocated space: near the water breed the black guillemots, shags and kittiwakes; above them nest the fulmars, common guillemots, razorbills and northern gannets. The top storeys are occupied by the puffins. All of them fear the predatory skua, which tries to steal prey from other birds with breathtaking aerial attacks, but also occasionally catches another bird.

Fish, whales and seals

In the inland waters there are no purely freshwater fish – here too the level of biodiversity is low. In some rivers however, there is a substantial quantity of salmon, trout, Arctic char, eels and sticklebacks. In the coastal waters, some **300 species of fish** find good living conditions; of those, cod, herring and capelin are of the most economic value. Other fish caught are plaice, halibut, haddock, turbot, hake and redfish. The coastal waters also harbour common seals and other types of seal, as well as several species of whale. On whale-watching safaris, which mainly depart from the Snæfellsnes peninsula and from Húsavik, visitors stand a good chance of seeing orcas, harbour porpoises, minke whales, humpback whales or fin whales. With a bit of luck, one of the extremely rare blue whales might even make an off-shore appearance.

One problem for whale tourism could prove to be the resumption in 2003 of **whaling, supposedly for research purposes**. Whale watching operators subsequently registered a collapse of bookings by 90 %. In this way, Iceland's insistence on whale hunting might seriously endanger whale tourism and thus an important economic factor. The WDCS whale and dolphin protection organization even goes as far as to claim that in Iceland whale hunting and whale tourism cannot coexist, as in the past minke whales were hunted near tourist boats. It has to be said that the Icelanders' stubborn refusal to give up old traditions is counterproductive economically, as today's commercial whaling has **no economic importance** any longer, and this situation is not going to change in the foreseeable future.

Whaling

People · Economy · Politics

The Icelanders are the direct descendants of the Vikings from Norway that settled the island in the North Atlantic. There is, however, also a dash of Celtic blood from Great Britain and Ireland flowing in the veins of today's Icelanders. Icelandic society is considered homogenous, with a low percentage of foreigners due to a restrictive immigration policy. Sometimes it even seems that everybody is related, which perhaps makes it less surprising that many Icelanders dedicate themselves with great patience and enthusiasm to **genealogical research**, and that everybody can trace back their lineage for many generations. Icelanders address each other by first names, as was already the case during the time of the Viking settlement – only that today a lot more people live in Iceland than in those days, which makes it hard work to look somebody up in Reykjavík's telephone directory, which is arranged by first names. For Icelanders, the first name is more important than the last name, which, following Old

Descendants of the Vikings

? DID YOU KNOW ...?

■ that Iceland has the lowest infant mortality rate in the world and that Icelandic men live longer than any other men?

Germanic tradition, is formed by adding a »-son« to the first name of the father, with sons, and a »-dóttir« in the case of daughters. Thus, Einar Jónsson is called Einar and is the son of Jón, while Guðrún Egilsdóttir, listed in the telephone directory under Guðrún, is the daughter of Egil.

From Poorhouse to Welfare State

For a long time, Iceland was one of the poorest countries in Europe. It was only in the 20th century that a rapid change took place – from a backward agrarian country to a modern welfare state. While agriculture was never particularly productive due to the small amount of available land and the short vegetation period, 100 years ago half of the population still lived on individual farms along the coast. Today, they are fewer than 10 %, with most farmers breeding sheep.

No prosperity without fish

The economic and social development of Iceland after the Second World War was shaped by the so-called **Reconstruction government**, consisting of a coalition of the bourgeois-conservative Independence Party, the Social Democratic Party and the People's Unity – Socialist party. The prime goal was to boost the economy and to improve living conditions for the population.

The biggest investment went into the fisheries and fish-processing companies. Thus, the country soon had one of the largest and most modern fishing fleets in the world. At one stage over 90 % of the country's exports came from this sector of the economy. Today, the main fish caught are still cod, herring, redfish, haddock and halibut. With the revenue from the fisheries, Iceland finances much of its basic commodities, food, fuel and machinery imports. Since the 1960s, in order to somewhat reduce dependence on the fish sector, some energy-intensive industries have been established with foreign help.

Towards the future

Between the mid-1990s and the financial-services meltdown in 2008, Iceland's economy was stable. After a few years of strong economic growth, the new millennium saw a short-term slowdown, but until 2008 Iceland ranked among the countries with the highest per-capita income in the world. The problem of Iceland having to spend a lot of money on importing most goods – excluding fish, energy and some agricultural produce produced cost-intensively in the country – will also probably remain an issue for a while. Today, **tourism** occupies the second position in terms of foreign exchange revenue, and if the country succeeds in attracting tourists outside the summer months too, the current rate of around 485,000 visitors should have room for expansion, especially as prices have come down now. The Icelanders' standard of living was until recently recognized as the highest in the world, and a factor that shouldn't be underestimated in discussions of the **high standard of living** is surely Iceland's nature, which is largely untouched, leaving each Icelander plenty of space for leisure activities. The world financial crisis, however, could be a danger to the living standard: In the fall of 2008 Iceland faced national bankruptcy.

This man is impervious to the Icelandic weather. →

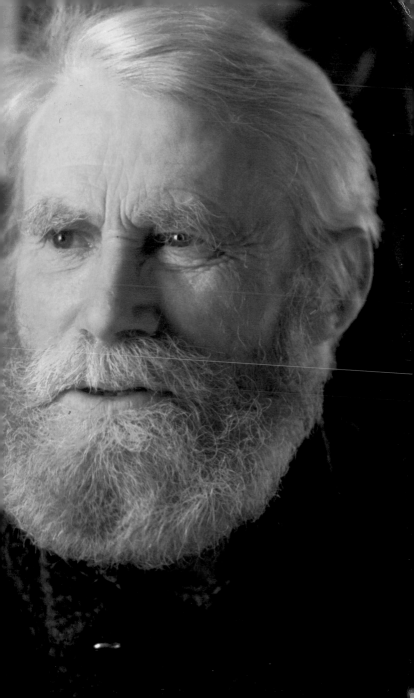

In the course of ongoing genetic research, the supposedly homogenous people of Iceland had to face new facts: Celtic blood flows through their veins too

THE PEOPLE WITH THE TRANSPARENT GENES

The human genome has been decoded. Now, scientists are hunting for active substances that may treat genetically conditioned diseases. For this, so-called »Bio Banks« are required, linking genetic information and health data. Iceland is the first country to have established such a database.

Human DNA might be decoded, but even with this knowledge we are still far from understanding the biological construct of a 'human being'. While we possess fewer genes than previously assumed, the interactions between them are much more complex. This is where the really difficult part begins: finding out the genetic differences between individual human beings in order to be better able to predict the **risk factors** leading to diseases. But the ultimate goal is another big step away: finding new active substances against diseases that have so far not been treatable – this is where phar-

maceutical companies are hoping to make big money. The first requirement for this complex task is **bio banks** containing the health data of the majority of the population – as complete as possible, and with as many blood samples as possible. The Icelanders were the first to start setting up such a bio bank, now Estonia and Britain have followed suit.

A long way to go

In this business speed pays dividends, but the Icelandic collection of blood samples probably only comprises a

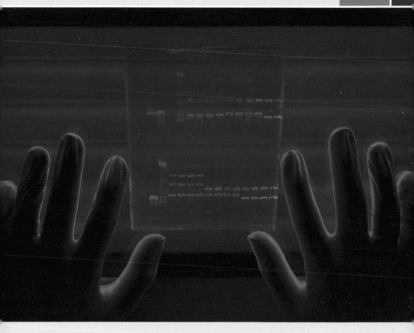

few thousand. The exact number is a company secret of **deCODE genetics**, but at this stage, science is still far from being able to check the genetic material of all Icelanders.

A handful of Vikings

There are good reasons why Iceland in particular was the first country to set up a bio bank: the Icelanders are a young people, as it was only some 1,000 years ago that the first Vikings came from Norway to settle the island in the North Atlantic. It can only have been a handful of people that landed at the time, and as there has been practically no further immigration the 300,000 people living on the island today should, in principle, nearly all be related. This would be the ideal population scenario for genetic scientists, and perfect for isolating hereditary diseases. That was the theory behind the foundation of the deC-

ODE genetics company in Reykjavík by Kari Stefánsson, a professor of medicine. The Swiss pharmaceutical giant Hoffmann-La Roche was so taken with Stefánsson's idea of cataloguing the Icelanders genetically and genealogically, that in 1997 they offered him collaboration and a lot of money.

Enthusiastic genealogical researchers

Since then, the first surprising results have come to light, one of them being that the Icelandic population is by no means as homogeneous as previously thought. On their way to Iceland, the wild red beards seem to have stopped in **Scotland and Ireland** to stock up on some women, who then appear to be responsible for the not-insignificant proportion of Celtic blood in Icelandic veins. The other reason that Iceland appeared particularly suitable for this

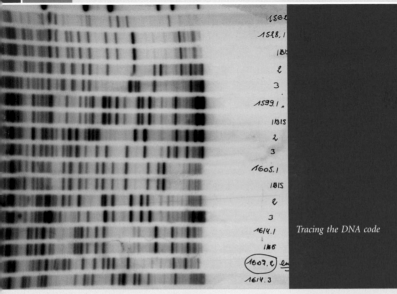

Tracing the DNA code

project was at least sound enough: Icelanders do research their ancestors with dedication and enthusiasm. And as their ancestors too indulged in this passion, the **National Register** comprises nearly all relationships on the island going back to the time of the Settlement.

Endangered privacy

Another piece of the puzzle is provided by Icelandic doctors, who over the past hundred years have collected dossiers of patients. Together with genetic research, these might be able to throw light onto the interaction of environmental and genetic factors in the **development of diseases**. A prerequisite for this was the 1998 law that allowed the entire **health records of all Icelanders** – living or dead – to be collected on a central database. A twelve-year licence for its setup and use went to the deCODE genetics company.

This was a law introduced quickly and which had far-reaching implications, allowing for the commercial use of the data, which was to lead to protests

»*Furthermore, Icelandic doctors have collected countless dossiers of patients over the past hundred years, which, together with genetic research, might be able to throw light onto the interaction of environmental and genetic factors in the development of diseases.*«

the past hundred years have collected dossiers of patients. Together with genetic research, these might be able to throw light onto the interaction of environmental and genetic factors in

later on. Icelanders were justifiably concerned that data would be handed over to private companies with no privacy protection or ethical control mechanism.

Outpost in the North Atlantic: Iceland's Politics

According to the constitution, the head of state is the president, elected directly by the people for a term of four years. In 1980, when **Vigdis Finnbogadóttir** became the first woman to take on the office of president, she was also the first woman worldwide to have been elected head of state. Reelected three times, she held office until 1996, when she renounced a further candidature. Her successor was Ólafur Ragnar Grímsson. The government consists of the prime minister and ten ministers. The parliament (Alþing) is elected every four years in eight electoral districts and consists of 63 members. The party-political landscape is dominated by the left-liberal Progressive Party, the conservative-liberal Independence Party, the Social Democratic Party and the Socialist People's Alliance. Since the founding of the Republic in 1944 no party has been able to govern alone – coalition governments have always had to be formed. The long-term coalitions of Conservatives

? DID YOU KNOW ...?

■ ... that despite membership of NATO Iceland has never had its own army?

and Social Democrats (1959–1971) led to domestic stability, while in the following years the coalitions changed more frequently. **Membership of NATO** and strong links with the US since the Second World War are the most important pillars of Icelandic foreign policy. In NATO, the country plays an important role as a strategic outpost in the North Atlantic zone. Following an agreement signed in 1951, the US maintained a somewhat controversial air base in Keflavík, which they gave up however in 2006.

[the fleet] found islands that were at the time still unknown, called Orcades, and pacified them. Far in the distance, Thule was spotted ...« Here, Tacitus used the name of Thule for the »most northern«. He was undoubtedly familiar with the writings of **Pytheas of Marseille**, who in the 4th century BC had made a journey into northern territories and whose notes circulated amongst geographers and explorers far into the Middle Ages, but only came down to us in the form of quotes of varying authenticity from other authors.

The writings of Pytheas

Pytheas gave the northernmost country that he found the name of **Ultima Thule**. He even described the midnight sun, although doubt has been cast on whether he saw it with his own eyes. According to current research, Pytheas probably reached central Norway around Trondheim or the northern end of the Gulf of Bothnia, but under no circumstances Iceland, as his Thule is a country with inhabitants. Since Pytheas, the name has been haunting the literature of the discoveries and is always picked up again when a name is needed for the absolute northernmost point in the known world of an era. In this way, Iceland became the »Thule« of the European Middle Ages; today an American air base in northeast Greenland bears this name.

First Written Documents by Word of Mouth

Irish monks looking for solitude

Apart from the writings of Pytheas and those that copy from him, it took until the 9th century for North Atlantic discoveries to be mentioned in literature. Around 825, the Irish **monk and geographer Dicuil**, teaching in France, wrote down what he had heard from colleagues on their travels at the end of the 8th century in the direction of the Faroe Islands and Iceland, without having taken part in them himself. His *De mensura Orbis terrae* tells of encounters of godfearing Irishmen with Norsemen on the Faroe Islands: »As early as a hundred years ago, the desire for the hermit's life led a few Irish monks to the many islands in the northern part of the British sea, which can be reached, provided the winds are favourable, in two days from the British Isles. The islands, uninhabited and nameless since the creation of the world have now, following the appearance of Nordic pirates, been abandoned again by the hermits«. Dicuil's writings showed furthermore that the monks visited Iceland, spending a summer there and even sailing on, »a day's voyage north, until they found the sea frozen over«.

Brendan's Voyage

According to legend, a monk named **Brendan, and other friars** from the Emerald Isle, cross the Northern Seas with small hide boats, or »currachs«, in the daredevil search for solitude. Doubts about whether Brendan, a monk born in Kerry in Ireland in 484 – and who is

Historic map based on the writings of Pytheas: →
could his »Ultima Thule« be Iceland?

OCEANVS · DEVCALIONIVS ·

THVLE INSVLA

VOLAS SINVS

LEMANONIVS
SINVS   CALCEDONI SILVA

Clotais est
Alabına

OCEANVS · GERMANICVS

MAGNAE · GRANIAE

· PARS ·

· GALLIAE BELGICAE ·

· PARS ·

credited with descriptions of geysers and »burning mountains« – really did reach Iceland, emerge from the long period of time between the alleged voyage in the early 5th century and its recording in the 9th century, when Iceland had already been discovered and these phenomena known. Today, many historians assume that the explorer Brendan is a composite figure who was invested with the dates of birth and death of a real man of the church. This figure then served as a canvas onto which true reports were projected, as well as legends and sagas about seafarers that are circulating in the Celtic world.

Documented History

12th century	Ari Þorgilsson writes the *Íslendingabók*.
around 870	Harald Finehair gains power over all Norway.
from 870 onwards	The permanent settlement of Iceland begins.

Ari Þorgilsson   A more reliable documented account of the history of Iceland and the whole North Atlantic was provided by Nordic settlers. In the early 12th century Ari Þorgilsson – one of the few historians of medieval Iceland known by name – wrote the Book of the Icelanders, the **Íslendingabók**, with the benefit of some 200 years of hindsight. As opposed to the sagas this work can lay claim to historical fact. Ari also confirmed the words of his Irish collegue Dicuil: the first Nordic »Icelanders« encountered Christians whom they calld »Papar«.

Archaeological evidence   Modern archaeology has proven however over the past decades that there were Nordic settlers on Iceland before the settlement documented in writing, and that they too lived alongside the Papar. However, the official story of Iceland, which also governs the national celebrations, continues to follow the *Book of the Icelanders* chronicle of Ari Þorgilsson, as well as the **Landnámabók**, the book by an unknown historian telling the story of the island's settlement.

Harald Finehair – Uniter and Expeller

Political upheaval in Norway   In the early 870s, Harald I Hårfagre, Harald Finehair, established autocratic rule in Norway and put an end to the oligarchic system of petty kingdoms, in which chieftains, farming large estates, ruled in their districts in the manner of small kings. Those who refused to pledge allegiance to the new central power leave their homeland and head for new shores. The Shetland and Orkney Islands, the Hebrides and Ireland could not serve as places of refuge for long, as according to the understanding of the time all these areas belongd to **Harald Finehair's Norway**, and soon after the subjugation of the Norwegian

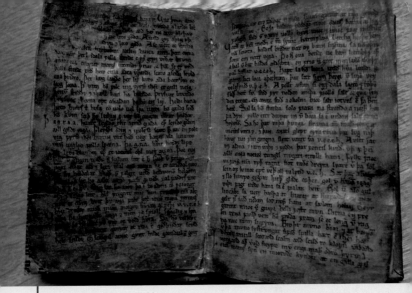

The beginnings of documented history

heartlands he asserted his claim to power here too, placing loyal men in important positions.

This is what Snorri Sturluson, of whom more in due course, wrote in his **Heimskringla**– a work on the Norwegian kings – of Harald Finehair's military expedition: »First he reached the Shetlands and killed all the Vikings there that had not taken flight in time. Then he sailed to the Orkneys and cleansed them too of all Vikings. Finally he took his army on to the Hebrides and slew many Vikings ... Then he battled in Scotland ... When he arrived on the Isle of Man, the story of all the battles that he had fought had already preceded him. Everybody fled to the interior of Scotland, and the Isle of Man was deserted.« The consequences of Harald's Western Island tour turn out to be the same as in the mother country: whoever did not want to accept the new balance of power had to flee.

Harald's tour of the Western Isles

Serendipitous Discovery

Fortunately, we have the tales of the voyages of two men. On their way to the Faroe Islands, strong winds blew a certain **Naddoður**– as well as a **Garðar Svavarsson**– off course, while looking for a country that his mother, blessed with a psychic gift, had described to him. Both arrive at Iceland's coast. Naddoður landed in the area of the eastern fjords, but soon set sail for the Faroe Islands. By circumnavigating Iceland, Garðar found out that the country he has discovered is an island, subsequently spending a winter in the north, the site of

Slaves as the first permanent settlers

today's town of Húsavík. After their return, both report on this new country that Naddoður called Snæland, Snowland, and Garðar, with the utmost modesty, Garðarshólmur. All these details of Iceland's settlement are told in the aforementioned Landnámabók. There, one particular episode is mentioned in an aside that is hardly picked up in other historiography: Náttfari, a slave, together with a maid, leaves Garðar Svavarsson's party and stays near Húsavík when his master sails back south. Their settling place is assumed to be on the small bay of **Náttfaravík**, on the banks of the wide Skjálfandi Bay opposite Húsavík. This would make an escaped slave and a maid the first (permanent) settlers in Iceland.

A freezing cold winter gives Iceland its name

The short visits of Naddoður and Garðar were soon followed by an attempt at settlement. **Flóki Vilgerðarson** started from the Norwegian Rogaland in the direction of Iceland. Preparing for a permanent settlement, he landed in the west of the island, on the northern shore of the Breiðafjörður. Neglecting to think about winter rations for the cattle with which he was travelling, Flóki promptly lost them all in the following winter. In the spring, he sailed back to his home country, but not without first giving the island a name: Iceland. After Thule, Snæland and Garðarshólmur, this fourth name proved to be the one that stuck.

Iceland's Settlement Progresses

Argument over a woman

The forbidding name didn't deter people: in 874 – as described in the Landnámabók – two Norwegians left their country to set about the final and permanent settlement of Iceland. **Ingólfur Arnarson and Leifur Hróðmarsson**, who grew up as brothers, fled: they killed someone in an argument over a woman, and both were threatened with the blood feud of the victim's family. Ingólfur, initially living in the south of Iceland on a spot that today bears his name, **Ingólfshöfði**, later moved to a bay where there is smoke – Reykjavík. According to tradition, on arrival Ingólfur threw two carved tree trunks into the sea off Iceland and has them searched for after landing. In the **Bay of Smoke** where they were washed ashore, he then established his new home.

Leifur and the men from the west

Leifur settled just below the Mýrdalsjökull at a place that today is called Hjörleifshöfð. However, he was not allowed to enjoy his new home, as the slaves that he brought over from the west beat him to death. Subsequently they fled on to the islands lying within sight of the coast, giving them their name: islands of the men from the west – **Vestmannaeyar**. They, however, did not live to a ripe old age either, as Ingólfur took bloody revenge for his foster brother. Thus Iceland's history began with murder and mayhem.

An imposing man and early settler of Iceland: Ingólfur Arnarson →

**Iceland –
a country of
immigrants**
Ingólfur was followed by a stream of people wanting to make a new life for themselves in Iceland. In roughly half a century, around 400 immigrant leaders arrived with their retinue. How many people came ashore in total can only be estimated; it is probably between 20,000 and 30,000, but a figure of 70,000 has been put forward too. »Ísland byggäist fyrst ýr Norvege á dogum Harallz ens hárfraga, Hálfdanar sonar ens svarta ...« (Iceland was first settled from Norway, during the time of Harald Finehair, son of Halfdan the Black ...), states the beginning of **Ari Þorgilsson's** *Íslendingabók*. The proven fact that many settlers came from the Norwegian possessions in Britain and Ireland does not invalidate Ari's statement; for him and his time, this was Norway. Genetic research confirms the Celtic influence: about every tenth Icelander of the founding generation is from the British Isles.

The Alþing, Parliament of All?

around 930	End of the conquest of Iceland. The first Alþing convenes.
982	Erik the Red discovers Greenland.
around 1000	Christianization. Leifur, son of Erik, discovers America.

**Emerging
political
structures**
In 930, Iceland's colonization was practically complete and the available lands distributed. The first political structures emerged, initially at local level with the **Goðorðs** – domains of influence controlled by chieftains, or goðar. The Goðar came from the ranks of rich landowners that ran a temple on their estates for the people of their region. In addition to looking after the temples, they were soon invested with secular powers, even the administration of justice. To support them, from around 900, regional Þing assemblies were established; these however were so autonomous that the law s interpreted differently in different parts of the country.

**Alþing in
Þingvellir**
In order to achieve a uniform regulation of society, the first national Alþing convened in 930. Three years previously, a group of nationally-minded Goðar had sent a legally trained man, **Úlfljótur**, to Norway to put together a body of laws. After his return, he reports his version of new Icelandic law orally at the Alþing. In so doing, Úlfljótur founded a tradition that was to endure until the written codification of law in the early 12th century: the elected legislative speaker reported the entire law orally at the annual assembly of the Alþing. This gave him a prominent position, as he could even – as long as there is no dissent – change the law by presenting laws in a different way or omitting them. A meeting place was chosen in the southwest of the country, east of Reykjavík: **Þingvellir, the field of the þing**.

Governing the issues of the largest state in the region with relative sovereignty, the Alþing of the Icelanders was the most important þing in the North Atlantic area. Although its assembly had legal and judicial powers, the first Icelandic Free State forgoes an executive arm. Its citizens could gain legal titles, and the enforcement of law was a private issue, including the **carrying out of death sentences**.

No executive powers

The parliament of today's Iceland is still called Alþing and sees itself in direct lineage to the assembly of the first Free State, and as such as the oldest existent national parliament in the world. However, the early Alþing represented an oligarchy, led by three to four dozen Goðar, whose **followers were free men**. In Iceland at that time, most people are either unfree, female or both, and hence not represented in the Alþing.

Oligarchy rather than democracy

For those who did have the right to make decisions there, the early Alþing was a symbol of their freedom from the Norwegian king, although contact with Norway is maintained; travelling back to the old country was a part of life. The language documents this: in Old Icelandic, a ship sailing from Norway to Iceland is said to be sailing

Voyage »from outside«

Here the law was proclaimed and judgments executed: Þingvellir, the field of the assembly

»út« – out – and in the other direction »útan« – from outside. For the sons of important Icelandic families, it was part of their career to have served at the king's court in Norway. **Harald Finehair's son Håkon** founde an elite brigade, where many young Icelanders served, pledging allegiance to the king. Despite all this, for half a century the Icelanders were able to withstand Norway's attempts to influence the decisions of the Alþing. King Olav I Tryggvesson changed this and had all Icelanders who happend to be in Norway at the time arrested and baptised by force. He held four sons of important families as hostages to force the Alþing to accept the blessings of Christianity in Iceland too. This came to pass in AD 1000.

Duality of faith Soon after the beginning of Christianization around 1000, the church gained influence without becoming overpowering. Bishoprics were established in Skálholt and Hólar. For a while, the old and new religions existed side by side, sometimes even within one family. The most famous case is told in the saga of Erik the Red, who lead the European **settlement of Greenland**. Whilst Erik worshipped the old gods, his wife Þjodhlíð embraces Christianity, to the extent that a small church was established in the grounds of their Brattahlíð estate in southwest Greenland, the first in the New World.

Leifur Eiríksson and his crew standing on American soil

Iceland as Stepping Stone to the New World

Erik was one of the most colourful figures of the young country of
Iceland. Early on he was forced to leave Norway together with his father Þorvaldur, settling in the Dalir district in West Iceland. There
too, further crimes made him an **outlaw** – in order to survive, he
had to leave the country. At the time, there were stories doing the
rounds that there was more land a bit further west. Erik discovered
it in 982, and called it Grønland, Greenland – for good publicity –
when he turned up again in Iceland three years later. »Because he
thinks people are more likely to want to move there if the country
has a nice name«, said Ari Þorgilsson and other saga authors, revea-
ling Erik's true intentions. His strategy bore fruit however: in 986, a
band of some 500 people followed Erik to the »New World«. Only
300 arrived though, as eleven of the 25 ships did't make it. Outlawed
in Iceland, Erik became the esteemed leader of the small colony. His
son Leifur, born in the Dalir district of Iceland, ensured that his and
his father's names become immortal: **Leifur Eiriksson** was credited
with discovering America around the year 1000. For a long time only
attested by quotes from various sagas, since the 1960s there has been
archaeological confirmation of this through finds in L'Anse aux Meadows in Newfoundland. A pronounced worsening of climatic conditions – examinations of Greenland's inland ice suggest an extended
cold spell between 1390 and 1550 – broke Iceland's connections to
the west around 1400, consigning them to historical oblivion.

To America

The End of the Free State

1262	Iceland is subjected to the Norwegian crown.
from 1302	Economic decline
1380	Iceland falls into Danish hands.
16th century	The Reformation leads to bloody conflicts.
1800	The Alþing is dissolved

From the end of the settlement of the island into the new millennium, Iceland experienced years of peace and prosperity. Then, the
Icelanders sealed their own fate, as disputes began between the powers that be. The Norwegian kings, initially welcomed as arbiters, later
meddled without being asked for their advice. From 1152 onwards,
on ecclesiastical issues Iceland was subject to the archbishopric of Ni-
daros, today's Trondheim. In 1238, for the first time, Norwegians oc-

From arbiter to ruler

cupied both Icelandic episcopal seats. In 1241, Snorri Sturluson – as writer and historian an indisputable authority, but as a power politician from one of Iceland's leading dynasties rather mediocre – fell victim to intrigue. In 1258, the Norwegian **King Håkon IV Håkonsson** managed to place a loyal administrator in Iceland – who received the title Duke of Iceland – and four years later, the work was done: the Icelanders pledged allegiance to the Norwegian king at the Alþing, with the duke becoming vice king. The Free State thus destroyed, Norway's power in the North Atlantic was at a peak, especially as the previous year the small colony of Greenland had already submitted itself to the Norwegian crown.

Economic decline
The new rule only brought the Icelanders peace and prosperity for a short time. After a few years the economic upturn was finished. Trade became dependent on foreign ships, the **former Vikings** having neglected their own seafaring. Foreign ships only came if they thought they could make enough profit. From 1302 onwards, the Norwegian king restricted trade with Iceland to Norwegians only, later only to merchants from Bergen. The latter mercilessly abused their monopoly, giving the Icelanders low prices for their goods and low-quality goods for their money.

Iceland falls into Danish hands
It is a woman who in 1376 shuffled the cards afresh in the north: Margaret, daughter of the late Danish king, and wife of the Norwegian king Håkon VI, ensured that in the **elective kingdom of Denmark** her six-year old son was chosen, as Oluf III Håkonsson, to be her father's successor. When Margaret's husband died in 1380, little Oluf automatically became, as Olav IV Håkonsson, king in the unelected kingdom of Norway and thereby ruler of the territories in the North Atlantic. The death of the young king at 17 brouht Margaret the formal regency which she had already been exerting in practice. The centre of the Nordic Empire, which also included Sweden as part of the Kalmar Union (1397 – 1448), rapidly shifted to Denmark.

Heads Roll in the Wake of the Reformation

Denmark's influence grows
As the Reformation spread north in the 16th century, Denmark officially became Lutheran in 1536, following a bloody civil war, and began imposing Lutheranism on its outlying possessions. Meanwhile, in Iceland, the two Catholic bishops used Denmark's internal problems to grab secular power. Violent clashes ensued, with loss of life on both sides. In 1541 the **bishopric of Skálholt** in the south was reformed by force, while in Hólar, in northern Iceland, the popular Jón Arason was the last bishop in the whole of northern Europe to remain faithful to Rome. Making the mistake of his life, he used force to usurp the episcopal throne after the death of his Lutheran rival in Skálholt, and reintroduced Catholicism. Soon afterwards he was overpowered and beheaded, together with two of his sons. As

Denmark gained substantial influence on the island with this bloody deed, Jón Arason was subsequently turned into a **martyr for Icelandic freedom**; his death was avenged with the murder of many Danes, while Arason's followers carried his mortal remains to Hólar.

Hard times

The Danes soon took trade completely into their own hands and eventually proclaimed the Northern Atlantic to be their state territory. In 1602, the Icelanders were even banned under threat of punishment from trading with third parties. The population was entirely dependent on the mercy of the monopolists appointed by the king. However, they were anything but merciful and the Icelanders went through hard times. At this stage, **Árni Magnússon**, having come to an arrangement with the Danes, safeguarded most manuscripts, ensuring that the Icelandic literature of the Middle Ages survived. He did not have much time, as the increasingly impoverished population used the skins that the manuscripts were written on for all sorts of things, and no longer just for reading. The manuscripts found their way to Copenhagen, where some of them fell victim to fires in the city.

Iceland on the Edge of the Abyss

Natural disaster

In Iceland even nature now seemed to turn against the island's inhabitants. Diseases, some affecting animals and some humans, famines, harsh winters and constant volcanic activity regularly claimed victims. The **peak of the natural disasters** was reached with the eruption of the Laki fissure in southern Iceland in 1783/4. This caused the Eldhraun, »fire lava«, at 560 square kilometres/216 square miles the world's largest contiguous lava surface in historical times. On top of that, toxic gases entered the atmosphere. Witnesses described sulphuric clouds spreading over all of Iceland, known as the Móðuharðindi, or »Mist Hardships«. 9,000 people died as a result of the eruption, while nearly all the livestock perished. 910 years after the settlement, colonial civil servants in Copenhagen planned the evacuation of Iceland to give the survivors a new home on the heather moors of Jutland. Many did not have to be resettled as, following the catas-

Almost no other country on earth has been so shaped by natural disasters

trophe, the island had fewer inhabitants than at any point since its settlement. In the end, the survivors were left where they were and the cheaper option was selected: in 1786, the Danes eased the trade monopoly. Slowly life returned to the country – economically at least. Politically, the following years remained gloomy. **Dependency on the central government in Copenhagen** increased. In 1798 the nearly irrelevant Alþing met for the last time before being formally dissolved in 1800.

The Path to Independence

1814	The Danish-Norwegian dual monarchy is dissolved.
1845	The Alþing convenes again.
1918	Iceland becomes an »autonomous« kingdom.
1944	Independence of Iceland; proclamation of the Republic
1986	Gorbachev and Reagan meet in Reykjavík.
2003	Iceland takes up whaling again.
2008	The world financial crisis almost causes national bankruptcy.

Renaissance of the Alþing After the Napoleonic Wars, which raged in Europe, the Danish-Norwegian dual monarchy was dissolved by the victorious powers – Denmark fought on the side of France – at the end of the war in 1814. Norway came under Swedish influence, then became independent. But its old colonies – Greenland, Iceland and the Faroe Islands – remained with Denmark. In the meantime, the early 19th-century nationalist movements extend to the far north. Gathering in Copenhagen, Icelandic students and intellectuals were supported by liberal Danes, united in their efforts for the preservation of Icelandic culture and language, which was being supplanted by Danish. Soon they turned political however, demanding the reinstatement of the Alþing and gaining followers in Iceland. The young **Jón Sigurðsson** (1811–1879), brought up as a pastor's son on a remote fjord in northwestern Iceland, eventually became their leader. Unlike the romantics of the early movement, who aimed to revive the historical Free State with a parliamentary assembly in Þingvellir, he was a political realist, envisaging a modern Iceland. He established this in 1845 when the Alþing convened as a modern **parliament in Reykjavík**, initially only in an advisory capacity. In 1874, a constitutional reform invested the Alþing with legislative powers, while the Danish king remained head of state. The latter appointed a governor who reported to an Iceland ministry in Copenhagen. In the eyes of the Icelanders this of course was only half the prize. In 1904, they were given more with the dissolution of the Iceland ministry. In Reykjavík, new political machinery took shape, reporting to the Alþing. From 1915, Iceland has flown its own flag and in 1918 a treaty of union made the country an autonomous kingdom – in personal union with Denmark.

The Turmoil of War Leads to Independence

In April 1940, the German Wehrmacht entered Denmark and Norway. British troops moved in to occupy formally neutral Iceland and pre-empt a putative **occupation by Germany**, which in previous years had shown a marked interest in the strategically positioned island. While protesting, Iceland's government still called on the population to stay calm and asked them to treat the British as guests. For the Icelanders this was easy: the soldiers brought money into the country and provided employment, overcoming the last consequences of the economic recession of the 1930s. In 1941, in order to ease the pressure on Great Britain, the Americans took on the role of occupying force protecting the island, this time with the approval of the Alþing who had demanded – and obtained – a declaration confirming the **sovereignty of Iceland** and promising a pull-out of the troops as soon as the war ended. The Americans brought in even more money, more jobs, new engineering techniques and much technical know-how. The country enjoyed a real boom and made a rapid leap forward in terms of development. Economically, the Icelanders also did well, especially as they got to supply Great Britain with fish. The country itself was spared acts of war, but not its merchant fleet, so that in proportion to its population Iceland suffered a high **death toll** in the war.

Allied troops in Iceland

In 1943, the **Act of Union**, signed 25 years previously between Denmark and Iceland, expired. The Icelanders did not extend it but dissolved it unilaterally. Whilst technically within their rights to do so, many Danes today still question whether under the circumstances it was morally justified as well. On 17th June 1944, the 133rd birthday of the hero of Icelandic freedom, Jón Sigurðsson, the Republic is proclaimed at historic Þingvellir. 682 years after Håkon IV Håkonsson took power, the Icelanders regained their freedom.

Proclamation of the Republic

Apart from a short break between 1947 and 1951, American soldiers remained stationed in the country. From 1951, they began to expand Keflavík to a large **NATO base** and, backed by a defence agreement, were responsible for Iceland's national defence. Iceland joined NATO in 1949, but without possessing an army of its own. The country's contribution consists exclusively of its strategic position.

NATO base at Keflavik

For a long time, the arguments over the **pros and cons of the American presence in the country and the Keflavík base** dominated the political discourse in post-war Iceland, leading to the worst political

American troops prove divisive

riots the country has ever seen in front of the Alþing in Reykjavík during the vote on joining NATO. At a later stage, left-leaning government coalitions twice tried to cancel the contracts with the Americans and persuade them to leave the country. In 1956, the Alþing actually voted accordingly. However, Warsaw Pact troops then invaded Hungary and the Icelanders did not follow up on this resolution. With the end of the Cold War in 1989/90, the presence of the Americans became less of an issue, and finally they closed the Keflavik base in 2006.

Reykjavík at the centre of world politics

Internationally, Iceland made few political headlines, apart from an event of global significance in 1986, when the two most powerful men in the world, **Ronald Reagan and Mikhail Gorbachev**, met for the first time – on neutral soil in Reykjavík. This was the beginning of a political development that was to change the world forever (see above). Five years later, as one of the consequences of these geopolitical changes, Iceland was briefly thrust into the limelight again: the country was one of the first to give the Baltic states diplomatic recognition, prompting Russia to recall its ambassador from Reykjavík.

Only in Iceland...

Reykjavík as the battleground of the dog lobby

Apart from exceptions of this kind, and until Iceland was propelled into the world spotlight in 2008 for all the wrong reasons, reports from Iceland tended toward the bizarre: When the finance minister threatened to pack it in and leave the country if he was not allowed to keep his dogs with him in Reykjavík, where a **dog ban** is in place. Soon after, keeping dogs was allowed on a trial basis, only to be banned again by referendum after the end of the trial phase. Generally, bizarre prohibitions – or indeed their lifting – continue to make headlines: the world's media looked on in 1989 as the prohibition on beer was dropped, having been routinely disregarded for 74 years. Since March 2002, it has been possible to stage boxing matches again, after a 45-year ban passed by the Alþing after a mass brawl outside a dancehall, involving professional boxers. The **whaling issue** (▶ p. 27), which isolated Iceland in the late 1980s, provides negative headlines on a regular basis. Between 1990 and 2003, Iceland renounced whaling before taking it up again for »research purposes«.

The ice is broken, the curtain falls: it is in Reykjavík that →
Ronald Reagan and Mikhail Gorbachev begin to change the world

Arts and Culture

When did the Icelandic sagas emerge? What exactly is skaldic poetry? Who wrote the first Icelandic novel? Which motifs are favoured by the painter Jóhannes Kjarval? What stood in the way of the development of sculpture in Iceland? All will be revealed on the following pages.

Iceland's Cultural Heritage

12th – 14th centuries	Emergence of the Icelandic sagas
1850	Publication of the first Icelandic novel.
19th century	The Icelanders begin to engage more intensively with painting.
First half of the 19th century	Jónsson and Sveinsson rise to become the most important sculptors in Iceland.
1950	Death of the most renowned Icelandic architect, Guðjón Samúelsson
1955	Halldór Laxness is awarded the Nobel Prize for Literature.

Iceland's early cultural tradition was influenced by Scandinavia, and Norway in particular. Early on, conscious engagement with language and literature had an important role to play and was valued by large parts of the population. It should come as no surprise then that literature going back to the Middle Ages became an essential part of the country's cultural heritage. One prerequisite for this was the **introduction of the Latin written language**, which entered the country together with Christianity. Living for centuries without political freedom and in abject poverty, the Icelanders, also hampered by their geographical isolation, were not in a position to participate in the new trends of European arts and culture until late, if at all. Instead they immersed themselves in the medieval manuscripts. These only started to be systematically collected from the 17th century, with Árni Magnússon (1663 to 1730), the first Icelandic university professor in Copenhagen, playing an important role. On his travels through Iceland he collected **old manuscripts** and had them brought to Copenhagen. There they remained until 1971; only then did the Danish give the remaining manuscripts – a large part had perished in the flames of the 1728 Copenhagen fire – back to the Icelanders. For Iceland this was a historic event, marking the definitive regaining of their cultural sovereignty.

Norwegian influences

Literature: from the Sagas to Laxness

Icelandic sagas belong to the outstanding works of world literature. Written between the 12th and 14th centuries, these works count among the most diverse medieval manuscripts in Europe – and all originating from a poor, remote island in the North Atlantic. It is as-

Sagas

← No-frills, basic and utilitarian: Icelandic architecture represents simplicity itself – but still knows how to please

sumed that the sagas were initially transmitted orally and only later written down. To this day it is not clear who wrote them; one of the reasons that attribution is difficult is that the originals no longer exist. Sagas are a combination of fiction and historiography and bear witness to the high artistic ability of their authors. Copies, as well as embellished and reworked versions, have been preserved since the 13th century. The kings' sagas describe ruling Nordic dynasties going back to the 9th century. The most important amongst these is the **Heimskringla by Snorri Sturluson**, which, for the first time, tells history chronologically. The Icelanders' sagas were written down around the middle of the 13th century, i.e. not until 200 to 400 years after the events they describe. Considered the masterpiece of this classic period of Old Icelandic prose, the **Njáls saga** deals with more or less all human and societal conflicts. The Sturlunga saga is a literary reworking of the end of the Icelandic Free State in all its details and cruelties. As the Icelandic language has hardly changed since the Middle Ages, the sagas are still understood today and many Icelanders are familiar at least with the content of the most important works.

Edda/ Skaldic poetry

Early Icelandic literature also encompasses the Edda songs and skaldic poetry. Skaldic poetry came to Iceland from Norway and Scotland, while the older Edda songs deal with the fates of the Scandinavian and Germanic gods. The Younger (or Snorra) Edda gives insights into **Old Germanic mythology**. Written by Snorri Sturluson (1179–1241), it is at the same time a primer for the complex skaldic poetry. This form of poetry got its name from the skalds, courtly poets who praised their patrons' deeds to the skies, usually with musical accompaniment. After Iceland lost its independence, its literature entered a period of crisis when, apart from ecclesiastical writings, hardly any prose literature appeared up to the early 19th century.

Towards modernity

The modern era begins with the publication of the first Icelandic novel in 1850: *Boy and Girl* by Jón Thoroddsen. A love story, the book is at the same time a realistic depiction of rural Icelandic life at the time. All in all, the 19th century was the time of **national romantic** literature, describing the traditional ways of life in Iceland. One of the most famous exponents of this movement is Gunnar Gunnarsson (1889–1975), whose most successful novel, *Guest the One-Eyed*, tells a rural family saga. Gunnarsson wrote much of his extensive work in Danish, which gave him a certain recognition outside Iceland too. With the awarding of the Nobel Prize to Halldór Laxness (▶Famous People p. 61) in 1955, Icelandic literature finally regained international recognition. The fact that today some modern Icelandic authors are read abroad can probably be credited to him, although the towering figure of Halldór Laxness may have made it more difficult for young authors to make their mark at home.

Painting and Sculpture

Only in the 19th century did the Icelanders engage in painting more intensively. In 1863 **Sigurður Guðmundsson** (1833–1874) founded the National Museum of Iceland, and in 1900, Þorarinn Þorláksson was the first Icelandic painter to have a solo exhibition of his landscape paintings. Modern Icelandic painting begins with **Ásgrímur Jónsson** (1876–1958), with his landscapes, portraits and still lifes characterized by wonderfully atmospheric light. Another master of capturing the seascapes and fishermen bathed in the northern light was **Jóhannes Kjarval** (1885–1972). Many works by one of the best-known Icelandic artists are exhibited in the municipal Kjarvalsstaðir Gallery in Reykjavík (►p. 255), which was named after him.

For centuries, sculpture was very much a marginal art form in Iceland. Among the reasons were the lack of wood and the difficulties in working the predominantly volcanic rock. The medieval **church door of Valðjófsstaður** in East Iceland, dating back to the 13th century and adorned with plant and dragon decorations, is one of the

A scarcity of wood

Einar Jónsson's affinity with Symbolism is plain to see

few remaining wood carvings from the Middle Ages. During the Reformation, many Catholic relics were destroyed or moved to Denmark. Only a few wooden sculptures, as well as chests and cabinets with pretty tendril patterns, have been preserved from the time after the Reformation.

Einar Jónsson and Ásmundur Sveinsson The fame of Einar Jónsson (1874 – 1954) rests on his sculptures, heavily influenced by Nordic, Greek and Asian mythology. Visitors can't miss his works in the centre of Reykjavík, representing Iceland's first settler Ingólfur Arnarson, and Jón Sigurðsson, the fighter for national independence. Further works by Jónsson may be seen in a **museum in Reykjavík** that he designed himself. Born in West Iceland, the most famous sculptor is Ásmundur Sveinsson (1893 – 1982), who created his works – some on a monumental scale – following motifs taken from the Edda. Like a lot of Icelandic artists, Sveinsson also spent many years abroad, studying in Paris and Stockholm, among other places.

Architecture: no Palaces or Castles

The magnificent churches, palaces and castles that can be found in their hundreds elsewhere in Europe were never built in Iceland, due to the lack of a rich upper class that could have financed this type of construction. Thus, all buildings were unadorned, simple and utilitarian. The oldest buildings still standing are two small churches in the south of Iceland dating from the 17th century.

For a long time, the buildings most associated with Iceland were **peat houses with grass sod roofs** and characteristic front gables. Small and offering little living comfort, they were at least well insulated against the winter cold by their walls, several metres thick. Today, some of these houses stand in open-air museums. The first stone house was built in 1755 near the capital and today belongs to the National Museum. Wood and other construction materials have always been scarce in Iceland and had mostly to be imported, significantly raising building costs. This is why, to save money, in the early 20th century many houses were clad with corrugated iron when they needed to be protected from the elements.

A good number of these houses characterize the urban image of Reykjavík. Together with the stone houses that were built later and the glass and concrete buildings, the capital does not exactly present a homogenous and architecturally successful cityscape. However, the brightly-painted houses do make it more attractive. A significant influence on Reykjavík's modern architecture was **Guðjón Samúelsson** (1887 – 1950), the architect who designed Hallgrim's church, the National Theatre, the University, the Catholic church and the Hotel Borg.

One of the most beautiful of its kind: the turf farmstead of Bustarfell →

Famous People

Singer Björk is world-famous, and Halldór Laxness is the brightest star in the Icelandic literary firmament. But who was Jón Arason, or Jón Sigurðsson? What is remarkable about Vigdís Finnbogadóttir? Did Leifur Eriksson really beat Christopher Columbus to America?

Jón Arason (1484 – 1550)

Beheaded, together with two of his sons, at Skálholt in southern Iceland in 1550, during the course of the Reformation, the last Catholic
bishop of Iceland owes his reputation as martyr and freedom-loving
nationalist to his **resistance against Danish rule**. As bishop of Hólar,
the northern of the two Icelandic sees, Jón Arason held extensive estates. Therefore his fight for the pope and Catholicism wasn't entirely
altruistic, as not only goods, fiefdoms and tithes, but also natural
land rights such as fishing and hunting, as well as the gathering and
use of driftwood, were claimed by the Reformation and seculariza-
tion or passed down to the Danish crown and its centralized administration. In early 2003, the start of the Íslendingabók Internet ge-
nealogy programme by Kári Stefánsson of the Íslensk erfðagreining
genetic research company yielded interesting new information on
Jón Arason: the majority of Icelanders can trace their ancestry back
to the bishop, born in 1484. As fertile as he was belligerent – Rome
was far away and Iceland had its own laws – the Catholic dignitary
had numerous children both with his wife and several concubines.

Bishop and »father« of the Icelanders

Björk (born 1965)

No other person from the island in the North Atlantic is currently
the object of so much international media attention as musician and
singer Björk. At the tender age of eleven, Björk Guðmundsdóttir
launched her first record, landing a hit straight away. Still only 13,
she formed her first band, *Exodus*, with girlfriends, followed by *Jam
80*, *Tappi Tikarrass* and the nationally successful band *KUKL*, before
starting to gain recognition outside Iceland too, with the legendary
Sugarcubes (1986 – 1992). The precocious maverick child star has
developed into an independent composer, singer and pop artist. Never in thrall to mainstream musical tastes, Björk joined forces with a
jazz trio in 1990 to release the album *Gling-Gló* in Iceland, a collection of songs in traditional interpretation – a long-running bestseller
in the island's record shops and a coveted Icelandic souvenir for her
fans all over the world. Leaving the Sugarcubes launched Björk's rise
to global stardom. The albums she since released as a solo artist have
met with much acclaim; her last, **»Volta«**, in 2007, was no exception.
What is more, her songs have been released in countless remixes,
with Björk herself in most cases collaborating on the new versions.
Time and again, Björk has also contributed songs and soundtracks
to films, amongst them *Tank Girl*, *The Young Americans*, *Mission Impossible* and *Being John Malkovitch*. In 1999/2000, she even dabbled
in acting under Denmark's eccentric star director **Lars von Trier**: in
the film musical *Dancer in the Dark*, Björk plays the central character

Musician and singer

← *Iceland's favourite elf: Björk on the cover of one of her
recent albums, »Medúlla«*

A contemporary Icelandic icon: Björk prefers singing to acting

of Selma, an immigrant in the US who is nearly blind through a hereditary illness. In her desperation to spare her child the same fate, she makes the ultimate sacrifice. Whilst the tabloid press relished the escalating arguments between the difficult director and the no less difficult pop star – Björk declaring she would never act again as she simply could not stand it – she was awarded Best Actress at Cannes 2000. Of course Björk also composed the music for *Dancer in the Dark* and interpreted all the songs herself; in 2000 the title song *I've Seen It All* was nominated for an Oscar as Best Original Song. The title of the whole soundtrack is ***Selmasongs***. Married to the US-American artist and former football star Matt Barney, Björk Guð-mundsdóttir has two children and divides her time between New York, London and Iceland.

Leifur Eriksson (c970 – c1020)

Discoverer of America
Leifur Eriksson, also called »Leif the Lucky«, must have come from a particularly feisty Viking family. Not only did his grandfather have to leave Norway and to go into exile in Iceland because of a murder, his father, Erik the Red, was also banished in 982, subsequently making tracks for Greenland with his son Leifur. Erik returned after three years to look for colonists that would accompany him to Greenland, eventually setting sail with 25 ships. Around the year 1000, Leifur

Eriksson himself set sail in the direction of Greenland, but, after losing his way a few times, eventually landed, in all likelihood, near Boston – which meant that he **discovered America before Columbus** by a long way. After his return, the Vikings launched further voyages to America and most probably also founded some settlements there.

Vigdís Finnbogadóttir (born 1930)

Born in Reykjavík, Vigdís Finnbogadóttir finished high school in 1949 and went on to study in Grenoble and at the Sorbonne in Paris, at Uppsala in Sweden, and at the University of Iceland. At the presidential elections in 1980, Vigdís Finnbogadóttir achieved victory over three male candidates by a slim majority. Her electorate was mainly to be found in the left-leaning sections of society and not least among women. Later on, she became a **president popular with all political camps**. As the world's first female head of state elected by the people, Vigdís Finnbogadóttir held office for four legislative periods, renouncing a new candidature after 16 years. During her presidency, Vigdís Finnbogadóttir was a tireless ambassador abroad for Icelandic culture – the visual arts and contemporary literature in particular – and worked hard for women's equality.

Former President of Iceland

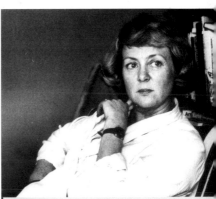
Still extremely popular today: Vigdís Finnbogadóttir

Halldór Laxness (1902 – 1998)

Over the course of a long writer's life, Halldór Kiljan Laxness authored 62 works – novels, drama, essays and short stories. What is more, he wrote countless newspaper articles to give his point of view on virtually any issue. For this small country he was not just the only Nobel Laureate but also the towering father figure of modern Icelandic literature, his extensive work shaping the 20th century. Born **Halldór Gudjónsson** in Reykjavík, he lived from the age of five on the Laxness farm near Mosfellsbær, later taking on this name. Never finishing high school, he started travelling, restlessly crossing the whole of Europe and also spending some time in America. In 1923 he fathered a daughter, converted from the Lutheran to the Catholic faith and took on the name of Saint Kilian. The novel *The Great Weaver from Kashmir* is a literary testimony to this period in his life. A long stay in the US turned Laxness into a staunch **follower of communism**, though he turned away from it again in the mid-1950s. The es-

Man of letters and Nobel Laureate

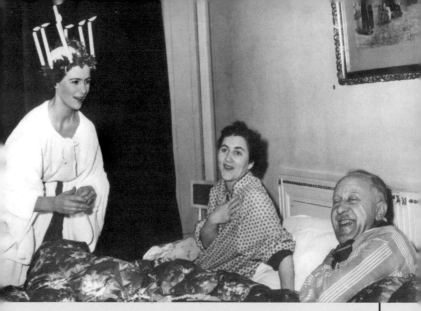

Lucia, Queen of Lights, congratulates the newly garlanded Nobel Prize winner Laxness and his wife in December 1955

say collection *The Book of the People* dates from this time. In the 1930s, Laxness wrote three epic novels that count among the most important books in Icelandic literature: using the fates of a girl living in a fishing community (*Salka Valka*), a farmer (*Paradise Reclaimed*) and a poet (*World Light*), he describes the problems and changes in Icelandic society. In the 1940s he wrote the novel *Iceland's Bell*, set in the 17th century, a time when Iceland was living in poverty and dependence on Denmark. In 1948, the novel *The Atom Station* was published, dealing with a controversial issue of its time: the agreement with the US that turned Iceland into a military base for the Americans. In 1955 Laxness was awarded the Nobel Prize for Literature.

Jón Sigurðsson (1811 – 1879)

Pioneer of Icelandic independence
No other Icelandic personality has been as continuously revered in Iceland as Jón Sigurðsson, pioneer of the country's independence. Born the son of a pastor in Hrafnseyri in the western fjords, Sigurðsson's role in securing the freedom of the country has made him an iconic personality and unassailable in every way. In 1833, he moved to Copenhagen to **study history and linguistics**. The revolutionary and democratic trends of Europe and America reached the Icelandic intellectuals living in Copenhagen, giving rise to *Ny félagsrit* (New Society Journal), an annual periodical published for the first time in 1841, edited by Jón Sigurðsson and appearing until 1871. Only in

1845 did Jón Sigurðsson return to Iceland, to take part in the resurrected Alþing as the elected representative of the Westfjords. Jón Sigurðsson was elected to be president of the parliament ten times, more often than any other parliamentarian in Iceland. His vehement commitment to independence for Iceland, and his indignant »**We all protest**«, which he flung in the face of the Danish monarchy, made him a cult figure. From 1852 onwards, Jón Sigurðsson led the Icelandic fight for freedom, again from Denmark. In countless letters, articles and contributions to almanacs he fired up his fellow countrymen in faraway Iceland. »The awakening of Denmark will make our position worse if we don't awaken too.« Thus, it was under his leadership that in 1855 the Danish trade monopoly over Iceland that had lasted for a good 250 years was ended. The constitution decreed by Denmark in 1874 for Iceland provided for a parliamentary monarchy under the Danish crown, leaving the country enough independence for Jón Sigurðsson to be able to call it »steps we can stand on«. Before reaching definitive independence in 1944, the country was to take quite a few more steps, but not Jón Sigurðsson, who died in Copenhagen as a result of an earlier bout of syphilis. The 17th of June, Jón Sigurðsson's birthday, is now Iceland's National Day, a major public holiday.

Ásmundur Sveinsson (1893 – 1982)

Sculptor

Influenced by cubism, and later on by expressionism, the sculptor Ásmundur Sveinsson spent his youth on the Kolsstaðir farm in the Dalasýsla district in the northwest of Iceland. Moving to Reykjavík in 1915 he began to work as a wood carver. Four years later, Ásmundur left Iceland to study at the State Academy in Stockholm. After finishing his studies in Paris and exhibiting several works at the Paris spring exhibition of 1929, he returned to Iceland. His interest in modern technology gave rise to metal works entitled *Electricity, Space Dragon, Flying Future* or *Yearning for Space*. In 1968, American astronauts, having trained in the lava deserts of Iceland and about to commence their journey to the moon, visited the visionary sculptor. Faithful to the school of thought that sees sculpture as part of the urban landscape, Ásmundur Sveinsson created large-scale sculptures that can be found at many places in Reykjavík, for instance *The Water Carrier* at the Meteorological Institute and *Mother Earth* in Sigtún, in eastern Reykjavík, home to Ásmundarsafn, the Ásmundur Sveinsson Museum, the artist's last residence and studio.

Practical
information

WHICH SPECIALITIES OF ICELANDIC CUISINE
SHOULD DEFINITELY BE TRIED? WHAT
ARE THE ROADS LIKE IN
ICELAND? WHICH ARE THE
ESSENTIAL ITEMS TO PACK? FIND ALL
THE ANSWERS HERE, PREFERABLY
BEFORE DEPARTURE!

Accommodation

Iceland offers a great variety of accommodation, from four-star and mid-range hotels to guesthouses, private rooms, youth and family hostels, holiday cottages, mountain lodges, farm holidays and sleeping-bag accommodation. Many hotels, guesthouses and farms are open in winter too, while campsites, the summer hotels belonging to the Edda Group and some youth hostels shut down for the winter months. During the main travel season there might be bottlenecks near the tourist highlights, so it's a good idea to phone ahead to enquire after free beds. Updated every year, the free *Áning/Places to Stay* brochure lists some 300 mainly smaller hotels and guesthouses, but also huts and campsites. The individual properties are presented with their address, photographs and a short write-up; however, prices don't appear either in the brochure or on the website (www.gisting.is) and have to be requested from each place individually.

Classification/ Price categories

For some years now all places offering accommodation can have themselves classified by the Icelandic Tourist Board and be awarded one to five stars for comfort. Classified houses show a blue-and-red symbol at the entrance; however, so far only a few establishments have requested classification. Due to fluctuating exchange rates, all prices here are given in Icelandic krona. The accommodation places listed in the red travel section have been divided into the following categories:

► **Budget**
up to 9,000 ISK per night/
2 people (double room)

► **Luxury**
over 18,000 ISK per night/
2 people (double room)

► **Mid-range**
9,000 – 18,000 ISK per night/
2 people (double-room)

Farm holidays

Icelandic Farm Holidays is an association of around 130 farmhouses with some 4,000 beds in all, spread over the whole of Iceland. Accommodation is very varied, featuring small **country hotels** as well as **bed and breakfasts**, holiday cottages and apartments. Everything from cheap sleeping-bag accommodation to en suite rooms is available, with prices ranging as widely. A double room without bathroom usually costs between 6,000 ISK and 10,000 ISK, and an en suite double between 8,000 ISK and 12,000 ISK. Lodges and holiday cottages are usually rented by the week. Icelandic Farm Holidays also offers comprehensive packages, from accommodation bookings to driving holidays with hire car.

Youth hostels Map

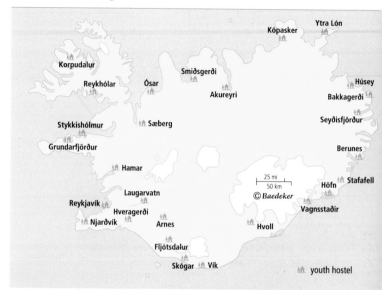

Kópasker
Ytra Lón
Korpudalur
Smiðsgerði
Húsey
Reykhólar
Ósar
Akureyri
Bakkagerði
Seyðisfjörður
Stykkishólmur
Sæberg
Grundarfjörður
Berunes
Hamar
25 mi
50 km
© *Baedeker*
Stafafell
Laugarvatn
Höfn
Reykjavík
Hveragerði
Vagnsstaðir
Njarðvík
Arnes
Hvoll
Fljótsdalur
Skógar
Vík
youth hostel

All 25 Icelandic youth and family hostels welcome guests of any age. Every hostel is different – some are based in former farmhouses, some in modern buildings – but they all offer relatively cheap accommodation in rooms with 2 to 6 beds. Apart from Fljótsdalur, all the hostels have **family rooms**. Every youth hostel has a well-equipped self-catering kitchen. Accommodation rates per person range from 1,700 to 2,550 ISK for members, to between 2,100 and 2,950 ISK. Breakfast costs around 900 ISK. Blankets and pillows are available in the rooms, but duvet covers or sleeping bags have to be brought or rented. Apart from this, all youth hostels offer many outdoor activities, ranging from fishing, hiking and horse riding to glacier tours. For more information, bookings or to get the *Hostelling in Iceland* brochure, contact the Icelandic Youth Hostel Association.

Family and youth hostels

The largest selection of hotels can be found in the capital Reykjavík and Akureyri, but there are many good mid-range hotels in the rural areas. Standards and prices vary greatly and not all rooms are en suite, although the ones that aren't tend to be cheaper. During the summer months (early June to end of August), numerous boarding schools and students' halls of residence are turned into summer hotels.

Hotels

In many smaller places, but also in Reykjavík and other towns and cities, guesthouses provide **relatively affordable accommodation**. Admittedly, their comfort levels vary, with prices differing accordingly.

Guesthouses

A patch of ground and a tent – there are few requirements for spending the night in Iceland

Camping Iceland has some 125 official campsites, which are usually open from early June to late August or mid-September. There are also many private camping options, usually attached to a guesthouse or a farm. Generally speaking, the campsites are fairly basic, with a reception and shop the exception rather than the rule, and the sanitary facilities limited to the bare necessities. At between 600 and 800 ISK per night however, the prices are unbeatably low. Booking ahead is not necessary; payment can be made at reception – if there is one – and in the highlands usually with the staff of the local hiking association lodges. Although **wild camping** is not prohibited outside the national parks and conservation areas, there is no real need for it as there are so many cheap campsites. Also, with the

! *Baedeker* TIP

A cheap bed

Visitors on a tight budget who don't fancy camping should ask for sleeping-bag accommodation. Many farms, guesthouses and youth hostels offer them, but Edda hotels, schools and community centres also provide rooms in the summer. Expect to pay from 1,800 ISK for a mattress in a communal dormitory. Sometimes traditional hotels also offer sleeping-bag accommodation in single or double rooms.

ACCOMMODATION

FARM HOLIDAYS

► **Icelandic Farm Holidays**
Siðumúli 13
108 Reykjavík
Tel. 570 27 00, fax 570 27 99
www.farmholidays.is

YOUTH HOSTEL ASSOCIATION

► **Icelandic Youth Hostel Association**
Sundlaugarvegur 34
105 Reykjavík
Tel. 553 81 10
Fax 588 92 01
www.hostel.is

CHAIN HOTELS

► **Fosshotel Iceland**
Tel. 562 40 00
Fax 562 40 01
www.fosshotel.is
14 tourist hotels, most of them
summer hotels, scattered around
the whole of Iceland, with three in
the capital Reykjavík

► **Hótel Edda**
Tel. 444 40 00
Fax 444 40 01
www.hoteledda.is
15 hotels all over Iceland, belonging to the Icelandair Hotels group

► **Icelandair Hotels**
Tel. 444 40 00
Fax 444 40 01
www.icehotels.is
Seven hotels, some top-of-the-range.

► **KEA Hotels**
Tel. 460 20 00, fax 460 20 60
www.keahotels.is
Five hotels, one in Reykjavík, four
in northern Iceland

nature of Iceland being so fragile, there are initiatives that would like to ban wild camping completely, mainly because some people don't stick to the golden rule: leave no trace! Camping on private grounds should be arranged with the owners.

► Sport and Outdoors, hiking p. 104   Hiking lodges

Arrival · Before the journey

Year-round air links with Iceland from Britain, the US, Canada, and   By air
major European hubs are provided by **Icelandair**. Icelandair flies
from London Heathrow, as well as Manchester and Glasgow, from
Boston, New York JFK, Minneapolis/St Paul, Orlando, Toronto-Pearson and Halifax, to Keflavík near Reykjavík. Apart from the traditional flight tickets, the airline often offers attractive excursion, family and group fares. Particularly good-value offers become available in

GETTING THERE

AIRLINES

▶ **Icelandair in Iceland**
Hotel Loftleiðir
IS-101 Reykjavík
Tel. 50 50 700, fax 50 50 701
www.icelandair.is

▶ **Icelandair in the United Kingdom**
Adam House, 2nd Floor – 1 Fitz-
roy Square, London
W1T 5HE
Tel. 0207 874 10 00, fax
0207 387 57 11
www.icelandair.co.uk

▶ **Icelandair in North America**
5950 Symphony Woods Rd – Suite
410
Columbia, MD 21044
Tel. 1 800 223 5500, fax
1 410 715 35 47
www.icelandair.com
www.icelandair.ca

▶ **Icelandair in Australia**
Level 7 – 189 Kent Street
Sydney, NSW 2000
Tel. 02 9087 0244
www.icelandair.com.au

▶ **Iceland Express**
Efstaland 26
IS-108 Reykjavík
tel. 55 00 600, 01 27 966 52 20
(UK), 03 54 550 06 00
(international)
www.icelandexpress.com

FERRIES

▶ **Smyril Line Iceland**
Terra Nova Sól
Stangarhýlur 3a
IS-110 Reykjavík
Tel. 591 90 00, fax 591 90 01
www.smyril-line.fo

▶ **Smyril Line UK**
Tel. 84 70 420 12 67
www.smyriline.co.uk

the low season. Budget carrier Iceland Express links London Stansted
(twice daily), and European cities such as Alicante, Berlin, Copenhagen and Warsaw with Keflavík, adding more services and cities in
peak season. Charter company JetX Airlines operates seasonal flights
from Montreal. Flight time from England is three hours, and five-
and-a-half hours from the east coast of the United States. Visitors
from Ireland, Australia, New Zealand and South Africa usually use
London as a gateway.

Airport bus | Keflavík international airport and Reykjavík are linked by an airport
bus, the journey taking about 45 min. The bus first heads for the
Hotel Loftleiðir at Reykjavík's city airport, and then stops at other
stations (campsite, youth hostel, more hotels) in the capital. The **Hotel Loftleiðir** is again the departure point for the airport transfer
some 2 hours before departure. Starting from here, guests are picked
up at their respective accommodation points. Travellers should make
sure they pass on their transport requirements in good time to the

A few hours and you're there!

hotel reception or their host, who will usually take care of everything. A one-way Flybus ticket for adults is about €14 and half price
for children up to twelve. By taxi, the drive from Keflavík to Reykjavík is around 8,000 ISK. Internal flights depart from Reykjavík city
airport.

Travellers crossing from Scandinavia can take advantage of the year-
round weekly ferry link established in 2004 between Hanstholm in
Denmark and Seyðisfjörður in East Iceland, and a link between Bergen in Norway, with a flexible return option via Denmark. The pas-
senger and car ferry of the **Smyril Line**, the *Norröna*, can transport up
to 800 cars and 1,500 passengers. In the summer, the *Norröna* sets
sail from Hanstholm on Saturday evening and, after 35 hours at sea,
reaches Tórshavn on the Faroe Islands early in the morning on
Monday. Here, onward passengers to Iceland have a two-day stop,
while the boat heads to Bergen and Scrabster near Thurso on the
northern tip of Scotland to pick up new passengers. On Wednesday
evening, the *Norröna* sets sail again from Tórshavn and heads for
Seyðisfjörður, arriving there Thursday morning. The return journey
begins Thursday lunchtime and goes direct via Tórshavn to Hanstholm, where the boat arrives on Saturday at 2pm. The link with Ler-
wick in the Shetland Islands was discontinued in 2008. The summer
sailing from Scrabster entails a mandatory 3-day stay on the Faroes

By boat

on the return journey. All the above information is liable to change, due to the financial crisis threatening to take Bergen and Scrabster off the schedule.

Entry and exit requirements

To enter Iceland, visitors from the United Kingdom, Ireland, the US, Canada, Australia and New Zealand do not require a visa, only a passport valid for three months after the planned date for leaving the country. Visitors from South Africa need to apply to the Royal Danish Embassy in Pretoria. Any other visa enquiries are also handled by the respective Royal Danish Embassies, not by the embassies of Iceland. In the UK, however, the Icelandic embassy is the point of call for any tourism-related enquiries, as there is no tourist board office. Duty-free import limits are 1 l of spirits and 1 l of wine, or 1 l of spirits and 6 l of beer, or 2.25 l of wine, plus 200 cigarettes or 250 g of other tobacco products. The legal age for alcohol is 20, and for tobacco products 18. Only 3kg/6.6lb of foodstuff per person may be brought into Iceland, with the import of eggs and dairy produce completely prohibited. Meat, poultry and sausages are only allowed in tinned form. Bringing pets into the country is more or less impossible, as entry regulations for live animals are very strict. The veterinary authorities usually demand that the animal be put into quarantine for several months. Travelling with **fishing and riding gear** is also subject to restrictions, as its geographical isolation makes Iceland particularly vulnerable to contagious diseases. Icelandic animals are not vaccinated, thus have no protection against pathogens brought into the country from abroad. Therefore used saddlery may not be imported at all, and used riding and fishing gear has to travel accompanied by paperwork proving proper disinfection. Icelandic customs operate a disinfection service.

Electricity

Electricity supply is 220 Volt, 50Hz. British three-pin plugs and US flat two-pin plugs will require an adapter to fit the power points.

Emergencies

► **Fire service, ambulance and police**
Tel. 112

► **Breakdown service**
F.I.B., tel. 5 112 112
VAKA, tel. 567 67 00

Etiquette and Customs

Even though in daily life Icelanders tend to act with Scandinavian reserve, sometimes visitors might feel that their hosts are the »Italians of the North«. Most are past masters in improvisation, and **punctuality** is not their strong point either. Thus, it is the rule rather than the exception that jobs only get done after a major last-minute effort.

A large part of the problem could be the weather – not the inclement variety as one might think, instead it's the short, unexpected periods of good weather that play havoc with schedules. These brief windows of opportunity must be taken full advantage of, being far too valuable not to arrange a picnic with friends or play a round of golf. Who knows when the sun will shine again, meaning any overtime will have to wait for the next shower of rain.

Blame it on the weather

At first glance, many Icelanders might seem a bit surly and taciturn, but once the ice is broken, visitors will be surprised by their **warmth and hospitality**. Even at times when the service might not be up to expectations, keep calm; loud criticism doesn't cut it with the proud Icelanders. Try to appreciate that in this country which is so sparsely populated, every tiny village offers travellers accommodation and that people will try to assist visitors with any problem. Often the petrol station attendant or the cashier at the supermarket also manage the tourist information centre, or the school kid, whose boarding school bed you are sleeping in, serves breakfast too. The tourist season is short, far too short to warrant keeping the infrastructure going all year round. So it's all a matter of improvisation!

Keep calm!

One of the best ways of meeting Icelanders are the hot tubs, available not only at every swimming pool, but also in the most remote places. Hot tubs take on the function of pubs, which are rare here. Sitting there up to the neck in relaxing warm water, even the Icelandic reserve melts. Don't be surprised if the person sharing the tub uses the familiar form of address; and when Icelanders ask for your name they always mean the first name. This is nothing to do with a lack of respect, but with different **linguistic habits**. So forget titles and formal terms of address, in Iceland everyone is on first-name terms.

Bath instead of pub

Visitors lucky enough to be invited into a home should take off their shoes before entering the house. Incidentally, the same is true for swimming pools and youth hostels, where there is usually a sign up to that effect. Be prepared also to **write in the guest book**, and don't forget to give the hosts a few words of thanks for their hospitality at the end of a visit. A sure way to **put your foot in it** is to discuss whaling with Icelanders, assuming you are against it, as are the great majority of people in most other countries. This is a topic where most Icelanders display a good deal of **stubbornness** and usually refuse to be swayed by even the best arguments. Visitors should also take into account the Icelanders' extremely strong national identity, pride in their cultural heritage and sense of independence.

Festivals · Holidays · Events

PUBLIC HOLIDAYS

▶ **1 January**
New Year

▶ **March/April**
Maundy Thursday,
Good Friday,
Easter Sunday and
Easter Monday

▶ **3rd Thurs in April**
Start of Summer

▶ **1 May**
Labour Day

▶ **May**
Ascension Day,
Whit Sunday and Monday

▶ **17 June**
National Day

▶ **1st Mon in August**
Commerce Day

▶ **24–26 December**
Christmas

▶ **31 December**
New Year's Eve (from midday)

Food and Drink

These days, Iceland's cuisine is surprisingly varied, ranging from international fast-food dishes to gourmet restaurants – at least in Reykjavík. When local produce such as fish or lamb is served, it tends to be very fresh indeed and of excellent quality. Travellers aiming to eat relatively cheaply should look out for the menus of the day, tourist menus or lunch buffets, which can be had for about 2,500 ISK.

PRICE CATEGORIES

▶ **Inexpensive**
Simple restaurant, with the cost of a main dish below 1,700 ISK.

▶ **Moderate**
Average restaurant, with a main

dish costing between 1,700 and 2,600 ISK.

▶ **Expensive**
Very good restaurant. Main dish from 2,600 ISK.

Pantomime in Reykjavík

FOOD, FUN AND BRASS BANDS

Even though the Icelanders usually seem to show Nordic reserve they do like a party too. Many festivals have music and dance, food and drink, and an excuse can always be found; religious feast days, celebrations predating Christian times, but also traditional customs and historical dates make up the calendar of festivities.

The new year has hardly begun when celebrations mark the end of the Christmas period, which for the Icelanders lasts 13 days and is seen off on 6 January with fireworks and campfires.

Take a close look at the menu

The Þorrablót midwinter festival, which has no fixed date, goes back to Viking times and is a welcome excuse to banish the melancholy of the dark season. Þorrablót refers to the month of Þorri, which, according to the old calendar, began between the 19th and 25th January and marked the middle of winter. Today, Þorrablót is a feast for the palate, but only really for the Icelanders. The few tourists that are on the island at this time should study the restaurant menu carefully and consider whether sheep

Dainty ankles on show at the Gay Pride Festival in Reykjavík

Easter is one of the musical highlights of the year, with many concerts being put on. Large chocolate eggs grace people's breakfast tables, and the occasion calls for roast lamb.

The third Thursday in April sees the celebration of the first day of summer, the start of the long bright days providing a welcome excuse for processions with brass band music and street parties.

In early June, all the boats gather in the harbour for Seamen's Day, where rowing and swimming competitions are held, plus some more processions of course. In some coastal towns, Seamen's Day, which highlights the significance of the sea and seafaring, is the most important celebration of the year.

offal sausage, blackened sheep's heads, fermented shark, whale lard, salt meat or mutton testicles in a sour marinade are really their cup of tea.

Carnival up north

Food plays an important role in the Icelandic carnival too. On the Monday, doughnuts filled with cream or jam are eaten, on the Tuesday massive portions of pea soup with salted lamb, while on Ash Wednesday children dress up to go from house to house and collect sweets.

Roast lamb and chocolate

Gourmets also have a field day at the annual Food and Fun Festival in February, as foreign and local star chefs present their creations in various restaurants.

Commemorating independence

On 17 June 1944, the birthday of freedom fighter Jón Sigurðsson, the Republic of Iceland was founded. Since then, Independence Day is celebrated annually on 17 June, with colourful pageants, solemn speeches, music and dancing. The streets of

A crackling midnight fire on the Ingólfsfjörþur

Reykjavík are particularly lively on this day. For all Scandinavians, and the Icelanders too, the longest day of the year (21 June) has a particular significance that can only be appreciated fully by someone who has lived through a long dark winter up north. Midsummer is a happy occasion which in rural areas is celebrated with dancing and music around a midsummer fire – a party of good cheer.

From party to party

The Monday following the first weekend in August is a bank holiday, and (nearly) all Icelanders take advantage of a long weekend in the great outdoors, many spending a few relaxing days in a holiday cottage or camping. Part of this involves visiting one of the numerous festivals happening on that weekend.

The three-day celebrations on Heimaey, the largest of the Westman Islands, attract particularly high numbers of visitors.

After a short working week, the next party is already lined up for the following weekend: during the Gay Pride Festival the homosexual and lesbian community lead a bright and colourful parade through Reykjavík city centre.

Sheep and snow grouse

With the sheep being brought down from their summer pastures and the return of the horses from the highlands in September, the summer is finally over, which the Icelanders use as another pretext for open-air parties with plenty of drink. Christmas is celebrated the traditional way: on Christmas Eve, the presents are spread out under the Christmas tree, followed by roast snow grouse. Christmas Day again sees traditional cooking, when smoked lamb is served.

The old year is finally seen off on New Year's Eve with large fires and fireworks. At midnight everyone is out and about to see in the New Year noisily.

The taste buds can occasionally be strained by Icelandic cuisine;
but if lamb is served, don't worry, just dig in!

Icelandic food

Typically Icelandic, to the point where it is nearly a national dish, is **skýr**, a mixture of yoghurt and low-fat curd cheese that is often blended with fresh fruit or cream. **Súrmjölk**, a thick sour milk, can also be found on every breakfast table. **Harðfiskur** is air-dried, salted fish that works well in a strong-smelling fish soup. Specialities popular with Icelanders but less so with foreigners are: **hangikjöt** (spicy smoked lamb), **svið** (singed half of a sheep's head, first boiled then browned in the oven), **hákarl** (putrefied shark) or **pungur** (ram's testicles in a sour marinade). Menus often show puffins, which are caught in the traditional way using nets. Visitors wary of eating the cute birds can at least rest assured that their stocks are not in danger. The Icelanders' national drink is coffee, drunk at any time of day or night. If the food was a bit too rich, it is washed down with one or several glasses of **svarti dauði**, the local brandy, which is not called »Black Death« for nothing.

Restaurants

The restaurants featured in the chapter »Sights from A to Z« are divided into three categories, giving an idea of the price and standard of the restaurant. The www.restaurants.is website is an excellent guide to the island's gastronomic scene.

Health

Health centres – joint practices grouping together various doctors and specialists – or hospitals can be found in all Iceland's larger towns. In an emergency call the national **emergency number 112**. Medicines are only available in pharmacies (apóteks), which can be found in every town and have the usual opening hours. Some pharmacies stay open at night.

The **quality of tap water** is good everywhere, while the water from streams and rivers is also usually drinkable. Be careful however in thermal areas, where the water may taste and smell of sulphur.

Highlands

Crossing the Icelandic highlands is still something of an adventure, as nowhere else in Europe has such vast **untamed wildernesses**. There are good reasons why nobody ever settled here for long. Regardless of the mode of transport, whether on foot, by mountain bike, on horseback or by car, a highland crossing should be planned well in advance. The only exceptions are the organized tours which give a good overview of this primeval landscape.

The two most important tracks connecting the north with the south are the Kjölur Route and the Sprengisandur. Of these two, the Kjölur is the easier option, and in favourable conditions is even manageable for **vehicles without four-wheel drive**. The Sprengisandur is more challenging and definitely requires a four-wheel drive.

Kjölur and Sprengisandur

Apart from these two main road links there are several other shorter highland tracks and connecting link roads. As a general rule drivers should never leave the tracks, as the soil and vegetation are extremely sensitive, with car tyres leaving imprints that, like wounds on the landscape, won't heal for years.

! *Baedeker* TIP

Geared up for the highlands

The Icelandic road authority issues a weekly overview map detailing the state of the highland tracks (www.vegagerdin.is). The state television's teletext service contains information on pages 483 to 485. Call tel. 1777 daily from 8am to 4pm to receive information on the state of the roads.

▶ APPROXIMATE OPENING TIMES OF THE HIGHLAND TRACKS

▶ **Skaftártunga – Eldgjá**
from 8 June

▶ **Kaldalsvegur (F 550)**
from 15 June

▶ **Kjölur (F 35)**
from 15 June

▶ **Sigalda – Landmannalaugar**
from 17 June

▶ **Landmannaleið (F 225)**
from 19 June

▶ **Askja (F 88)**
from 20 June

▶ **Laki Fissure (F 206)**
from 20 June

▶ **Landmannalaugar – Eldgjá**
from 28 June

▶ **Sprengisandur (F 26)**
from 1 July

▶ **Southern Route
(F 210,
»Behind the mountains«)**
from 5 July

▶ **Eyjafjörður Highlands (F 82)**
from 9 July

Planning

When planning a drive into the highlands one thing should be borne in mind: the highland tracks are closed until well into the spring, as rivers in spate and mud make them impassable. Depending on the state they are in, the routes are then gradually opened.

Maps   It is essential for drivers to familiarize themselves with the planned route before departure. Petrol stations are sources of information too. Good maps and a **compass** are essential equipment during a tour through the highlands.

Fords   Rivers and streams without bridges require maximum concentration, as the points where **glacier rivers** ford the road can change quickly. Solo travellers should take their time and only cross glacier river fords once another vehicle comes into sight. Due to the lower water level, a river crossing is easier in the morning than in the evening.

Provisions   Sufficient provisions, water and petrol have to be brought along, as there is hardly any opportunity to stock up or fill the tank along the way. Apart from (very few) lodges, camping is the only **accommodation** en route. The weather being unpredictable, visitors should be prepared for strong winds, rain and snow showers. The weather forecast issued by the Meteorological Office in English also contains

the **highland weather**. Up to the end of June, and sometimes even later, visitors should be prepared for the highland tracks to be closed
still where rivers or mud have made them completely impassable.
Once these tracks are opened to traffic, most are only manageable by
jeep. Some of them should really only be attempted in convoy with
at least two vehicles.

Information

TOURIST INFORMATION IN THE UK

► **Brochure request line**
POSTCODE
tel. 020 7 636 96 60
www.visiticeland.com

TOURIST INFORMATION IN THE US

► **Icelandic Tourist Board**
655 Third Avenue
New York N.Y. 10017
Tel. 212 885 97 00
Fax 212 885 97 10
www.icelandtouristboard.com

TOURIST INFORMATION IN ICELAND

► **Reykjavík**
Tourist Info Center Reykjavík
Aðalstræti 2
IS-101 Reykjavík
Tel. 590 15 50, fax 590 15 51
www.visitreykjavik.is

► **Keflavík**
Tourist Information Center
Leifur Eiríksson Airport
IS-235 Keflavík
Tel. 425 03 30, fax 421 61 99
www.reykjanes.is

► **Reykjanes Peninsula**
Tourist Information Center
Kjarninn – Hafnargata 57
IS-230 Keflavík
Tel. 421 67 77, fax 421 31 50
www.reykjanes.is

► **East Iceland/Höfn**
Tourist Information Center
Nýheimar
IS-780 Höfn
Tel. 478 15 00, fax 478 16 07
www.east.is

► **South Iceland/Hveragerði**
Tourist Information Center
Sunnumörk 2 – 4
IS-810 Hveragerði
Tel. 483 46 01, Fax 483 46 04
www.south.is

► **West Iceland**
Tourist Information Center
Brúartorg
IS-310 Borgarnes
Tel. 437 22 14, fax 437 23 14
www.west.is

► **Western fjords**
Tourist Information Center
Aðalstræti 7
IS-400 Ísafjörður
Tel. 456 80 60, fax 456 51 85
www.vestfirdir.is

► **North Iceland**
Tourist Information Center

Hafnarstræti 82
IS-600 Akureyri
Tel. 550 07 20, fax 550 07 21
www.nordurland.is

► **East Iceland**
Tourist Information Center
Kaupvagur 6
IS-700 Egilsstaðir
Tel. 471 23 20, fax 471 18 63
www.east.is

**EMBASSIES AND
CONSULATES**

► **British Embassy Reykjavik**
Laufásvegur 31
IS-101 Reykjavík
(postal address:
PO Box 460, 121 Reykjavík)
Tel. 550 51 00, fax 550 51 05
www.britishembassy.gov.uk/
iceland

► **Honorary Vice-Consulate
Akureyri**
Central Hospital (Fjordungssjuk-
rahusid a Akureyri
v/Eyrarlandsveg
IS-602 Akureyri
(postal address:
PO Box 380, IS-602 Akureyri)
Tel. 436 01 02, fax 436 46 21

► **Irish Honorary Consulate**
Laufásvegur 31
IS-210 Gardabaer
Tel. 554 23 55
Fax 568 65 64
davidcsh@islandia.is

► **Irish diplomatic representation
via Irish Embassy, Denmark**
Ostbanegade 21
2100 Copenhagen
Tel. 550 51 00
Fax 00 45 35 43 18 58
irlemb_dk@yahoo.com

► **American Embassy Reykjavík**
Laufásvegur 21
IS-101 Reykjavík
Tel. 562 91 00
www.iceland.usembassy.gov

► **Embassy of Canada Reykjavík**
Túngata 14
IS-101 Reykjavík
Tel. 562 91 00
rkjvk@international.gc.ca

► **Australian diplomatic
representation via
Australian Embassy, Denmark**
Dampfaergevej 26, 2nd floor
2100 Copenhagen
Tel. 70 26 36 76, fax 70 26 36 86
www.denmark.embassy.gov.au

► **Australia/New Zealand diplomatic representation (via PR
of China)**
Landmark Tower 1, # 802
8 Dongsanhuan Bei Lu 100004
Beijing
Tel. 10 65 90 77 95/6, fax
10 65 90 78 01
www.iceland.org/cn

► **Embassy of Iceland UK**
2a Hans Street, London SW1X 0JE
Tel. 020 72 59 39
99, fax 020 72 45 96 49
www.iceland.org/uk

► **Icelandic Consulate in Ireland**
Cavendish House, Smithfield
Dublin
Tel. 01 87 29 299
Fax 01 87 29 877

► **Embassy of Iceland in the US**
1156 15th Street, NW, Suite 1200
Washington DC 20005-1704
Tel. 202 265 66 53
fax 202 265 66 56
www.iceland.org/us

► **Consulate General of
Iceland in New York**
800 3rd Avenue, 36th floor
New York, NY 10022
Tel. 212 593 27 00, fax
212 593 62 69
www.iceland.org/us

► **Embassy of Iceland in Canada**
Constitution Square
360 Albert Street, Stuite 710
Ottawa, Ontario
K1R 7X7
Tel. 613 482 19 44, fax
613 482 19 45
www.iceland.org/ca

► **Consulate of Iceland
in Australia**
16 Birriga Road, Bellevue Hill
Sydney 2000, NSW
Tel. 2 936 57 345
Fax 2 936 57 328
Iceland@bigpond.net.au

► **Consul of Iceland in
Auckland, New Zealand**
Eric Francis Barratt
c/o Sanford Ltd
22 Jellicoe Street
Auckland
Tel. 9 379 47 20
Fax 9 309 95 45
www.sanford.co.nz

► **Consul of Iceland in
Nelson, New Zealand**
Sigurgeir Pétursson
5 Noel Jones Drive, Atawahi
Nelson
Tel. 3 545 29 44
Fax 3 545 29 42
geiri@xtra.co.nz

ICELAND ON THE NET

► **www.visiticeland.com**
Website of the Icelandic Tourist
Board in several languages

► **www.icelandair.com**
Alongside extensive flight details
the site also contains a lot of
practical information on Iceland.

► **www.geysir.com**
Private Icelandic information
service

► **www.iceland.org**
Extensive background information
on Iceland

► **www.iww.is**
General information on Iceland

► **www.travelnet.is**
Practical information on Iceland

► **www.destination-
iceland.com**
Practical information, region by
region

► **www.exploreiceland.net**
Information on Iceland and its
activities

► **www.visitreykjavik.is,
www.reykjanes.is**
Information on the capital and the
southwest

► **www.whatson.is**
Events, restaurants, hotels and
background information on
Reykjavík

► **www.south.is**
Information on South Iceland

► **www.west.is**
Information on West Iceland

► **www.northwest.is**
Information on Northwest
Iceland

Language

The official language is Icelandic, a Germanic-Nordic language
which, due to the country's isolated position, has remained more or
less the same since the island's settlement by Norwegian immigrants,
unlike the other northern European languages which have changed
much over the course of the centuries. **Linguistic identity** is an important part of Icelandic culture, which tries to avoid overloading
the language with foreign words. Instead, modern concepts that
aren't available in the Old Icelandic vocabulary are formed by para-
phrasing. Thus, the word »tölva« (computer) was put together from
the words »tala« (number) and »völva« (clairvoyant). The Icelandic
alphabet has the special characters þ, ð, and æ, but the letters c, q, w
and z are missing. Apart from that, the vowels a, e, i, o, u and y occur with and without accents, resulting in differing pronunciations.
Icelandic pronunciation is relatively difficult, and few tourists master
it straight away. Luckily many Icelanders speak good English, so there are few problems with communication.

ICELANDIC LANGUAGE GUIDE

Pronunciation

a	as in 'art', but before ng or nk like 'ow', before gi like 'I'
á	like 'ow'
e	like an open e
é	as in 'share'
ý, í	as in 'it'
ó	as in 'no'
u	as in German 'über'
ú	as in 'zoo'
au	approx. as in 'purr'

æ	as in 'I'
ei	as in 'pray'
ð	like the voiced 'th'
f	at the beginning of a word and before k, s and t like f, otherwise like a v
r	rolled
v	like v
þ	like the unvoiced 'th'

Basic words

yes	já
no	nei

Getur þú hjálpað mér? Can you help me?

please	gjörðu svo vel
thanks	takk
Good morning/Good day	Góðan dag
Good evening	Gott kvöld
Good night	Góða nótt
Good bye	Vertu sæll/vertu sæl
Excuse me	Afsakið
I don't speak Icelandic	Ég tala ekki íslensku
I don't understand	Ég skil ekki
Do you speak English?	Talar þú ensku?
How much is it?	Hvað kostar þetta?
Can you help me?	Getur þú hjálpað mér?
Where is ...?	Hvar er ...?
I need	Mig vantar
I'd like	Ég ætla að fá

Accommodation

Do you have a room?	Er laust herbergi?
breakfast	morgunmatur
dinner	kvöldmatur
double room	tveggja manna herbergi
guesthouse	gistiheimili
hotel	hótel
lunch	hádegismatur
room	herbergi
shower	sturta
single room	eins manns herbergi
sleeping bag	sumarhús
youth hostel	farfuglaheimili

Food and drink

beer	bjór/öl
low-alcohol beer	Pilsner
butter	smjör
cheese	ostur
dried fish	harðfiskur
Icelandic quark (low-fat curd cheese)	skyr
milk	mjólk
restaurant	veitingastaður
sandwich	samloka
shark	hákarl
smoked lamb	hangikjöt

tourist menu .... sumarréttir
white/red wine .... hvít-/rauðvín

On the road

arrival / departure .... koma / brottför
bank .... banki
blind road .... blindhæð
bus station .... umferðarmiðstöð
city bus .... strætó
drive carefully .... akið varlega
ferry .... ferja
garage .... verkstæði
harbour/port .... höfn
hillside .... brekka
hospital .... sjúkrahús
information .... upplýsingar
mortal danger .... lífshætta
one-way street .... einstefna
open-air pool .... sundlaug
overland bus .... rúta
petrol station .... bensínstöð
plane .... flugvél
police .... lögregla
post .... póstur
round-trip .... fram og tilbaka
street, path .... gata, braut, vegur
taxi .... leigubíll
telephone .... sími
ticket .... miði
timetable .... ferðaáætlun
to the left / right .... til vinstri / hœgri

Geographical terms

east .... austur
west .... vestur
north .... norður
south .... suður
mountain .... fjall
mountain range .... fjöll
bay .... vik
cave .... hellir
farm .... bær
fjord / fjords .... fjörður / firðir

Talar þú ensku? Do you speak English?

forest	skógur/mörk
glacial outwash plain	sandur
glacier	jökull
gravel plain	melur
hot spring	hver
island	ey/eyja
lake	vatn
lava field	hraun
plain	völlur
pond	tjörn
river	á
river bank	bakki
sandbank	eyri
small island	hólmi, hólmur
valley	dalur
warm spring	laug
waterfall	foss

Weather

The weather is good	veðrið er gott/fínt/ágætt
calm	logn
cloudy	skýað

fog	þoka
rain	rigning
storm	stormur/rok
sunny	bjart
sunshine	sólskín
weather forecast	veðurspá
wind direction	átt
wind speed	vindstígur

Days of the week

Monday	mánudagur
Tuesday	þriðjudagur
Wednesday	miðvikdagur
Thursday	fimmtudagur
Friday	föstudagur
Saturday	laugardagur
Sunday	sunnudagur

Numbers

0	núll
1	einn, eitt
2	tveir
3	þrir
4	fjórir
5	fimm
6	sex
7	sjö
8	átta
9	níu
10	tíu
11	ellefu
12	tólf
13	þrettán
14	fjórtán
15	fimmtán
16	sextán
17	sautján
18	átján
19	nítján
20	tuttugu
30	þrjátíu
40	fjörutíu

50	fimmtíu
60	sextíu
70	sjötíu
80	áttatíu
90	níutíu
100	hundrað
1000	þúsund

Literature

► Baedeker Special p. 92

Media

Newspapers For a quick check on the weather forecast, take a look at one of the three national daily newspapers (Morgunblaðið, DV or Dagur Tíminn); English-language newspapers are available, at least in the summer and with the usual delays, at some larger newsstands. The English-language magazine **Iceland Review** is published four times a year and is well worth getting for its excellent photographs and features on many aspects of Icelandic life (www.icelandreview.com).

? DID YOU KNOW ...?

■ ... that until 1983 Icelandic television took a break in July, and until 1987 one day a week was kept free of television?

A round-up of the news in English is broadcast on the public-service **radio** from 1 June to 1 September Mon – Fri at 7.31am on 92.4 and 93.5 FM. The BBC broadcasts on 90.9 FM. Foreign films on Icelandic **television** and in cinemas are shown in the original version with subtitles. Many hotels also have satellite TV receiving English-language programmes.

Midnight sun

Due to its position just below the Arctic Circle, summer nights in the whole of Iceland are light-filled and short. In the north, it's even possible to see the midnight sun. To be precise, it is not really the midnight sun, as the Icelanders take liberties with their time zone.

This would be a beautiful sunset – if the sun did actually go down...

Iceland runs on Greenwich Mean Time all year round, even though the island really lies one or two time zones further west. As a result, at midsummer (21 June) the sun can be seen until after midnight in Akureyri, but then disappears for a short time below the horizon. Visitors who want to see the real midnight sun have to take a trip to Grímsey Island, situated exactly on the Arctic Circle around 100km/ 62 miles north of Akureyri. In the winter, the days are extremely short; in December and January, the sun only appears for 3.5 to 4.5 hours. Due to the shifted time zone, at this time of year the sun only comes up around midday. By early March however, the days have over ten hours and by early May as much as 17 hours.

Money

The unit of currency is the **Icelandic krona** (króna, ISK). Coins in circulation have values of 1, 5, 10, 50 and 100 krónur. All coins show Iceland's four guardian spirits on the front and sea animals on the back. The National Bank of Iceland issues notes of 500, 1,000, 2,000 and 5,000 krónur.

Currency

The rate of exchange in Iceland is more favourable than elsewhere. The airport and all banks have ATMs where money can be withdrawn using a bank card. Paying

i	Exchange rates
■	£1 = 210 ISK
	US$1 = ISK
	€1 = 175 ISK
	1CAN$ = 1.5 ISK
	1AUS$ = 90ISK
	1ZAR = 13 ISK
	(November 2008).

ISLAND OF POETS AND WRITERS

Allegedly one out of every ten Icelanders will write a book sometime in their lives! And when they are not writing, they buy books – on average four per year – and probably get round to reading quite a few of those during the dark winter months.

In terms of literature, Iceland has a lot more to offer than just Halldór Laxness. These days, a few titles of modern Icelandic literature are being translated into English. Here is a small selection:

A bitter testament

Written in a lively style, the historic novel *The Sacrifice* by Vilborg Davidsdóttir is set in 14th-century Iceland and is based on a true story. At her mother's death bed, the 18-year old Katrin is told about a bitter testament. Her inheritance is going to the church, and she herself has to enter a convent. In doing this, her mother is expiating an old sin. Katrin acquiesces in order to appease God; however, this is only the beginning of her difficulties. Earlier books, such as *The Well of Fates* and *The Witches' Judgement*, telling the story of a slave in the Viking era, were influenced by Icelandic sagas.

Angels of the universe

Another novel in translation, Guðbergur Bergsson's *The Swan* is the award-winning story of a nine-year old girl sent to a remote country farm to serve her probation for shoplifting, and discovering her own kind of freedom in her new environment. Also worth reading is Einar Már Gudmundsson's *Angels of the Universe*. Set in the

1960s, the bleak story of a young man's mental illness unfolds, as Paul describes his life growing up in a working-class family and frequent retreat into a fantasy world of his own, as well as his stay in a psychiatric hospital. *Brushstrokes of Blue* is a recommended collection of modern Icelandic poetry that also includes some of Bergsson's poems.

The Icelandic Wallander

Arnaldur Indriðason's *Silence of the Grave* is the second detective novel featuring the melancholy Inspector

A testament to terror, broken families, living 'n subterranean squalor – Icelandic contemporary literature is just like real life.

Erlendur from Reykjavik, with an extremely high level of suspense. Human bones are found in a con-struction site, and more and more gruesome details are gradually un-earthed. Nearly an Icelandic version of Henning Mankell's much-loved Swedish Inspector Wallander! Readers who have become fans of Indriðason through this novel will equally love his previous book, *Jar City* , recently made into a successful film.

Over the top

The novel *Devil's Island* by Einar Kárason is a crazy story about a fairly eccentric but lovable family living in Camp Thule, a problematic social housing project near Reykjavík. The novel charts the cultural clashes with the American popular culture brought by US troops when Iceland became a strategically important NATO out-post. Britain's popular *Mastermind* gameshow host, the late Magnus Magnusson, provided the introduc-tion. Remember Magnusson's famous catchphrase? 'I've started so I'll finish.'

by credit card (Visa and Mastercard) is no problem in Iceland, while American Express cards are less readily accepted. With the value of the currency falling amidst the country's near-bankruptcy in the credit crisis of 2008, the notoriously expensive destination has seen its prices go down – good news for tourists.

National Parks

Iceland's four national parks count amongst the most beautiful and most popular natural landscapes on the island and offer many opportunities for hiking tours.

Jökulsárgljúfur

At 25km/15.5 miles long, 0.5km/0.3 of a mile wide and over 100m/328ft deep, the Jökulsá Canyon in the northeast of the island is one of the most impressive erosion gorges in Iceland. Jökulsárgljúfur National Park (120 sq km/46 sq miles) was established in 1973. A particularly spectacular view of the gorge can be had between the **Dettifoss** and the Syðra Þórunnarfjall. The hiking trail from the Dettifoss to the campsite at Ásbyrgi runs along wide stretches of the gorge. Alongside the gorge, the Dettifoss and some other waterfalls are worth seeing. The best access routes to the area are the [F 862] west of the **Jökulsá á Fjöllum** and the [864] east of the valley. Information can be picked up in Ásbyrgi.

The Svartifoss in Skaftafell National Park

The Skaftafell national park (4,800 sq km/1,850 sq miles) was established as early as 1967 and has been extended several times since then. It stretches from the Grímsvötn amidst the **Vatnajökull** in the north, to the Skeiðararjökull or Skaftafellsjökull in the south. The mountain ridge of the Skaftafellsheiði forms the core of the national park. A pretty view of the Skaftafellsjökull can be had from the Gláma mountain viewpoint at 600m/1,968ft high. Its position right on the ring road and the large campsite make access to the national park easier.

Skaftafell

The relatively small Snæfellsjökull lies at the top of the **Snæfellsnes Peninsula** in the west of Iceland. The national park (167 sq km/65 sq miles) was established in 2001 to protect the lava formations, the spectacular coast and traces of old settlements. The Snæfellsjökull, a volcanic cone that is glaciered over but still active, is considered the king of Icelandic mountains. There are many hiking trails in the national park, of which some are waymarked. Information can be picked up in the Hellissandur post office.

Snæfellsjökull

Established in 1930, Þingvellir National Park is the oldest in the country, comprising 50 sq km/19 sq miles. The park's proximity to the capital Reykjavík (50km/31 miles to the east) and its historic significance make it one of the most-visited tourist destinations in Iceland. The particular interest of the area lies in its numerous tectonic fissures and faults, which give an **insight into the geology of the island**. The information centre is located at the junction of the [36], [52] and [361], near the campsite, and has information on the national park, as well as maps with marked hiking trails and sights.

Þingvellir

Personal Safety

Iceland is one of the world's safest destinations. Whilst the crime rate is rising in the capital Reykjavík, compared to most Western countries it remains very low. In the countryside there is **hardly any crime**. Women travelling on their own should experience no problems in Iceland. However, while many Icelanders don't lock their cars or houses, tourists travelling with cars packed to the brim should exercise a modicum of caution in order to avoid unpleasant surprises.

Post · Telecommunications

Post offices can be found in every larger community and are usually open Mon–Fri from 8.30am–4.30pm. Sending airmail letters (up to

Post offices, postage

► DIALLING CODES

► **From Iceland …**
… to Britain: 00 44
… to the US/Canada: 00 1
… to Australia: 00 61
… to New Zealand: 00 64
… to South Africa: 00 27

The zero of the following local dialling code is dropped.

► **Calling Iceland**
00 354 (followed by the 7-digit number)

20 g) and postcards within Iceland and to Scandinavia costs ISK 65, letters and postcards to Britain and other European countries ISK 80/90, and to the US and worldwide ISK 90/120, depending on whether it is sent by B (economy) or A (priority) post.

Phone boxes   Iceland is not exactly littered with phone boxes; post offices and petrol stations offer the best chance of finding one. All phones offer direct dialling within Iceland and abroad, and most are **card and coin-operated**, with credit card phones less common. Phone cards to the value of ISK 500 and 1000 are available from post offices. Calling within Iceland requires dialling the 7-digit number; there are no local dialling codes.

Mobile phones   Multi-band mobile phones with activated roaming may be used on Iceland's GSM network in populated areas. Telecom Iceland (www.siminn.is) hires out mobile phones which can access the NMT network, which covers the interior and more remote areas. C-network mobile phones may only be imported with authorization. While Iceland has the highest number of mobile phones per capita in the world, there is no signal in the highlands; there are also some reception dead zones along the ring road.

Prices

Living costs in Iceland are substantially higher than most visitors will be used to. Alcoholic beverages in particular are very expensive.

► WHAT DOES IT COST?

Double room:
from 4,000 ISK

Main dish:
from 1,000 ISK

1 litre of petrol:
150 ISK

Glass of beer:
650 ISK

Shopping · Souvenirs

Even smaller villages nearly always have a grocery store or supermarket; larger petrol stations also often sell groceries. The choice of fruit and veg is significantly smaller and more expensive than in other countries, with almost everything **imported or grown under glass**. Shops are   usually open Mon – Fri 9am – 5pm or 6pm, Sat 9am – 1pm or 4pm. Large supermarkets often stay open longer and also at weekends, sometimes even up to 11pm. In the summer, souvenir and craft shops will sometimes open at weekends too.

Opening times

The classic souvenir is the Icelandic jumper made from thick sheep's wool with a characteristic pattern. In Reykjavík, they are sold on nearly every corner, and elsewhere they can be found in almost all souvenir shops. Alongside woollens, other recommended souvenirs are silver jewellery, ceramics and crafts made from natural materials.

Icelandic jumper

The classic souvenir: an Icelandic jumper

VAT refund   Foreign shoppers can claim a refund for certain items bought in Iceland, which can be as much as 15 % of the selling price. For this, the item needs to have been bought in a shop displaying the »Tax-Free-Shopping« symbol and be accompanied by a Tax-Free-Cheque made out at the till. However, the lowest sum per till receipt for a tax refund is 4,000 ISK. Visitors leaving the country no later than three months after purchase may reclaim Tax-Free vouchers up to a value of 5,000 ISK directly at the counter of Landsbanki Islands at Keflavík airport. Otherwise the purchases, apart from woollens, have to be shown at customs (for more information see: www.icelandrefund.com).

Shopping in   In Reykjavík, shopaholics will be in their element, as the capital has a
Reykjavik   surprisingly large selection of fine fashion and designer outlets.

Sport and Outdoors

Iceland is a **paradise for active holidaymakers**, offering opportunities for a great variety of sports and activities. Visitors who don't fancy walking or horse riding on their own can have specialist tour operators put together a tailor-made programme for them or join a group holiday. There is a wide variety of activities ranging from glacier tours, fishing and horse riding trips, deep-sea fishing, hiking and rafting tours, to bird and whale watching excursions amongst others.

Fishing   Iceland is famous for its excellent salmon and trout fishing. The salmon season starts around mid-June and lasts until mid-September, while trout is fished from April/May to late September, depending on the stretch of water. End of May to late August is the best time for **deep-sea fishing**. Salmon fishing licences have to be applied for in good time from the National Angling Association (▶ p. 102) and are extremely expensive. Including accommodation and a local guide, one day at a good salmon river costs on average 100,000 ISK. Licences for trout angling are much cheaper (around 7,000 ISK) and may be purchased at short notice too.

Glacier tours   The glaciers of Langjökull, Mýrdalsjökull, Snaefellsjökull and Vatnajökull can be explored by ski, snow mobile or »Super Jeep« (tour operators ▶ p. 102).

Golf   All Iceland's golf courses, of which there are over 60, are available to guests paying a green fee of 3,500 to 7,000 ISK. Some courses, such as the one in Hafnarfjörður and on the Westman Islands lie in a spectacular volcanic landscape. At the end of June, the Akureyri golf club (▶ p. 103) organizes the Arctic Open, an international tournament played by the light of the midsummer sun – if it shows its face.

Where to now? On the glacier road conditions are slightly different

Bikes for shorter rides can be rented in Reykjavík and many other places. For information and rental, BSÍ Travel (► p. 108) is a useful contact.

Longer tours and highland crossings in particular should be planned carefully and are best done on your own bike, which needs to be ready for this severe test. It is not just the equipment that has to take a lot of strain however, but the rider too: **steep climbs, gravel roads, the rain and cold and the relentless wind**, which attacks without mercy and has ground down many a rider, are permanent company. Despite all this, there are cyclists everywhere taking the challenge and being rewarded for their efforts with unforgettable experiences. Conditions are most extreme in the highlands, where endless gravel tracks present a tough challenge to even the best equipment and the highest fitness levels. Cycling in the highlands is not made any easier by the fact that the bike is heavily laden and there is no bike shop anywhere nearby should there be a problem. A helpful contact for the preparation of bigger trips is the Icelandic Mountainbike Club in Reykjavík. Every Thursday evening from 8pm their clubhouse is open for people to swap experiences (►p. 103). The club also runs a website with many useful links.

> ## ! *Baedeker* TIP
>
> ### 42 km or less
>
> Admit it: The first thing you think of when you hear the name Iceland is marathons. Then Reykjavík in the second half of August is the right place for you to take part in the international Reykjavík marathon. If the whole 42km/26mi is too much for you, you can run the half marathon or 10km/6mi. The organizers of the Mývatn Run and the Highland Marathon between Landmannalaugar and Þórsmörk are always happy to have international participants as well. Infos and registration for the Reykjavík marathon at: marathon@marathon.is, www.marathon.is

Cyclists in Iceland have to contend with all that nature throws at them

Rafting   Excursions with rafting boats for beginners and advanced levels are available on the Hvítá glacier river in southern Iceland and some glacier rivers in northern Iceland (tour operators ► p. 103).

Horse-riding   From time immemorial, the relatively small but robust Icelandic horses have been the ideal means of transport for Icelanders. Now a variety of farms and tour operators (► p. 103) offer tourists too the chance to go for **rides on Icelandic horses**. There is a wide choice, from hacks by the hour to a challenging two-week highland crossing on the historic Kjölur Route.

! *Baedeker* TIP

Landsmót

In 1950, aficionados of Icelandic horses met for the first Landsmót at the historical spot of the Alþing in Þingvellir. It was an opportunity to hold races at a gallop or »flying pace« (skeið), to judge breeding stock and to present competition horses. Initially only around 100 horses took part; today, over 1,000 animals come together for the largest competition event in Iceland, taking place every other year at varying locations (the last was in 2008 in Vindheimamelar near Varmhalíð, the next will be in 2010). The Landsmót is an unmissable event for horse lovers, who will not see so many Icelandic horses in one place anywhere else. For more information, see: www.landsmot.is

Icelanders love **skiing**, but very few tourists visit in the wintertime. The alpine centres with around 100 ski lifts in all are usually small and don't compare to the ski circus in the Alps. Après-ski opportunities are very limited, but cross-country skiers exploring away from the regular pistes have the chance to really **experience nature**. There are ski

Hiking lodges Map

Norðurfjörður

Tröllabotnar   Tunguhryggur
    Barkardalur

Þúfnavellir   Glerárdalur   Breiðavík
    Austurdalur   Suðurárbotnar   Húsavík
        Bræðrafell   Herðubreiðar-
    Dyngjufjalla-   lindir   Vöðlavík
Lambahraun   dalur
        Askja   Snæfell
Þjófadalir   Laugafell   Geldingafell
Þverbrekknamúli   Kverkfjöll   Kollumúlavatn
    Hvítárnes   Nýidalur   Lónsöræfi
    Hagavatn   25 mi   Geithellnadalur
Hlöðuvellir   50 km
        ©Baedeker
    Landmanna-
    laugar
Álftavatn   Hrafntinnusker
Emstrur   Hvanngil
    Þórsmörk

centres in Bláfjöll, Ísafjörður, Siglufjörður, Ólafsfjörður, Dalvík, Akureyri and Húsavík. Summer skiing is possible on the Langjökull and the Kerlingarfjöll from late June to late August. Equipment can be hired locally.

Nearly all towns, even the smallest, have an **open-air or covered pool**. Thanks to the abundant geothermal energy, the water in the open-air pools is heated to a comfortable 28–30 °C/82–86 °F even in winter, making the swimming pool a stand-in for the often non-existent local pub as a place to meet with friends and acquaintances. Of course, nearly every swimming pool has a **hot pot** with water of at least bathtub temperature – a perfect place to survive cold and rainy days.

Swimming

At least ten different bird rocks lure birdwatchers to the coasts of Iceland every year. The Westman Islands are worth seeing for the diversity of birdlife and the large colonies of puffins, the Mývatn for its various types of duck, and the **Látrabjarg, one of the biggest bird rocks in the world**, in the western fjords. More birdrocks can be found on the Reykjanes Peninsula, for instance the easily accessible Hafnaberg.

Birdwatching

To see a whale surface right next to your boat is an unforgettable experience. The chances of spotting a whale in the waters around Iceland are not bad, and often two or three different types of whale can be seen during an outing. The most frequently observed are **minke**

Whale watching

▶ SPORT AND OUTDOORS

FISHING

▶ **The National Angling Association**
Bolholt 6
105 Reykjavík
Tel. 553 15 10, fax 568 43 63
www.angling.is

GLACIER TOURS

▶ **Glacier Tours**
Hafnarbraut 15
780 Hornafjörður

Tel. 478 10 00, fax 471 21 67
www.glaciertours.is

▶ **Allrahanda Excursions**
Funahöfði 17
110 Reykjavík
Tel. 540 13 13, fax 540 13 10
www.allrahanda.is

▶ **Icelandic Adventure**
Álftaland 17
108 Reykjavík

The chances of seeing a whale in Iceland are very high. Whether the creature in view will also dive and show off its tail fin is less certain however.

Tel. 577 55 00
Fax 577 55 11
www.icemail.is

GOLF

► **Akureyri Golf Club**
P.O. Box 600
Akureyri
Tel. 462 29 74
Fax 461 17 55

CYCLING

► **BSÍ Travel**
Vatnsmýrarvegur 10
101 Reykjavík
Tel. 591 10 20, fax 591 10 50
www.dice.is

► **The Icelandic Mountainbike Club**
Brekkustígur 2
Reykjavík, Tel./fax 562 00 99
www.mfjallahjolaklubburinn.is

RAFTING

► **Activity Tours**
P.O. Box 75
560 Varmahlíð
Tel. 453 83 83, fax 453 83 84
www.rafting.is

► **Nonni Travel**
Brekkugata 5
P.O. Box 336
602 Akureyri
Tel. 461 18 41, fax 461 18 43
www.nonnitravel.is

HORSE RIDING

► **Íshestar**
Sörlaskeið 26
220 Hafnarfjörður
Tel. 555 70 00, fax 555 70 01
www.ishestar.is

► **Pólar Hestar**
Grytubakki 2
601 Akureyri

Tel. 463 31 79
Fax 463 31 44
www.polarhestar.is

► **Hestasport/Activity Tours**
P.O. Box 75
560 Varmahlíð
Tel. 453 83 83
Fax 453 83 84
www.riding.is

WHALE WATCHING

► **Sæferðir**
Smiðjustígur 3
340 Stykkishólmur
Tel. 438 14 50
Fax 438 10 50
www.saeferdir.is

► **Norður Sigling/ North Sailing**
Gamla Baukur
P.O. Box 122
640 Húsavík
Tel. 464 23 50
Fax 464 23 51
www.nordursigling.is

► **Elding**
At Reykjavík and Hafnarfjörður harbours
Tel. 555 35 65, fax 554 74 20
www.elding.is

HIKING

► **Ferðafélag Íslands**
(Icelandic Touring Association)
Mörkin 6
108 Reykjavík
Tel. 568 25 33, fax 568 25 35
www.fi.is

► **Útivist**
Laugavegur 178
105 Reykjavík
Tel. 562 10 00
Fax 562 10 01
www.utivist.is

and humpback whales, but dolphins, harbour porpoises and killer whales also exist off Iceland. In the waters around Ólafsvík on the Snæfellsnes peninsula, even one of the extremely rare blue whales sometimes puts in an appearance – a possibility offered by very few places on earth.

Hiking

Ferðafélag Íslands

Hiking is the best way to experience the spectacular nature of Iceland. Founded in 1927, the Icelandic Touring Association (Ferðafélag Íslands; ▶ p. 103) has taken it upon itself to support walkers in their expeditions into remote areas. The association manages 34 simple mountain lodges spread over the whole country, some of which are serviced by a lodge manager. However, all require walkers to bring their own food. The association also organizes tours and manages the upkeep of the waymarked trails. Hiking tours are on offer all year round, in the winter usually restricted to day or weekend tours, but in the summer extending to longer hikes. Longer tours have to be booked a month in advance, weekend tours four days ahead, while day trips can usually be arranged on the day. Participants have to bring their own food and gear for the sleeping-bag accommodation. Independent travellers should check ahead as to whether the lodge of their choice is being used by a larger group, as capacities are limited. They tend to be simple mattress accommodation; usually there are some cooking facilities, and some have nearby grounds that can be used for camping. Depending on the cabin's standards, accommodation prices range from 2,000 ISK to 3,000 for members (2,500 to 3,300 ISK for non-members; membership costs around 5,000 ISK).

Útivist

Útivist (▶ p. 103) also runs six mountain lodges and organizes various tours. Hikers wanting to use the Útivist lodges should book early as these huts also only have a limited number of beds. The orange-coloured refuges in the highlands and on the coast are only intended to be used in emergencies.

Time/Time and Date

Iceland is on **Greenwich Mean Time** (GMT) all year round.

Tour Operators

A number of tour operators feature an extensive Iceland programme, ranging from Fly and Drive via hiking, cycling and horseback riding holidays to tailor-made tours.

▶ **Icelandic Travel (UK)**
Whitehall House, Nenthead
Alston, Cumbria, CA9 3PS
Tel. 01 434 38 14 40
www.icelandic-travel.com

▶ **Iceland Saga Travel (US)**
3 Freedom Square
Nantucket, MA 02554
Tel. 1 866 423 72 42/508 825 92 92
Fax 508 825 99 33
www.icelandsagatravel.com

▶ **Exodus UK**
Grange Mills, Weir Road
London, SW12 0NE
Tel. 02 08 675 55
www.exodus.co.uk

▶ **The Nordic Company (US)**
5930 Seminole Center Court
Suite C
Madison, Wisconsin 53711
Tel. 888 806 72 26, fax
608 288 80 71
www.nordicco.com

▶ **The Great Canadian
Travel Company (Canada/US)**
158 Fort St
Winnipeg, MB, R3C 1C9
Tel. 1 866 949 01 29

333 N. Michigan Avenue
Suite 711
Chicago, IL 60801
Tel. 888 806 72 26
Fax 608 288 80 71
www.iceland-experience.com

▶ **Nordic Travel (Australia)**
Suite 4B, 600 Military Road
Mosman (Sydney), NSW 2088
Tel. 02 99 68 17 83
Fax 02 99 68 19 24
www.icelandic-travel.com

▶ **Wild Earth Travel (NZ)**
538 Montreal Street
PO Box 7218, Christchurch
Tel. 3 365 13 55
Fax 3 365 13 00
www.wildearth-travel.com

▶ **Isafold Travel Ltd.**
Sudurhraun 2 B
IS-210 Gardabar
Tel. 544 88 66, fax 544 88 69
www.isafoldtravel.is

▶ **Iceland Total/Icelandair**
Skúturogar 13A
104 Reykjavík
Tel. 585 43 78, fax 28 38 72
www.icelandair.de

Transport

By air

Iceland boasts a fairly comprehensive network of domestic flight routes. Particularly popular are the flights from Reykjavík to Akureyri and to the Westman Islands. **Domestic flights** depart in Reykjavík from the city airport. The main routes are served several times a day by the two largest companies, Air Iceland and Íslandsflug. All in all the following destinations are served: Akureyri, Egilsstadir, Ísafjörður, Hornafjörður, Bíldudalur, Gjögur, Sauðárkrókur, Vopnafjörður,

Bridge to nowhere: the omnipresent fog makes driving difficult

Grímsey and Heimaey. A one-way ticket from Reykjavík to Akureyri starts at 8,700. Visitors wanting to fly more often should get an **Air Iceland Pass** with four, five or six coupons. Within its 30-day validity, any destination served by Air Iceland can be booked. The Air Iceland Pass is available at any branch of the airline outside Iceland. Also on offer is the »Fly As You Please« Pass, valid for twelve days and for any number of flights on all domestic Air Iceland routes. Several smaller companies such as Mýflug offer charter and sightseeing flights which, on a clear day, give great views of the island's glaciers and volcanoes. For more information, contact the airlines (▶ p. 108).

By ferry

The ***Baldur*** ferry takes passengers and cars from Stykkishólmur via Flatey to Brjánslækur, considerably shortening travel times to the Westfjords.
The ***Herjólfur*** ferry runs between Þorlákshöfn and Heimæy, and takes passengers and cars on to the Westman Islands.

By bus

Scheduled coaches can take visitors to nearly every town and village in Iceland. In summer, even the **highland routes** are served by buses suited to uneven terrain. Tickets are available from the bus driver or the bus station; there is no need to book ahead. The buses are in principle only obliged to take a limited number of bikes (often max 5).

Most of the country can be accessed by bus. One-way tickets are expensive however, with the 400km/248 miles from Reykjavík to Akureyri costing around 8,700 ISK. Children under 4 travel free, and
those between 4 and 11 pay half-fare. Taking the bus becomes much
cheaper with one of the bus passes. The »Full Circle« or »Ring Pass«
(Hringmiði, €305) is valid for one **circuit of the island** on the ring
road with as many stop-offs as pass holders want, but the direction
of travel (east or westwards) must be set at the beginning of the tour
and then stuck with. This pass has no time limit, but in the winter
the connection between Akureyri and Höfn is suspended.

The Ring Pass including the Western Fjords is similar to the regular
Ring Pass, but allows travellers to explore the Westfjord circuit as
well. This pass is only valid between early June and late August.
The Omnibus passport (1 week €350, 2 weeks €490, 3 weeks €630,
4 weeks €700) can be used on nearly all scheduled Icelandic bus services up to a period of four weeks. Not included in this are the highland buses, e. g. to Landmannalaugar or Þórsmörk. With this option,
routes may be travelled several times, and there is no restriction on
direction of travel. Another option is the Full Circle Passport which
includes trips into the interior (€365). All bus passes are valid between early June and 31 Aug; in the wintertime only a limited range
are on offer. The bus passes are available in Reykjavík from the Trex
company, from the tourist information and the youth hostel, as well
as at the bus station in Akureyri and Seyðisfjörður.

By car

With a length of just under 1,400km/870 miles, the ring road forms
Iceland's most important lifeline and is the centrepiece of the overall
road network, which covers more than 10,000km/6,200 miles. With
a lot of financial expenditure and years of hard work, the ring road
has become a near-complete and quite easily negotiable tarmacked
route. The gravel sections become shorter year on year, meaning that
these days drivers can use any car to go round the island. Drivers leaving the ring road however, can expect substantially more **gravel
stretches, corrugated-iron tracks and potholes**. These slow travellers
down substantially, jarring the passengers and leaving their mark on
the car at the end of the holiday. Where the gravel cover is loose,
stones thrown up by oncoming and overtaking cars are always a risk
to the paintwork and the windscreen. Due to the required river crossings, the highland tracks – with the exception of the Kjölur and Kaldidalur – are only suitable for four-wheel-drive vehicles. In the winter, the main roads are the first to be cleared of snow, while the minor roads can take a bit longer to be passable again.

The quality of the roads may be gauged more or less by their num-
bering. The ring road deservedly bears the number 1, the other main

▶ TRANSPORT

AIRLINES

▶ **Air Iceland**
Reykjavík Airport
Tel. 570 30 30, fax 570 30 01
www.airiceland.is

▶ **Íslandsflug**
Reykjavík Airport
Tel. 570 80 30, fax 570 80 31
www.islandsflug.is

▶ **Mýflug**
Reykjahlíð Airport
Tel. 464 44 00
Fax 464 44 01
www.myflug.is

FERRIES

▶ **Seatours/Ferry Baldur**
Smiðjustígur 3
340 Stykkishólmur
Tel. 438 14 50, fax 438 10 50
www.saeferdir.is

▶ **Herjólfur**
Básaskersbryggja 900
Vestmannaeyjar
Tel. 481 28 00, fax 481 29 91
www.herjolfur.is

BUS COMPANIES

▶ **BSÍ (umbrella organization)**
Vatnsmýrarvegi 10
101 Reykjavík
Tel. 562 10 11
www.bsi.is

▶ **Trex**
Hesthals 10
110 Reykjavík
Tel. 587 60 00
Fax 567 49 69
www.trex.is

▶ **Reykjavík Excursions**
BSÍ bus station

Vatnsmýrarvegur 10
101 Reykjavík
Tel. 580 54 00
Fax 552 30 62
www.re.is

▶ **Bustravel South**
Skógarhlíð 10
105 Reykjavík
Tel. 511 26 00
www.bustravel.is

TRAVELLING BY CAR

▶ **Breakdown service**
Félag Íslenskra Bifreiðaeigenda
Borgartúni 33
105 Reykjavík
Tel. 414 99 99, fax 414 99 98
www.fib.is
Breakdown service (Mon – Fri
8.15am – 4.30pm): tel. 5 112 112
Outside these times: VAKA break-
down service, tel. 567 67 00

▶ **Information on the
current state of the roads**
Tel. 17 77 (daily 8am – 4pm) or at
www.vegagerdin.is

CAR RENTAL

▶ **Alp Car Rental**
Vatnsmýrarvegur 10
101 Reykjavík
Tel. 562 60 60
Fax 562 60 61
www.alp.is

▶ **Bílaleiga Akureyrar**
Tryggvabraut 12
600 Akureyri
Tel. 461 60 00
Fax 462 64 76
www.bilaleigaakureyrar.is

▶ **Budget Car Rental**
Malarhöfði 2, 110 Reykjavík

Tel. 567 83 00, fax 567 83 02
www.budget.is

Fax 505 06 50
www.hertz.is

► **Icelandair Hertz
Car Rental**
Reykjavík Airport
101 Reykjavík
Tel. 505 06 00

► **Rás Car Rental**
Víkurbraut 17
240 Grindavík
Tel. 426 71 00, fax 426 81 62
www.rascar.com

transit roads can be recognized by their two-digit numbers. The quality of the three-digit roads is worse, whilst roads marked by an »F« or paths without a number are usually only passable by four-wheel drive.

The ring road boasts a comprehensive network of petrol stations, while filling-up early is recommended. In Reykjavík and in towns with more than 800 inhabitants, at least one petrol station stays open till 11.30pm. In smaller towns shorter opening hours are quite common. Self-service petrol pumps allow payment by notes or credit cards outside opening hours. There are no opportunities for filling-up in the highlands, only emergency petrol pumps such as the one in Hveravellir, which should not be factored into the planning. Therefore it's best to fill up in good time and consider bringing spare cans. A breakdown service is provided by the Icelandic Automobile Association »Félag Íslenskra Bifreiðaeigenda« (► p. 108).

Petrol/Gas stations

The speed limit in built-up areas is 30mph/50km/h, on gravel tracks 50mph/80km/h and on tarmacked roads 55mph/90km/h. Off-road driving is prohibited. Headlights have to be switched on even in the daytime, and seat belts must be worn by everyone, including those in the back seat. **The permitted blood alcohol level is 0.0**! Penalties for traffic violations are higher than most visitors will be used to. Traffic signs warn of danger spots, but most don't explicitly ask drivers to reduce speed. Do bring relevant car insurance documentation; car insurers issue a Green Card proving that drivers are insured to drive in Iceland. If an accident happens, be sure to notify the police. Visitors unfortunate enough to have accidents involving sheep or horses have to pay compensation.

Traffic regulations

Foreign diesel vehicles have to pay a diesel tax – graded according to the vehicle's weight – for each week or part of a week, counted from the day of arrival to the day of departure. Payment is due when leaving the country; what counts is the amount of time between the arrival of the ferry and the verifiable departure of the boat according to the ticket. For further information, email the customs office (tollstjori@ tollur.is) or go to www.tollur.is.

Diesel tax

Car rental Hire cars can be rented from various Icelandic and international companies through travel agents, airlines, at airports and numerous other places. The choice ranges from small cars all the way to four-wheel drives. Prices however are significantly higher than most visitors might expect. A small car costs around €10,000 ISK per day and 60,000 ISK per week. **Four-wheel drive vehicles** will set the budget back by on average 20,000 ISK per day and 125,000 ISK per week. Booking a hire car together with the flight can get you significant discounts. The minimum driving age is 20, and for jeeps usually 23–25. The driving licence must have been held for one or two years, and a credit card is required for security. Highland tracks may only be attempted by jeep, which means that during high season it is a good idea to reserve four-wheel drives in good time.

Travellers with Disabilities

Travellers with disabilities should plan their holiday to Iceland carefully. A useful contact is the **Sjálfsbjörg Disabled Association** (Hátúni 12, 105 Reykjavík, tel. 550 03 00, www.sjalfsbjorg.is). All airlines are geared up for wheelchair users, as are many hotels, restaurants and supermarkets. More problematic are older public buildings, scheduled buses and off-the-beaten-track destinations in the highlands.

Wellbeing · Spa City Reykjavík

Many countries might have thermal spas, but nowhere else does warm water come as cheap as in Iceland – thanks to the abundance of heat in the ground. This is why most pools are open-air and no one is worried about wasting energy, even if the swimming pools in winter are shrouded in thick clouds of steam. Water temperatures hover around a very pleasant 29 °C/84°F, whilst the **thermal water pools** with temperatures of 37 °C to 42 °C/98°F to 108°F, pull in most visitors. Thankfully, a visit to the swimming pool counts among the few cheap pleasures on offer in Iceland, as some 350 ISK visitors to splash around in the warm water for as long as they like. No wonder that the swimming pools attract 1.5 million visitors each year and that for some time now, Reykjavík has been rightly promoting its excellent spa facilities.

▶ THE THERMAL SPAS OF REYKJAVÍK

▸ **Árbæjarlaug**
Fylkisvegur, tel. 510 76 00

One of the finest swimming pools in town, with sauna, sunbed, thermal pools, whirlpool and water slide. Also a play area for children, making it ideal for families. Many hiking trails in the surrounding area.

► **Gravarvogslaug**
Dalshús, tel. 510 46 00
Very beautiful pools with, of course, hot pots, whirlpool and steam bath. Hiking trails, golf and horse riding nearby.

► **Kjarneslaug**
Kléberg, tel. 566 68 79
Outside Reykjavík in Kjalarnes. Swimming pool, hot pots, steam bath, sunbed and gym. In the surrounding area there are opportunities for hiking along the coast and climbing the Esja for its splendid views.

► **Vesturbæjarlaug**
Hofsvallagata, tel. 551 50 04
Some 20 min on foot from the centre of town. Swimming pool, hot pots, steam bath and sauna. Pretty beach trail nearby.

► **Laugardalslaug**
Laugardalur, tel. 553 40 39
50-metre pool, hot pots, whirlpool, steam bath, sunbed and an 86m/282-ft water slide. Around the pool are good fitness and walking trails, and in the winter cross-country ski tracks.

► **Breidholtslaug**
Austurberg, tel. 557 55 47
Open-air swimming pool in the middle of a residential area, with hot pots, whirlpool, steam bath and an additional covered swimming pool.

► **Bláa Lónið (Blue Lagoon)**
44km/27 miles southwest of Reykjavík near Grindavík, tel. 420 88 00, www.bluelagoon.com. This ultramodern thermal spa complex with various treatment options, rehabilitation clinic, restaurant, shop, mail order spa treatments, conference centre and geological information centre was considerably extended in 2007.

When to go

The first thing many people think about when it comes to Icelandic weather is the Icelandic low-pressure area that brings Europe bad weather. These low-pressure areas can form all year round when, south of Greenland and near Iceland, the continental American **cold air mass meets the Gulf Stream**. Statistically it rains about every other day in Iceland; however, thanks to the fact that the wind is usually blowing these are often only showers, and they seldom turn into the kind of rain that carries on relentlessly for days. And another bit of good news: the months with least rain are the main travel months of May, June and July; only August can be a bit wetter. The south sees a fair bit more rain as the prevailing **southern and western winds** bring a lot of moisture from the sea, depositing it at the mountains and glaciers. Thus, precipitation on the southern coast re-

The Iceland low-pressure area

gisters as much as 3,000mm/118 inches per year, while the highlands north of the Vatnajökull only receive 400mm/16 inches. If the wind is coming from the north however, which is more unusual, it is probably raining in the northern part of the island. The rule of thumb is: if the weather is good in the south, it will be raining in the north and vice versa.

Water/air-temperatures   The island location creates a steady climate, at least in the coastal regions. Winters are mild, with average temperatures around 0 °C/32°F in Reykjavík and around -2 °C/28°F in Akureyri. In summer, average temperatures hover around 10 °C/50°F, while daily highs of 20–25 °C/68–77°F in June, July and August are a definite possibility. In the highlands, temperatures in the winter sink far below zero and even in summer it is perceptibly colder than on the coast. At higher altitudes, snow may stay on the ground up to June, and snow showers may occur even in summer. As a general rule, the weather changes faster and more violently than most visitors might be accustomed to. With longer tours in particular, always be prepared for bad weather and cold winds. Considering the northerly position of Iceland **near the Arctic Circle**, temperatures are very pleasant here thanks to the Gulf Stream, as this gigantic warm-water heating system provides much friendlier temperatures than in Siberia or Alaska,

Iceland in high season – weatherproof clothing a must!

which lie on a comparable latitude. However, even the Gulf Stream doesn't manage to warm the sea to a bearable swimming temperature; even in the summer, don't expect anything much above 10 °C/50°F.

The best months for visiting are June, July and August, although June may still be problematic for crossing the highlands. During these three months all the tourist facilities are open, while for the rest of the year the choice is much more limited. The long days in summer allow more or less round-the-clock open-air activities. In September, the sheep being driven down from their mountain pastures and the resplendent autumn colours are two high points before the country goes into hibernation: ferries stop running, buses run far less frequently, the highland tracks are impassable, and even the ring road can be blocked at short notice. Outside the **main travelling months** few tourists come to Iceland, even though airlines and hotels advertise special offers. The low season offers the more independent traveller interesting options such as dog sleighing or ski tours. Even in summer, clothes should be able to withstand any kind of weather – including wind, rain and cold. Visitors should also bring a pair of sturdy walking shoes.

Three months of high season

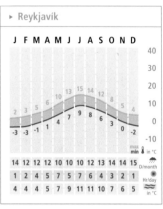

▶ Reykjavik

	J	F	M	A	M	J	J	A	S	O	N	D	
					10	13	15	14	12				40
				6						8			30
	2	3	5								5	4	20
				4	7	9	8	6					10
	-3	-3	-1	1						3	0	-2	0
													-10

max/min in °C

14	12	12	12	10	10	10	12	13	14	14	15	D/month
1	2	4	5	7	5	7	6	4	3	2	1	Hr/day
4	4	4	5	7	9	11	11	10	7	6	5	in °C

Tours

A WHOLE CIRCUIT OF ICELAND – OR JUST STICKING TO THE SOUTHWEST? LOOKING FOR SOLITUDE IN THE NORTHEAST OR PLUNGING INTO THE NIGHTLIFE OF REYKJAVÍK? WE TAKE YOU ON A TRIP SHOWING ALL THE DIFFERENT ASPECTS OF ICELAND.

TOURS THROUGH THE COUNTRY

Not sure yet where to head? Our suggested routes take visitors to the most beautiful stretches of the country and give tips for the best bases for exploring

▬▬ **TOUR 1**   **A good all-rounder**
Doing a circuit around Iceland on the almost fully-tarmacked ring road is the easiest way to explore many of the island's sights. Visitors with a bit more time on their hands can add little side trips to the highlands or into the Western fjords.   ► **page 120**

▬▬ **TOUR 2**   **Into the wild west**
On the Snæfellsnes Peninsula and the extremely sparsely populated Western fjords, an abundance of natural spectacles await the visitor. The magical Snæfellsjökull, mighty fjords and magnificent sandy beaches never fail to work their magic.   ► **page 122**

▬▬ **TOUR 3**   **Volcanoes, glaciers and geysers**
This tour leads to some of the most famous highlights in Iceland and, even outside the main tourist season, can easily be combined with a short visit to Reykjavík.   ► **page 125**

▬▬ **TOUR 4**   **Iceland for specialists**
Starting at Seyðisfjördur ferry harbour, this round trip leads to the extreme north, where Arctic foxes outnumber people. Taking in Húsavík, Goðafoss, Akureyri, Mývatn, Ásbrygi and Dettifoss, this tour encompasses some of Iceland's greatest sights.   ► **page 126**

Ísafjörður

Patreksfjörður   Hólmavík
           Brjánslækur
✶✶
Látrabjarg

         TOUR 2

Ólafsvík   Stykkishólmur

Arnarstapi

         Borgarnes   ✶✶
         TOUR 1   Þingvellir
         Akranes   National Park
      ✶✶ Reykjavík
      ✶✶ Blue
         Lagoon   Selfoss
Blue Lagoon   Grindavík
Wellness paradise

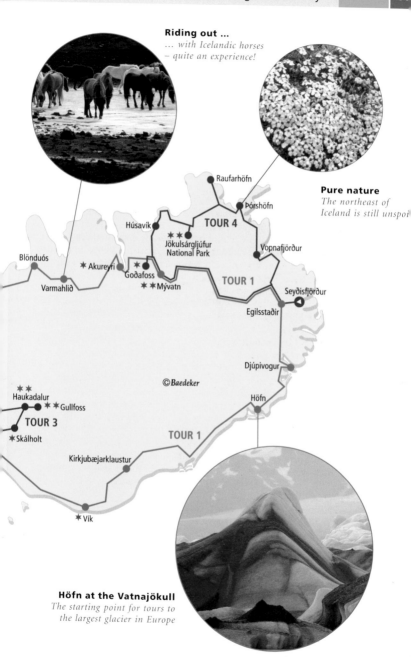

Riding out ...
... with Icelandic horses – quite an experience!

Pure nature
The northeast of Iceland is still unspoi

Raufarhöfn

Þórshöfn

Húsavík

TOUR 4

★★
Jökulsárgljúfur
National Park

Vopnafjörður

Blönduós

★ Akureyri

★
Goðafoss

TOUR 1

Seyðisfjörður

Varmahlíð

★★Mývatn

Egilsstaðir

Djúpivogur

© *Baedeker*

★★
Haukadalur

★★Gullfoss

Höfn

TOUR 3

TOUR 1

★Skálholt

Kirkjubæjarklaustur

★ Vík

Höfn at the Vatnajökull
*The starting point for tours to
the largest glacier in Europe*

Out and About in Iceland

Partying in Reykjavík

For the past few years insiders have been raving about **Reykjavík's pub scene**, and rightly so – prepare to be amazed at what goes on at summer weekends in the city! It seems like rivers of beer – and not just beer – flow through Reykjavík, and the whole city seems to be out and about, as if the light-filled summer nights have to make up for the long dark winter. Gastronomically, Reykjavík also has plenty to offer: visitors undeterred by the high prices have the choice between a surprising number of first-class restaurants. However, few visitors just come for a **city break to Iceland** – most are attracted by the spectacular nature of the Atlantic Ocean island.

Sublime scenery and few people

It is the combination of fire and ice – the intensity of which no other country in Europe can match – that is the biggest draw of a holiday to Iceland. Where else to find such a **sparsely populated country** that offers such extreme landscapes? Only the coast is settled to any degree; often many kilometres lie between the farmsteads, and even settlements that on the map seem to promise a modicum of urban flair turn out to be villages with no more than 100 or 200 inhabitants. Visitors leaving the narrow, often green, coastal strip and driving into the **highlands**, find themselves after only a few kilometres in a landscape devoid of people, desert-like in places and only negotiable during a few months in summer by all-terrain vehicles with a high clearance. But even those keeping »only« to the ring road will not tire of the landscape, large swathes of which are pretty extreme. A drive through Iceland presents all conceivable **forms of volcanic activity**, as if the country were an open textbook. There are lava fields, sometimes black and hostile, sometimes covered by thick green cushions of moss, plus steaming fields of solfataras, that with their rich colours and inhospitable terrain could serve as **film sets for science fiction movies**. Contrasting beautifully with this are the largest glaciers in Europe, with countless jagged breaks and tongues; even lagoons can be found here, with dozens of icebergs swimming in them. Few countries can offer this kind of variety.

Hot spots and fjords

Visitors looking for extreme volcanic landscapes will find what they are looking for along a line between the Reykjanes peninsula and the Mývatn, as this is the location of the **island's hot spots** – most of the geothermally active areas. Life is quieter if no less spectacular in the Western fjords and on the fjord coast of east Iceland. Here, the **mighty fjords** dominate the landscape, carved by the glaciers of the last Ice Age. Surprisingly, many of these bays consist of sandy beaches stretching for miles, some of which do merit the sobriquet »dream beach«. No matter where travels might lead, don't forget to pack hiking boots and swimming togs. Even visitors to Iceland who are no great fans of extensive **trekking tours** have countless opportunities

This is Iceland not Egypt: travelling in the highlands

for shorter and simpler walks, often leading to the most beautiful waterfalls, gorges and areas of geothermal activity. The endless empty beaches are also ideal hiking territory. To make up for the somewhat chilly sea, which even the hardy Icelanders never set foot in, nearly every town has a public swimming pool. As there is little shortage of hot water, the pools are nearly always cosily warm, and the hot tubs that form part of every public pool have at least bath-tub temperature. An ideal place, where even the legendary Icelandic low pressure area cannot drag you down.

Choosing the Right Transport

The most comfortable way to travel in Iceland is of course by car. Visitors can either bring their own car – which means arriving in the east of the island, at the Seyðisfjörður ferry terminal – or, for shorter stays, consider the time-saving option of **arriving by plane** in Reykjavík and hiring a car. All routes described below may be negotiated without problems in a regular saloon car, while bearing in mind that longer sections off the ring road have not been tarmacked yet. It has to be said that the Icelanders are investing a lot of money in road improvements, so that every year many kilometres of gravel road are covered with asphalt. It is also possible to take the ring road around Iceland by bus, although travellers will need to factor in more time. A visit to the **Þingvellir National Park** and the **Geysir and Gullfoss** is no problem without a car, as they can nearly always be reached as day trips from Reykjavík. In principle, a trip into the **Western fjords** and around the Melrakkaslétta peninsula is also doable by public transport, if somewhat cumbersome. Here, a hire car opens up a lot more options for detours to more far-flung sights.

Tour 1 A Good All-rounder

Length of tour: 1,375km/854 miles   **Duration:** min 14 days

Full of variety, at some points running right next to the sea, at others heading inland for a stretch, the ring road leads to many of Iceland's best sights. There's something for everyone along the way: the vibrant capital Reykjavík at the start and end of the tour, and in-between volcanoes, glaciers, lonely plateaus and beaches, as well as steaming solfatara fields.

Either the capital ❶＊＊ **Reykjavík** or the airport at **Keflavík** can serve as starting points for a trip around the island on the ring road. Heading north out of Reykjavík, the road passes the relatively densely populated suburbs of Kópavogur and Mosfellsbær, soon reaching the Hvalfjörður, which can either be crossed in a tunnel, thereby saving time, or rounded by the scenic route. Located at the point of a peninsula, ❷ **Akranes** is worth a stop for its extensive Garðar local museum and to climb the mountain of Akrafjall, which gives great views.

✔ DON'T MISS

- Reykjavík: good museums, great pub culture, excellent restaurants
- Reykholt: in the footsteps of Snorri Sturluson
- Glaumbær: the open-air museum gives a glimpse into the life of times past.
- Mývatn: volcanism in all its variations and a paradise for birdwatchers
- Vatnajökull / Skaftafell: endless expanses of ice and nature at its purest

In ❸ **Borgarnes**, all the streets are named after heroes of the Egillssaga, and at the Borg farmstead, a few kilometres further north, a statue of Ásmundur Sveinsson honours the saga hero Egill. At Borgarnes, the ring road swings inland and offers, after a few kilometres, the opportunity for a worthwhile detour to ＊ **Reykholt**, one of the most historic places in Iceland and inextricably linked with the great poet, historian and mighty »goði« Snorri Sturluson. Following the minor road from Reykholt in an easterly direction, visitors soon reach the impressive lava flow of **Hallmundarhraun** with its caves and the **Hraunfossar**, Iceland's most beautiful waterfalls.

Back on the ring road, the drive soon passes the imposing lava field of Grábrókarhraun. On the way to ❹ **Blönduós** on Húnaflói Bay visit the church of the once important Þingeyrar estate, near which the first convent in Iceland was founded in 1133. After heading into the interior of the country, the road eventually leads to the small town of ❺ **Varmahlíð**, with many sights waiting to be explored in the surrounding area. The nearby Viðimýri church ranks among the most beautiful turf churches in the country, while another must-see is the

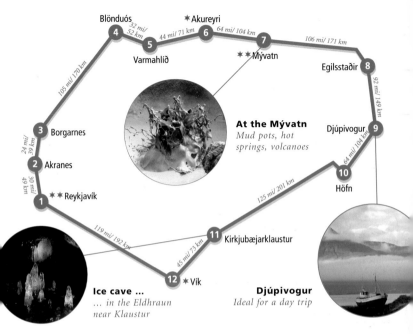

Blönduós
32 mi/ 52 km
Akureyri
4
44 mi/ 71 km
5
64 mi/ 104 km
6
7
106 mi/ 171 km
Varmahlíð
**Mývatn
Egilsstaðir 8
105 mi/ 170 km
92 mi/ 149 km
3 Borgarnes
Djúpivogur
9
24 mi/ 39 km
At the Mývatn
Mud pots, hot springs, volcanoes
2 Akranes
64 mi/ 104 km
30 mi/ 49 km
10
**Reykjavík
1
Höfn
125 mi/ 201 km
119 mi/ 192 km
11 Kirkjubæjarklaustur
45 mi/ 73 km
12 *Vík

Ice cave ...
... in the Eldhraun near Klaustur

Djúpivogur
Ideal for a day trip

turf museum of * **Glaumbær** with its large »baðstofa« (literally meaning »bathhouse«, this is the communal dwelling and sleeping area) and historic furniture. The pretty little town of **Sauðárkrókur** is the largest settlement on the Skagafjörður and the centre of the nationally famous stud farm. Also worth a visit in the area around Varmahlíð is **Hólar**, the most important bishopric in northern Iceland.

The next stop is ❻ * **Akureyri**, the undisputed capital of northern Iceland, which boasts numerous museums and an interesting cultural scene, alongside some historic buildings. On the way to ❼ ** **Mývatn** and its touristic centre **Reykjahlíð**, consider taking a look at the * **Goðafoss** – the »waterfall of the gods«, one of the most spectacular waterfalls in Iceland – which lies in the immediate vicinity of the ring road. Visitors with a bit more time on their hands should also make the detour to **Húsavik** to take in a ** **whale watching safari**. Try to schedule in a few days for the Mývatn, as nowhere else presents so many different forms of volcanic activity. Mighty lava flows, pseudo craters, solfatara fields and the Krafla volcano turn the area around the Mývatn into a fairytale landscape.

From the Mývatn, the ring road leads through the country's interior to ❽ **Egilsstaðir**, which lies on the elongated Lagarfljót lake. Egilsstaðir makes an excellent base for trips to the east coast of Iceland,

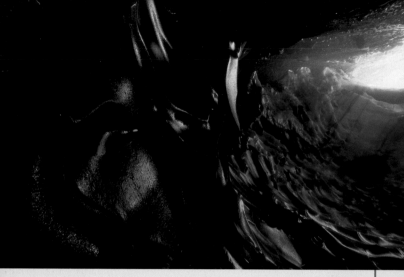

characterized by deep fjords, which stretch to the south of **❾ Djúpi-vogur**. By the time the road reaches the coastal town of **❿ Höfn**, the surrounding area is already influenced by the huge **✳ ✳ Vatnajökull**, its glacier tongues and sandar (broad plains of glacial outwash) offering a fantastic natural spectacle. The highlights of the drive along the southern coast are the glacier lagoon of **✳ Jökulsarlón** with its icebergs, and **✳ ✳ Skaftafell National Park**, which offers numerous hiking opportunities. The small town of **⓫ Kirkjubæjarklaustur** is the best base for a trip to the Laki fissure. The remaining route along the southern coast, via **⓬ ✳ Vík í Mýrdal** and **Hveragerði** back to **Reykjavík** , is also characterized by glaciers such as the Mýrdalsjökull. Here there are petrified lava flows and huge sandar, but also green meadows making for a beautiful contrast to the volcanic mountains.

Tour 2 Into the Wild West

Length of tour: 1,185km/736 miles   **Duration:** min 10 days

Tiny colourful villages against a backdrop of deeply-cut fjords, mighty mountains and gorgeous sandy beaches to enchant any nature lover. Here, climate and landscape are even harsher than elsewhere in Iceland, and the solitude boundless.

This circular tour also takes the capital of **❶ ✳ ✳ Reykjavík** as its starting point. Leaving Reykjavík in a northerly direction follow the

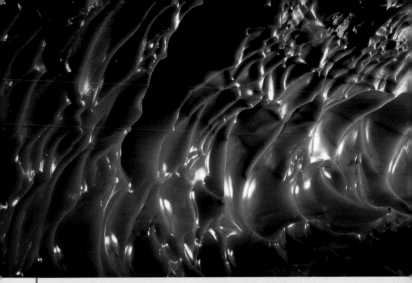

… in an ice cave at the Vatnajökull

ring road to the town of ❷**Borgarnes**, which is closely linked to the Egillssaga. Immediately after Borgarnes, the [54] road branches off from the ring road and, just before turning west towards the Snæfellsnes Peninsula, leads through the lava field of **Eldborgarhraun**, from which the red »fire castle« (Eldborg) rises up. From here the road runs along the sparsely populated southern coast of the Snæfellsnes Peninsula to ❸**Arnarstapi**. This small village is one of the best bases from which to explore the glaciated volcanic cone of ✶✶ **Snæfellsjökull**, credited by some with magical powers. Due to its location on the steep coastal cliffs fringed by bird rocks, Arnarstapi itself is well worth a visit.

Rounding the tip of the peninsula provides many opportunities for both short and longer walks, before the old trading centre of ❹**Ólafsvík** is reached. Driving along the northern coast brings visitors to the fishing town of ❺**Stykkishólmur**. From here, a ferry crosses the Breiðafjörður to ❻**Brjánslækur**, significantly shortening the drive to the Western fjords. Heading west from Brjánslækur, serpentine roads wind past lonely, sandy beaches against the backdrop of mighty fjords, leading to Iceland's most impressive bird cliff, the ❼✶✶ **Látrabjarg**, which shelters millions of breeding sea birds in the summer.

 DON'T MISS

- Snæfellsjökull: a picture-book glacier at the western end of the Snæfellsnes Peninsula
- Látrabjarg: millions of seabirds breed on a cliff reaching up to 440m/1,144ft in height, creating an extraordinary natural spectacle.

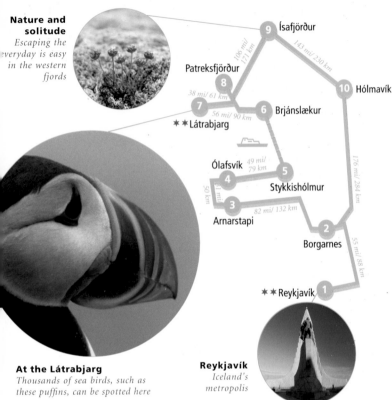

Nature and solitude
Escaping the everyday is easy in the western fjords

Ísafjörður
143 mi / 230 km
Patreksfjörður
106 mi / 171 km
Hólmavík
38 mi / 61 km
56 mi / 90 km
Brjánslækur
★★Látrabjarg
176 mi / 284 km
Ólafsvík
49 mi / 79 km
Stykkishólmur
50 km
41 km
Arnarstapi
82 mi / 132 km
Borgarnes
55 mi / 88 km
★★Reykjavík

At the Látrabjarg
Thousands of sea birds, such as these puffins, can be spotted here

Reykjavík
Iceland's metropolis

From here, continue along partially-gravelled roads snaking their way through a grandiose, extremely sparsely populated landscape of fjords to 8 **Patreksfjörður**, which was already a trading post at the time of the Hanseatic League (an alliance that monopolized trade along the coast of Northern Europe from the 13th to 17th centuries, it took control of trade with Iceland in the 16th century). On the way to 9 **Ísafjörður**, the largest town in the Western fjords, visitors really should make a stop at the Dynjandi waterfall. Ísafjörður, worth seeing for its blend of historic and modern houses, presents a near-urban bustle. The maritime museum reminds visitors of the hard life of fishermen. The reward for a lengthy drive along many deeply-carved, lonely fjords is 10 **Hólmavík**, with its biggest attraction, the unusual Icelandic Museum of Sorcery and Witchcraft. Having taken in part of the western bank of the **Húnaflói Bay** and the **Hrútafjörður**, the tour eventually rejoins the ring road and heads back to its starting point of Reykjavík.

Tour 3 Glaciers and Geysers

Length of tour: 350km/217 miles   **Duration:** min 3 days

This tour is well suited for a short trip to Iceland – and not only in the summer high season, as the sights along the route are accessible in winter too. In fact, covered in snow and ice, the Gullfoss is at least as spectacular as in the summer.

Starting in ❶ ✳ ✳ **Reykjavík**, take the [36] via Mosfellsbær to the Þingvallavatn and the national park of ❷ ✳ ✳ **Þingvellir**. For Icelanders Þingvellir is a magical place inextricably linked with their history, as it was here that the first Alþing convened over 1,000 years ago. In the **Almannagjá Gorge**, running through the landscape like a gaping wound, visitors can experience up close the fact that Iceland lies right on the border of two tectonic plates. The 60km/37-mile drive around the Þingvallavatn on the winding, hilly road is very rewarding for the pretty views it repeatedly offers of the lake and the surrounding mountains.

From the Þingvallavatn, the road leads to the small village of Laugarvatn, with its natural saunas and hot tubs, and on to the geothermal area of ❸ ✳ ✳ **Haukadalur** and then to the ❹ ✳ ✳ **Gullfoss**. Virtually every tour bus stops for the most famous Icelandic geothermal field at Haukadalur. Steam and hissing sounds emerge from various fissures, but the still, blue pools of hot water are remarkable too. The biggest attraction here though is the »**Strokkur**«, a fountain geyser which erupts several times an hour, sending a mighty column of water skywards. The large »**Geysir**« nearby, which gave its name to all erupting springs, was completely inactive for a long time; however, since an earthquake in 2000 the original geyser does surprise visitors with occasional eruptions.

DON'T MISS

- Þingvellir: the historical assembly site of the oldest parliament in the world is part of the UNESCO World Heritage.
- Haukadalur: don't miss Strokkur Geyser.
- Gullfoss: the »Golden Falls« – beautiful and mighty!
- Blue Lagoon: a warm bath is always welcome!

On the way back, consider taking a detour along the Hvítá river to the former bishopric of ❺ ✳ **Skálholt**, which for centuries was an important centre of power. Road [35] eventually leads to ❻**Selfoss** and the ring road. Drivers with time to spare before their return to Reykjavik can make a detour on the ring road to **Vík** (135km/84 miles), worth seeing for its impressive plunging coastline, a beach which has been described as one of the most beautiful on earth, and its proximity to the Mýrdalsjökull. It might also be worth considering a short stop en route at the ✳ **Skógafoss** or a detour to the

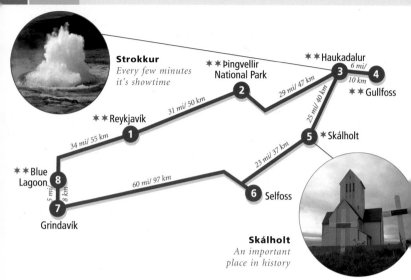

Strokkur
Every few minutes it's showtime

Þingvellir National Park

Haukadalur 6 mi/

Gullfoss

Reykjavík

Skálholt

Blue Lagoon

Selfoss

Grindavík

31 mi/ 50 km

29 mi/ 47 km

25 mi/ 40 km

10 km

34 mi/ 55 km

23 mi/ 37 km

60 mi/ 97 km

5 mi/

8 km

Skálholt
An important place in history

✶✶ Þórsmörk Valley, particularly popular with hikers. Drivers heading directly for ❼ **Grindavík** and on to Reykjavík from Selfoss should not miss taking a dip in the ❽ ✶✶ **Blue Lagoon**.

Tour 4 Iceland for Specialists

Length of tour: 705km/438 miles   **Duration:** min 10 days

On this tour, lonely hikes on the Langanes Peninsula and a drive around the practically uninhabited Melrakkaslétta Peninsula contrast with the popular tourist attractions of Húsavik, Goðafoss and Mývatn.

For those taking the ferry and their own car to Iceland, ❶ **Seyðisfjörður** on the east coast is the first point of contact with the island. They could not wish for a more beautiful introduction, as the town with its colourful houses and the fjord with its green mountain slopes and peaks flecked with snow even in summer, form a magnificent backdrop. From the ferry harbour, the road leads over a pass to ❷ **Egilsstaðir**, the busy hub of the region with its extensive East Iceland Heritage Museum. Before heading north, consider a drive around the **Lagarfljót** lake, with a walk in Iceland's largest forest and a hike up to the **Hengifoss** waterfall.

A drive north via ❸ **Vopnafjörður** leads to ❹ **Þórshöfn**, an ideal starting point for hikes on the abandoned **Langanes Peninsula**, one of the loneliest corners of Iceland. Afterwards, the [85] road leads around the **Melrakkaslétta Peninsula**, hugging the coast practically all the way. The extreme north of Iceland is sparsely populated and the coastline, littered with driftwood, has a rugged, austere beauty. Visitors looking for solitude but not wanting to forgo all comforts, should put up in the hotel of ❺**Raufarhöfn**. After a drive around the peninsula, ❻ ✶ ✶ **Jökulsárgljúfur National Park** offers good hiking options; don't under any circumstances miss the enormous, horseshoe shaped canyon of ✶ ✶ **Ásbyrgi** or the largest waterfall in Europe (in terms of volume of water), the ✶ ✶ **Dettifoss**.

From the national park, return to the coast and drive to ❼**Húsavik**, to take part in a ✶ ✶ **whale-watching safari**. A good stopping-off point on the way to the Mývatn is at the ❽ ✶ **Goðafoss**. A drive around the ❾ ✶ ✶ **Mývatn** really requires at least two days, in order to explore the solfatara field at the Námafjall, the geothermal area shaped by the numerous eruptions of the Krafla volcano, the black lava towers of Dimmuborgir and of course the lake with its rich birdlife. A good base for exploring is the small town of **Reykjahlíd**. The ring road eventually leads back to Egilsstaðir, and after another 21km/13 miles to the tour's departure point at Seyðisfjörður.

✔	DON'T MISS

- Langenes: A hike on this deserted peninsula is balm for the soul.
- Jökulsárgljúfur National Park: Unique canyon landscape with Ásbyrgi canyon as the highlight
- Mývatn: Craters, solfatara fields and our feathered friends await visitors.

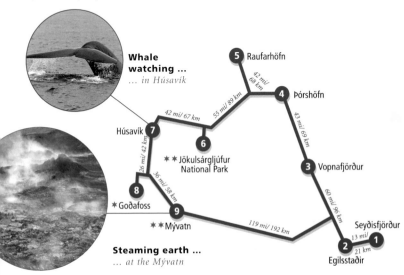

Whale watching ...
... in Húsavik

Steaming earth ...
... at the Mývatn

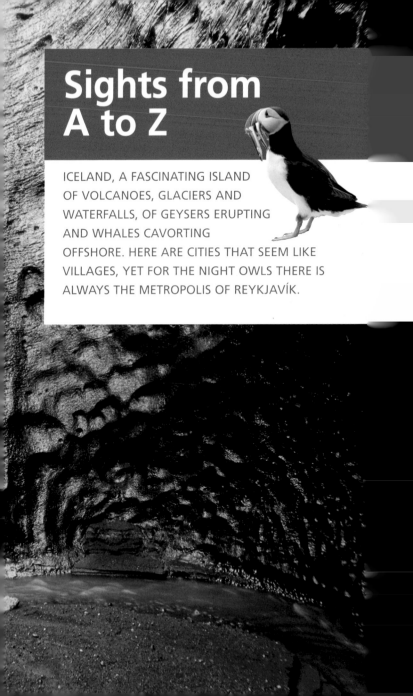

Sights from A to Z

ICELAND, A FASCINATING ISLAND OF VOLCANOES, GLACIERS AND WATERFALLS, OF GEYSERS ERUPTING AND WHALES CAVORTING OFFSHORE. HERE ARE CITIES THAT SEEM LIKE VILLAGES, YET FOR THE NIGHT OWLS THERE IS ALWAYS THE METROPOLIS OF REYKJAVÍK.

Akranes

D 5

Region: West Iceland   **Population:** 5,600

Akranes, formerly known as Skagi, lies at the end of the peninsula of the same name, between the Hvalfjörður fjord, reaching deep inland, and Leirárvogur Bay. According to the *Book of Settlement*, the region was settled around 880 by two Irish brothers, Ketill and Þormóður Bresason.

What to see in Akranes

Wandering around town, the two **lighthouses** on the tip of the promontory catch the eye, while the old harbour quarter is also worth a detour. The long sandy beach has its charms, with only the nearby factory spoiling the view somewhat. The **church of Akranes** dates back to the year 1896. Inside, look out for the golden baptismal font, the altar piece by Sigurður Guðmundsson, and the painted ceiling and walls executed in 1966 by Greta and Jón Björnsson.

Garðar museum complex

East of the town centre lies one of the largest regional museums in Iceland, with its four sections. Opened in 1959 and housed in the former Garðar farmstead, the **Folk Museum** forms the oldest part of the museum complex. On display is an extensive collection of items connected to the history of Akranes, including a rowing boat dating back to 1874, various model ships, a fully equipped blacksmith's workshop, the town's oldest wooden house (1875) and its first concrete house, the small school building from the early 20th century, as well as the restored *Sigurfari* coastal sailing boat.

The **rock and minerals collection** is the most extensive in Iceland, with thousands of items. Next to it is an exhibition telling the story of the Hvalfjörður Tunnel, which, since its construction in 1998, has considerably shortened the road link with Reykjavík. The **Sports Museum** looks at the history of Icelandic sport, showing photographs, sporting equipment and trophies. In addition, since 2003, the National Land Survey of Iceland has been presenting the history of cartography and the latest land survey techniques. Opening times: mid-May – mid-Sept daily 10am – 6pm, otherwise daily 1 – 6pm, www.museum.is.

Around Akranes

Akrafjall

Behind the town, the prominent basalt mountain of Akrafjall is divided in two by the Berjadalur. The southern peak, **Háihnjúkur** (555m/1,821ft), can easily be reached in an hour from the parking area at the foot of the mountain near the geothermal power plant. Climbing the western peak of **Geirmundartindur** (643m/2,110ft)

▶ VISITING AKRANES

INFORMATION

In the Garðar Museum
Tel. 431 55 66
Fax 431 55 67
www.akranes.is

WHERE TO EAT

► Expensive
Restaurant of the
Hotel Glymur
Hvalfjörður, tel. 430 31 00
The hotel is well known for its
excellent cuisine, with the extensive
Italian buffet a speciality. More af-
fordable is the superb buffet lunch
(non-residents need to book ahead).

► Inexpensive
Maríukaffi
Garðar, tel. 431 55 66
A good spot for a cup of coffee and a
slice of freshly baked cake. The shell
and sand compositions under the
glass panes covering the tables are also
worth a look.

WHERE TO STAY

► Luxury
Hotel Glymur
Hvalfjörður
Tel. 430 31 00, www.hotelglymur.is
An establishment that impresses
through attention to detail, and offers
a fantastic view across the fjord, an
extensive library for cosy reading
sessions, plus hot tubs with a view.

► Mid-range
Hótel Barbró
Kirkjubraut 11
Tel. 431 42 40, www.barbro.is
Small family hotel in the town centre,
open all year round.

► Budget
Gistihúsið Móar
Tel. 431 13 89, fax 431 13 87
Situated 7km/4.3 miles east of Akranes on the [51], with five imagi-
natively designed doubles in a cosy
guesthouse.

does not take much longer. Both peaks offer views of Faxaflói Bay
and the mountain ranges on the Reykjanes peninsula.

Penetrating inland for some 30km/18.5 miles, the Hvalfjörður,   **Hvalfjörður**
4–5km/2.5–3 miles wide, is the longest fjord on the southwestern
coast. It also counts amongst the most beautiful fjords in the country, due to its steep rock walls and the high massifs on its banks. In
the Second World War, both the British and the Americans maintained naval bases here, of which some traces can still be seen. After
the war, the fjord became well known for its large shoals of herring
and its **whaling station**. Since the opening of the tunnel, the interior
of the fjord has been fairly quiet, but the spectacular landscapes
make for a worthwhile detour on the 60km/37-mile [47], which is
often narrow and bendy. In **Saurbær** the small church is worth seeing, built in honour of Hallgrímur Pétursson (1614 – 1674), who was
pastor here while working on his Passion Hymns. At the end of the
fjord, a track leads into the **Botnsdalur**, with its impressive dense

birch forest. From the car park, a path takes about an hour to lead to the tallest waterfall in Iceland, the **Glymur**, some 200m/655ft in height. Options for longer walks are the Herringfishers Trail (Síldarmannagötur) and the rather worryingly named Legbreaker Trail (Leggjabrjótur), which also begin at the end of the fjord.

✴ Akureyri

G 3

Region: North Iceland   **Population:** 16,000

Whilst the capital of the North lies nearly within the Arctic Circle, it has an exceptionally mild climate with little rain, and surprises with vegetation that by Icelandic standards is positively lush. Some good museums, a long Summer Art Festival, fine old wooden houses, and good shopping options are combining to steadily increase the number of visitors.

At the end of the Eyjafjörður, which reaches far inland, and at the beginning of the green valley of the same name, this is Iceland's largest urban area outside the capital. Probably the first settler was **Helgi the Lean**, who settled around 10km/6.2 miles south of today's town in the 9th century, calling his farmstead Kristnes. He is commemorated by a statue north of the centre at the end of the Brekkugata, from where visitors have a good view of the town. Even at the time, the favourable climatic conditions and the relatively fertile soils allowed for productive agriculture. The first document mentioning Akureyri – today a university town but then only a village – dates back to 1562.

▶ VISITING AKUREYRI

INFORMATION

Central bus station
Hafnarstræti 82
Tel. 462 77 33, fax 461 18 17
www.eyjafjordur.is

TRIPS

The Ferðafélag Akureyrar hiking club (23 Strandgata, tel. 462 27 20) offers day trips and longer trekking tours to many sights: Goðafoss, Mývatn, Reykjavík via Kjölur, Dettifoss, Ásbyrgi, Hljóðaklettar, Vatnajökull, Kverkfjöll, Askja, Húsavík. In the summer there are numerous daily tours, with departures often at 8.30am from the bus station in Hafnarstræti. There are also scheduled flights to various destinations with Air Iceland (tel. 460 70 00), and a ferry to Hrísey from Árskógsströnd (8 x daily). The ferry to Grímsey (Mon, Wed, Fri) departs from Dalvík – half an hour northeast of Akureyri – at 9am, with a crossing time of 3.5hrs, plus a 3-hr stay.

EVENTS

At the end of July, the officially

northernmost 18-hole golf course in
the world hosts the international
Arctic Open tournament in the light
of the midnight sun.

WHERE TO EAT
► Expensive
① *Rosagarðurinn*
89 Hafnarstræti, tel. 460 20 00
The Rosagarðurinn on the ground
floor is a top restaurant in the best
hotel in town. The wine list is
impressive too. The dining room is
relatively large if not particularly cosy.

② *Fiðlarinn á Þakinu*
Skipagata 14, tel. 462 71 00
First-class restaurant in the town
centre. The view from the dining
room across the fjord is worth the
money alone.

► Moderate
③ *La Vita è Bella*
Hafnarstræti 92, tel. 461 58 58
Classic Italian restaurant with tasty
pizza and pasta dishes. Good wine list
and fresh home-made bread.

► Inexpensive
④ *Bláa Kannan*
Hafnarstræti 96, tel. 461 46 00
A wonderfully cosy interior, with lots
of wood, and a terrace on the main
shopping street. Serving tasty (cream)
cakes, rather pricey coffee, fresh bread
in the mornings, a nicely-priced soup
of the day and daily specials.

⑤ *Bautinn*
Hafnarstræti 92
Tel. 462 18 18
Located in one of the oldest and most
beautiful houses in Akureyri. On cold
days, visitors can enjoy the views from
the veranda. The salad bar is famous
and every main dish comes with soup
and salad.

⑥ *Blómahúsið*
Hafnarstræti 26, tel. 461 32 00
Cream cakes, sandwiches and tasty
snacks with views across the water.
Subtropically warm due to its location
in the middle of a large plant market,
a revelation on cold days.

WHERE TO STAY
► Luxury
① *Hótel Kea*
Hafnarstræti 87–89
Tel. 460 20 00, fax 460 20 60
www.hotelkea.is
This four-star hotel was built in 1944
in the town centre and is considered
one of the best establishments of its
kind outside Reykjavík.

► Mid-range
② *Gistiheimili Akureyrar*
Hafnarstræti 104
Tel. 462 55 88, fax 461 46 82
www.nett.is/guest
19 light-filled rooms, furnished in a
modern style, plus a fantastic buffet
breakfast every morning on the top
floor, giving a splendid view over the
town!

③ *Hótel Edda*
Hrafnagilstræti, tel. 444 49 00
www.hoteledda.is
Summer hotel in a high school, rooms
with or without bathroom, serving a
hearty buffet and à la carte meals in
the evening.

► Budget
④ *Farfuglaheimili Akureyri*
Stórholt 1
Tel. 462 36 57, fax 461 25 49
storholt@simnet.is
Cosy youth hostel with modern
furnishings just north of the town
centre, with rooms of various sizes
and two pretty summer cottages each
sleeping eight.

What to see in Akureyri

Akureyrarkirkja

Perched on a hill in the centre of town and visible from afar, the cathedral, with its tall towers, is the symbol of Akureyri. From the outside, the visual impact of the concrete edifice – designed by Icelandic architect **Guðjón Samuélsson** and consecrated in 1940 – is not exactly delicate, and the interior, too, is kept very simple. Similarly to Hallgrim's Church in Reykjavík, the towers are reminiscent of basalt pillars.

The stained-glass windows here are remarkable: the one in the chancel is 400 years old and was brought here from Coventry Cathedral, which was subsequently destroyed in the Second World War. The windows in the nave show events from the life of Christ and Icelandic ecclesiastical history. Opening times: June – Aug daily 10am – noon and 2 – 4pm.

Historic centre

Akureyri may be the second-largest city in Iceland, but it can easily be explored on foot. A good starting point for a stroll is the **Aðalstræti** at the southern end of the city, which forms the original core of Akureyri. Heading further north on this road leads to the heritage museum, the Nonnahús and several lovingly kept, old wooden houses. The southern part of the next street, **Hafnarstræti**, is also characterized by traditional wooden houses, which are around 100 years old. The conspicuous light-blue building at no. 3 Hafnarstræti used to be the city's phone exchange.

A little bit further north lies the inconspicuous **Laxdalshús** of 1795, which is considered to be the oldest house in Akureyri. At the beginning of the 20th century, Hafnarstræti merited its name, as the houses were still by the water; however, subsequent earth deposits have meant that the shoreline has moved a fair distance away from the harbour road. The northern parts of Hafnarstræti, Rádhustorg and Brekkugata, are mainly pedestrianized, forming the **town's commercial centre**, with numerous shopping opportunities, restaurants and pubs. From an architectural point of view, this part is less interesting, as the few old houses are virtually crushed by the surrounding modern concrete architecture.

Botanical Gardens

Lying high above the town and the fjord, the Botanical Gardens (Lystigarður Akureyrar), or »Pleasure Garden«, are also a public park. Locals like to use this **tranquil green oasis** for a short stroll or a picnic. 4,000 foreign and 400 indigenous types of plant thrive in the park.

On a warm sunny day, the colourful flowerbeds in bloom and the trees offering shade suggest much warmer climes, belying the city's proximity to the Arctic Circle. The park was originally laid out in 1911 by women who wanted to beautify Akureyri; in 1957 the botanical gardens were integrated into the park. Opening times: June–Oct weekdays 8am – 10pm, Sat/Sun 9am – 10pm.

Akureyri Map

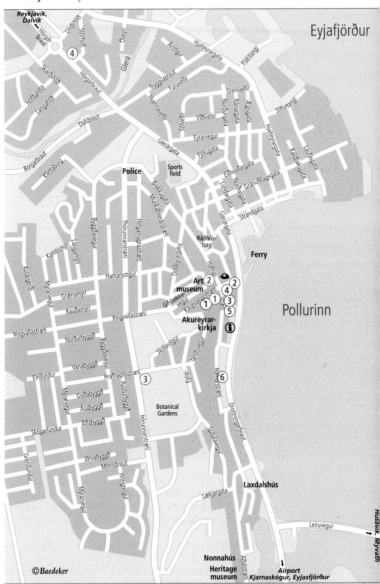

Where to stay
1. Hótel Kea
2. Gistiheimili Akureyrar
3. Hótel Edda
4. Farfuglaheimili Akureyri

Where to eat
1. Rosagarðurinn
2. Fiðlarinn á Þakinu
3. La Vita é Bella
4. Bláa Kannan
5. Bautinn
6. Blómahúsið

Walks in and around Akureyri

The town and its surroundings offer many hiking opportunities. For longer walks, the map issued by the Akureyri hiking club (Ferðafélag Akureyrar) – which also lists hikes in the **Glerárdalur** valley and on the **Vaðlaheiði** plateau – comes recommended. One popular way-marked route leads up to the local mountain, **Súlur**, whose pyramidical summit area often has pockets of snow even in summer. Beginning at the parking area of the municipal waste disposal site, the path to the summit ascends around 900m/2950ft, becoming rockier and steeper along the way. Allow at least 5 hours for the return trip. In good weather, hikers can see as far as Grímsey Island from the summit.

Winter sports in Akureyri

The Eyjafjörður region counts among the best skiing areas in Iceland, both for cross-country and alpine skiing. The ski centre, with its four lifts, is situated at the **Hlíðarfjall** mountain, only 7km/4.3 miles west of the city, and lies at an altitude of 500 – 1,000m/1,640 – 3,280ft.

Museums and exhibitions

Nonnahús

A life-size statue of the writer and Jesuit priest **Jón Sveinsson** (Jon Svensson), better known as Nonni (1857 – 1944), stands directly on the road in front of the red house belonging to the Zonta Club. Visitors have to pass this house however to see the small, black-tarred Nonnahús (Aðalstræti 54) where he lived. Inaugurated in 1957 to honour the centenary of Nonni's birth, the museum shows the constricted conditions of Jón Sveinsson's childhood. The interior is fitted out with 19th-century furniture and shows Nonni's books in many different languages (including Chinese and Esperanto!), as well as photos and memorabilia. Today, the memory of Nonni books such as *At Skipalón, An Icelandic Boy's Adventures in the mid-19th century* or *Nonni's Voyage Around the World* is somewhat faded; fifty years ago however, they were bestsellers. Opening times: June – Aug daily 10am – 5pm, otherwise by appointment, tel. 462-35 55, www.nonni.is

! Baedeker TIP

A long summer of the arts

»Listagil«, the »art canyon« in Kaupvangsstræti is the city's artistic and cultural centre. The former factories now house the art museum, the school of art, galeries and studios. From the middle of June to late August the heart of »Listasumar«, the summer of art, beats here with performances and exhibitions by local and foreign artists. The highlight of the summer of art is the Akureyravaka festival in August, which combines art and entertainment (www.listagil.is, only in Icelandic).

Heritage museum

Akureyri's heritage museum (Minjasafnið á Akureyri) is housed in the **Villa Kirkjuhvoll** (Aðalstræti 58), built in 1934, and shows two worthwhile permanent exhibitions on the history of the city and the Eyjafjörður area from the first settlement to the present day. Some

The great children's author Jón Sveinsson, aka Nonni, lived here as a child

100 years ago, the first tree nursery in Iceland was established here, on the site of today's museum garden. The small wooden church was erected in 1846 at Svalbarð, on the fjord's eastern banks, and has been standing in the **museum gardens** since 1970. Every Friday during the summer, the church is the starting point for a historic city walk. (tickets from Aktravel, Rádhústorg 3, tel. 460 06 00). Opening times museum: June – mid-Aug daily 11am – 5pm, otherwise Sun 2 – 4pm, www.akmus.is

Akureyri Art Museum

Since the nomination of Hannes Sigurdsson a few years ago as director of the art museum (Listasafnið á Akureyri), the dynamic Icelander's exhibits have put the efforts of big cities in the shade. For instance, in 2002 he brought a major exhibition of Dutch masters including 30 Rembrandts to Akureyri, while the presentation of 80 Goya drawings was a minor sensation. It remains to be seen which works by Icelandic and foreign artists he will in future choose for the display space of the former dairy (Kaupvangsstræti 24). Opening times: daily except Mon noon – 5pm.

Safnasafnið

Since 2001, the white house on the eastern banks of the Eyjafjörður (Svalbarðsströnd), with a view of Akureyri, has been home to a lovingly put together selection of modern Icelandic folk art. On display are drawings, sculptures, dolls, toys and much more. The imaginative figures outside the entrance alone merit a closer look. Opening times: mid-May – early September daily 10am – 6pm.

Around Akureyri

Vaglaskógur

In the fertile valley of **Fnjóskadalur**, branching off the ring road some 30km/18.5 miles east of Akureyri, spreads Vaglaskógur, one of the most beautiful birch forests in Iceland.

✱
Laufás

As far back as pre-Christian times there was a settlement at Laufás on the eastern banks of the Eyjafjörður. With Christianization, the place became a parish with a rectory, while today's church dates from 1865. The oldest parts of the neighbouring farmstead, which was inhabited up to 1936, are thought to date back to the 16th and 17th centuries. This typical Icelandic **grass sod farm** is much larger than most farms worked at the time and occupies a beautiful position between fjord and fell.

The frontage, clad with white clapboard and built sometime in the late 19th century, seems to suggest that Laufás at that time was a rich estate. Not only was the rectory surrounded by fertile soil, fishing and the sale of eiderdown brought in additional money. The eider duck on the roof of the storehouse is a reminder of this sideline. On average, there were 20 to 30 people living on the farmstead, as the large estate required a lot of labour. Today, Laufás is run as a regional museum, with the interiors reflecting the time around 1900. Opening times: mid-May – mid-Sept. daily 10am – 6pm, otherwise by appointment: tel. 463 31 96.

Goðafoss, the Fall of the Gods: as illustrious …

Its position directly on the Arctic Circle lends the island of Grímsey **Grímsey**
– 5.3sq km/2 sq miles in area and 41km/25 miles off Iceland – a certain cachet. The barely 100 inhabitants of this northernmost settlement in Iceland share the verdant island with a large number of seabirds, for whom the rocks of the eastern coast (up to 105m/344ft
high) make ideal nesting conditions. The islanders live first and fore-
most by fishing and fish processing, but since the island has had an
airport and regular ferry connections, many tourists join them,
drawn here by the »real« **midnight sun**.

Some 50km/31 miles east of Akureyri, the Skjálfandafljót river forms ✱
the Goðafoss waterfall, which might boast only a modest height of **Goðafoss**
10m/33ft, but the way the water gushes over a lip 30m/98ft wide into
the gorge below is highly photogenic. As the **»Fall of the Gods«** occupies a logistically strategic position on the ring road, it counts among
the most popular sights in Iceland. The fall got its name from the
Goði Þorgeir, who converted to Christianity at Þingvellir in the year
1000, whereupon he threw his statues of pagan gods into the waterfall.

The **extensive peninsula** between Eyjafjörður and Skjálfandi used to **Látraströnd**
be densely populated, but nowadays is completely abandoned.
Hardly in use now, the paths provide a good option for longer walks.
One pretty stretch leads from Grenivík and hugs the coast all the
way to Gjögurtá at the furthest tip of the peninsula.

… as the gods that created it

Aurora borealis in green – not an uncommon sight in the Icelandic winter

LUMINOUS PAINTINGS IN THE SKY

The Northern Lights count among the most impressive natural phenomena in the Nordic countries. Iceland, Northern Scotland, Lapland, Greenland, Canada, Alaska and North Siberia offer the best chances of seeing them. These areas all lie on the polar auroral oval, a circular zone around the South Magnetic Pole.

Here, polar lights appear frequently, sometimes even daily, especially at times of **heightened solar activity**. If the sun is particularly active, relatively weak polar lights might even be seen in the night sky further south. As it never gets really dark in the northern parts of the world between mid-April and late August, the polar lights can only be seen in the wintertime.

Awestruck wonder

The inhabitants of the far north have been living with the Northern Lights for aeons, but even for them the bright night sky never loses its power to amaze, and so superstition and awestruck wonder always accompanied the **nightly glow in the sky**, as for millennia all earthly attempts to explain it failed. Anyone who has seen these mostly green, but sometimes blue or red, veils of light continually and soundlessly changing shape will understand that this phenomenon unsettled many. For hours, the veils, beams,

draperies, arcs, clouds and swirls dance across the sky to disappear again all of a sudden or to culminate in an **aurora** looking like a crown seen from below.

Bad omen

In the Middle Ages, the polar lights, in the same way as the appearance of a comet, were taken to signal impending war, famine and disease. In **Norse mythology** and the myths of the Northern American Indians and Inuit, the polar lights played an

In the Middle Ages, the polar lights, in the same way as the appearance of a comet, were taken to signal impending war, famine and disease.

important role too. They were often interpreted as a dance of the virgins and Valkyries, or as the struggle between the gods and spirits, but also as a message to the living from fallen warriors. In Finland, a mythical

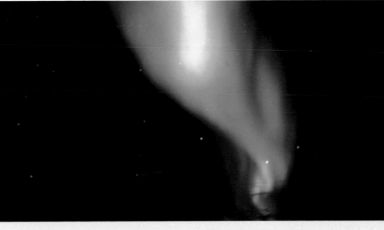

creature – Repu the fox – is said to be responsible, whipping up snowflakes that cover the sky with glittering light. They have also been taken to herald a change in the weather: thus on the Faroe Islands, low-lying Northern Lights signalled good weather, whereas Northern Lights standing high in the sky heralded bad weather. And if they were flickering, then wind was brewing.

There's an explanation for everything

Nowadays we know all this isn't true and that the mysterious lights in the night sky are down to a **reciprocal interaction of the sun and the earth's magnetic field**. Every eleven years the sun shows an exceptionally high number of spots, a sign of heightened sun activity manifesting itself in particularly violent eruptions – so-called »protuberances«. During these eruptions, X-rays travelling at the speed of light are expelled, as well as electrically charged particles such as protons and electrons, which are much slower and only reach the earth as a sun wind a few days after an eruption. The **sun wind particles** hit the earth's magnetic field, compress it

and move along the magnetic lines of force towards the magnetic poles. By doing so, they penetrate the uppermost layer of the earth's atmosphere where they hit gas molecules such as oxygen or nitrogen. This changes a part of their kinetic energy into light, with the collisions with oxygen leading to green northern lights, those with nitrogen to a red tinge in the sky. As the sun wind particles migrate from all sides in the direction of the magnetic poles, polar lights always form around both poles at the same time. The northern lights are called **Aurora borealis**, its southern equivalent **Aurora australis**. If the **sun wind** becomes a magnetic storm, the magnetic field is even more compressed, and the sun wind comes into contact with the earth's atmosphere earlier than the magnetic poles. This is why during periods of intense sun activity polar lights can also be seen in Central Europe. Summer visitors to Iceland will not see polar lights because of the bright nights. A small compensation is offered by the multimedia show at the Geysir Center (p. 169), which, while not as fascinating as the real thing, does give an idea of the beauty of the luminous night sky.

Möðruvellir The farmstead of Möðruvellir, situated 1km/0.6 miles north of Akureyri in the Hörgárdalur valley, is one of the most historic places in northern Iceland. From 1296 up to the Reformation there was an **Augustine monastery** here; afterwards it served as the seat of the provincial governor. Today, Möðruvellir houses an agricultural research institute and a handsome church dating from the year 1865. It is also the birthplace of the writer Jón Sveinsson (»Nonni«).

Dalvík Dalvík on the western banks of the Eyjafjörður was almost completely destroyed by a major earthquake in 1934 and rebuilt in a modern style. The **heritage museum** shows a pretty decent natural history collection. The museum also honours the memory of Jóhann Pétursson, who was born in 1913 in Dalvík and at 2.34m/7.6ft remains, to this day, the tallest man Iceland has ever known. Opening times: June–Aug daily 11am–6pm. Dalvík is also the point of departure for **whale-watching tours** (information: tel. 863 25 55; www.hvalaskodun.is) and trips to the island of Hrísey.

★★ Askja · Kverkfjöll

J 4/5

Region: Highlands north of the Vatnajökull

Icelandic highlands at their best! The area north of the Vatnajökull with the prominent table mountain of Herðubreið, the crater cauldron of Askja, the volcanic crater of Víti – which invites travellers to take a bath in its milky-white water – and the geothermal area at the Kverkfjöll, is among the most interesting regions of Iceland, and will stay in the memory of any visitor.

[F 88] and [F 910] Not all paths lead to the caldera of Askja, but many do. Most drivers choose the **Öskjuleið** [F 88], which turns south off the ring road 30km/18.5 miles east of Reykjahlíð am ► Mývatn. Running parallel to the raging glacier river **Jökulsá á Fjöllum**, the [F 88] is – along with all other access roads to the Askja – only passable by jeep. Visitors travelling west on the ring road from ► Egilsstaðir are best served by the [923], turning off 34km/21 miles past Egilsstaðir. This access road first leads through the **Jökuldalur to Brú**, where it joins the [F 910], which can be followed briefly north, then westwards to the Askja. Sandy passages and a few easy fords have to be negotiated on the [F 910], while the raging **Kreppa** is bridged. The scenic beauty on both sides of the [F 910] is unforgettable: an area characterized by pumice deserts, basalt formations and dark expanses covered in volcanic ash, where sea lyme grass and sea starwort, oyster plant and sea campion maintain tender islands of vegetation. Alternatives to the [923] as access road to the [F 910] are the [901] and [F 905], or indeed the [901] and [907]. A general recommendation is to get to

Aerial shot of the Jökulsá á Fjöllum glacier river in winter

experience both the [F 88] and the [F 910], one of them on the way there, the other on the way back.

✳ Herðubreið – the »broad-shouldered«

This mountain dominates the scenery of an entire region, being ever-present on the horizon here: the Herðubreið, or »broad-shouldered«, table mountain displays its distinctive outline in the east of the lava desert **Ódáðahraun**. Whether approaching the Askja area from the north on the [F 88] or from the east on the [F 910], the Herðubreið is a constant presence and **point of reference** on the way to the highlands north of the Vatnajökull. Standing at 1,682m/5,518ft tall, the mountain towers above the high plateau at its base by some 1,000m/3,280ft, making it an unmissable landmark which is often shrouded in cloud.

<table>
<tr><td>❓ DID YOU KNOW ...?</td></tr>
<tr><td>■ ... that in Norse mythology the Herðubreið – under the name of Asgard – is the seat of the divine dynasty of the æsir (Norse gods)? However, the first people to reach the sacred summit area were the German Hans Reck and the Icelander Sigurður Sumarliðason in 1908.</td></tr>
</table>

With its abundant vegetation, the oasis of Herðubreiðarlindir makes a pleasant contrast to the barren countryside east of the Herðubreið: a speck of land blessed with a wealth of plant life amidst an expanse

Herðubrei-
ðarlindir

⏵ VISITING ASKJA · KVERKFJÖLL

INFORMATION
▶Egilsstaðir
▶Mývatn, Reykjahlíð

EXCURSIONS
In high season (15 June – 31 Aug), Destination Iceland offer excursions to the Askja three times a week (Mon, Wed, Fri), becoming daily between 15 July and 15 Aug. Duration: approx. 12hrs. Departure in Reykjahlíð at Mývatn. The same company sets off twice a week for the three-day »Ice and Fire Expedition« heading for Askja and Kverkfjöll. Departures from Reykjahlíð, Akureyri and Húsavík. For more information, contact: tel. 591 10 20, www.dice.is

WHERE TO STAY
▶ Budget
Herðubreiðarlindir:
Þorsteinskáli lodge/campsite
Tel. 462 27 20
(book ahead for lodge!)
Lodge (floor mattresses, cooking facilities) and campsite in a green oasis on the [F 88] dirt road near the Herðubreið.

Askja/Dyngjufjöll:
Dreki lodge/campsite
Tel. 462 27 20

(book ahead for lodge!)
Small lodge in an impressive location at the entrance to the Dragon Gorge; campsite somewhat exposed to the wind and on stony ground, but offering good sanitary facilities, partly adapted to special needs.

Kverkfjöll:
Sigurðarskáli lodge/campsite
Tel. 853 62 36 (book ahead for the lodge at the Ferðafélag Ísland Icelandic hiking club: tel. 568 25 33, www.fi.is)
Lodge at the northern edge of the Vatnajökull. Grass areas set up for tents.

of desert landscape. Herðubreiðarlindir lies right on the [F 88], 60 km/37 miles south of the turning off the ring road, and is the starting point for hikes and tours at the foot of the »Queen of Mountains« – another name for the Herðubreið. Accommodation is provided by a lodge with campsite run by the Akureyri hiking club. Waymarked trails lead through the surrounding countryside, including one to a lava cave where the legendary outcast **Fjalla Eyvindur** is said to have spent the harsh winter of 1774/75. Herðubreið may also be climbed from Herðubreiðarlindir, but the route is considered very

The Herðubreið: seat of the gods?

difficult. Even those with alpine hillwalking experience and the right equipment should check the conditions on the mountain with the staff at the lodge before setting out.

✴ ✴ A bath in the volcano: Askja

Our next stop is anything but a green oasis such as the one at the Herðubreið. In harsh surroundings at the foot of the Dyngjufjöll massif, 30km/18.5 miles southwest of Herðubreiðarlindir, there is just a mountain hut and campsite. The Dreki lodge lies at the entrance to the Drekagil, the **Dragon Gorge**, which ends with a waterfall plunging down a rock face. A trail leads through the entire gorge.

Drekagil

The Dreki lodge is the start of the [F 894], a dead-end road leading through a lava field which only appeared in 1961 – this is a volcanic area that remains active to this day! – to a parking area at the northeastern edge of the Askja caldera. The Askja's **crater cauldron** (caldera) was formed just under 5,000 years ago by the emptying of a magma chamber and the subsequent subsidence of the ground. From the car park a footpath offers a 20-minute stroll to the interior of the caldera, and on to the Víti crater and the Öskjuvatn. Both are much younger than the Askja caldera: following a major eruption in 1875, the southeastern part of the Askja subsided further and gradually filled with water – giving birth to the Öskjuvatn. At the same time, further eruptions formed the Víti crater. A bath in its milky-

✴ ✴
Víti crater, Öskjuvatn

Crater landscape: the Öskjuvatn with the Víti crater in the foreground

white, lukewarm water is a very special experience. A monument at the crater's edge honours the memory of the geologist **Walther von Knebel** and the painter **Max Rudloff**, who in 1907 as part of a research trip set out to the Askja area, and despite advance warning put out on the Öskjuvatn in a canvas boat. Neither of them was ever heard from again.

✳ ✳ Kverkfjöll: hot springs in the eternal ice

The Kverkjökull glacier with the Kverkfjöll mountain is a textbook example of the combination of volcanic activity and glacial phenomena, of **fire and ice**. Whilst volcanic activity below Iceland's glaciers is not unique by any means and other geothermal extrusions from the perpetual ice do exist elsewhere, it is only at the Kverkfjöll that they are accessible with relatively little effort.

Two tracks lead to the Kverkfjöll, so that one can be used for access and the other as the return road. Starting from the Askja, drive east, and later southeast, on the [F 910], until reaching the [F 902] (Kverkfjallaleið). Three kilometres/1.8 miles further on, the [F 903] (Hvannalindavegur) turn off south,

and changing exhibitions featuring well-known textile artists. Part of the museum, the Halldórustofa, is dedicated to **Halldóra Bjarnadóttir** (1873–1981), the oldest Icelandic woman on record. Opening times: ⊙ June–Aug daily 10am–5pm, www.simnet.is/textile

Consecrated in 1993, the **parish church of Blönduós** was designed by Maggi Jónsson. Taken to symbolize the surrounding nature, the conspicuous concrete building has excellent acoustics and is often used for concerts. The altarpiece is the work of Jóhannes Kjarval.

Blönduósskirkja

Around Blönduós

It was in 1133 that in Þingeyrar, 25km/15.5 miles southwest of Blönduós, the first **Benedictine monastery** in Iceland was founded. Remaining active for some 400 years up to the Reformation, the monastery held a lot of land in the surrounding countryside. It was also an important cultural centre where many historic books were written. Thus, the abbot **Arngrímur Brandsson** wrote down the history of Bishop Guðmundur the Good, containing the oldest known description of Iceland. Various sagas of the Húnavatn region, such as the Heiðarvíga Saga, were also recorded in this monastery. Today, the stone church built between 1864 and 1877 in the Romanesque style is the only reminder of this once important religious site. Inside, look out for the **alabaster altarpiece**, probably dating back to the 13th century, the pulpit (1696) and the silver baptismal font.

Þingeyrar

Situated between the Víðidalsfjall (993m/3,258ft) and the Vatnsdalsfjall (1,018m/3,340ft), the green valley of Vatnsdalur, 25km/15.5miles

Vatnsdalur

 VISITING BLÖNDUÓS

INFORMATION
Brautarhvammi
Tel. 452 45 20, www.northwest.is

WHERE TO EAT
▶ **Inexpensive**
Við Árbakkann
Húnabraut 2, Tel. 452 46 78
Conspicuous blue house with terrace in the centre of town, serving snacks such as sandwiches and pancakes.

WHERE TO STAY
▶ **Mid-range**
Hótel Blanda
Aðalgata 6
Tel. 557 61 00
Fax 557 61 08
www.gladheimar.is
Small hotel in the historic centre of Blönduós right on the ring road.

Glaðheimar
Brautarhvammur 11
Tel. 452 44 03
Fax 452 49 13
www.gladheimar.is
Seven well-appointed holiday cottages sleeping 3 to 8, most of which have hot tubs and a sauna. Further accommodation is available in the Blöndubyggð guesthouse.

long, has a lot of good pasture and is traversed by the Vatnsdalsá river. Rich in salmon and with its source in the highlands, the river forms a deep gorge and numerous waterfalls on its way to the sea. At the exit of the valley, near the ring road, lie a bizarre group of hills (Vatnsdalshólar), formed by a massive avalanche from the **Vatnsdalsfjall** long before the settlement of the country. The hills have different colours and shapes, some quite conspicuous. North of the ring road, three hills (Þrístapar) lie close together. This is where, on 12 January 1830, the last execution in Iceland took place. Waymarked hiking trails lead through the Vatnsdalshólar.

Skagi Peninsula

From Blönduós, consider a drive around the sparsely populated Skagi Peninsula, on the [74], [744] and [745] (length of drive around 140 km/87 miles). On the coast at **Skagaströnd** near **Spákonufellshöfði** some fine basalt pillars can be found. One of the most striking mountains in the area is the Spákonufell (646m/2,119ft), which got its name (»Mountain of the Seeress«) from the clairvoyant Þórdís who in the 10th century lived on the farm of the same name at the foot of the mountain. From the **Brandaskarð** farm, a hiking trail leads to the summit, with good views in all directions. Also north of Skagaströnd, between Króksbjarg and Kálfshamarsvík, there are cliffs of up to 50 metres/165ft in height, featuring basalt pillars that are worth seeing. In the north of the peninsula, at **Selavíkurtangi**, seals can often be spotted on the rocks from the shore.

! Baedeker TIP

A visit to the King of Country

The Kántrýbær country music restaurant in Skagaströnd is unique in all of Iceland. Owner Hallbjörn Hjartarson calls himself the only cowboy in Iceland, running his own radio station (FM 96.7 and 100.7) and often organising live performances in his rustic venue. Hólanesvegur, tel. 452 29 50.

Borgarnes

D 5

Region: West Iceland   **Population:** 1,770

Borgarnes appears as far back as the Egil saga under the name Digranes, which is why all the roads here are named after personalities from this saga. With the construction of the bridge over the Borgarfjörður in 1980, the town became a transit hub between Reykjavík and the North.

What to see in and around Borgarnes

Skallagrímsgarður

In the small Skallagrímsgarður park in the town centre a burial mound shelters the remains of Egil's father, **Skallgrímur Kveldúlfs-**

● VISITING BORGARNES

INFORMATION
Hyrnan, Brúartorg
Tel. 437 22 14, fax 437 23 14
www.vesturland.is, www.west.is
or: Borgarbraut 59 (Esso petrol station), tel. 437 15 29

EVENTS
The Reykholt Festival in July sees classical music performed on historic soil. www.reykholt.is.

WHERE TO EAT
► Expensive
Restaurant in the Borgarnes Hótel
Egilsgata 14-16
Good Icelandic cuisine

► Inexpensive
Esso petrol station
Borgarbraut 59
Large selection of good fast food dishes

WHERE TO STAY
► Mid-range
Fosshotel Bifröst
Tel. 433 30 90, www.fosshotel.is
Summer hotel on the campus of the business college, in a pretty location amidst a lava field at the foot of the volcanic cone of Grábrók. Good hiking opportunities.

Hótel Reykholt
Tel. 435 12 60
Fax 435 12 06
hotelreykholt@simnet.is
Modern hotel near the museum, also offering spaces for sleeping bags. Open all year round.

► Budget
Guesthouse Bjarg
Tel. 437 19 25,
Fax 437 19 75
bjarg@simnet.is
Old farmstead a little outside Borgarnes, with a total of 14 beds, amongst them a studio apartment.

Feraþjónustan Húsafelli
Tel. 435 15 50, fax 435 15 51
www.husafell.is
Cabins with spaces for sleeping bags, and a pretty campsite in the birch forest of Húsafell, open all year round. With swimming pool, horse-riding, hiking and golf.

Milli vina
Tel. 435 15 30/861 32 90
www.millivina.is
Guesthouse on farm with six doubles. Garden with hot pot. Snooker and darts available. Breakfast and dinner on request. No credit cards.

---

son, who was buried, Viking-style, with his horse and weapons. A relief by the Danish artist Anna Marie Brodersen shows Egil with his dead son Böðvar, who is also said to have been buried here.

The Safnahús museum complex (Bjarnarbraut 4–6) houses the **Art Museum**, showing works by Icelandic artists, the **Natural History Museum** with an extensive collection of stuffed birds, as well as the **Heritage Museum**, showing historical dress and tools of daily life from the region. Opening times: Mon – Fri 1 – 6pm, Tues to 8pm.   Safnahús

Borg à Mýrum The Borg à Mýrum farm at the end of Borgarvogur Bay, west of Borgarnes, is the birthplace of the famous skald (poet) **Egill Skallgrimsson** (900 – 983). In front of the small wooden church (1885) stands the *Sonatorrek* (Lament for the Sons) sculpture by **Ásmundur Sveinsson**, representing the loss of Egill's two sons Gunnar and Böðvar. The great poet **Snorri Sturluson** (1178 – 1241) also lived for a while in Borg before moving to Reykholt.

Deildar- Some 20km/12 miles north of Borgarnes, the [50] branches off the
tunguhver ring road, leading through a wide, green agricultural valley, surrounded by gently rising hills. Shortly after the **Hvitá** river crossing, the Deildartunguhver thermal spring, with a length of several hundred metres, produces around 11,000 litres/2,905 gallons of near-boiling water per minute. This makes it the most productive hot water spring in Iceland, but not the only one, as these gently steaming springs – tamed these days – can be seen everywhere, providing the farmers with cheap energy.

Viðgelmir lava After this detour, head back across the Hvitá and follow the [523]
cave leading along the northern banks of the river. There, the **Fljótstunga farmstead** is the starting point for a visit to the Viðgelmir lava cave, one of the largest lava caves in the world. As a protected site, the cave may only be visited as part of a guided tour. At the **Kalmanstunga farm**, a track branches off to two other caves, **Surtshellir and Stefánshellir**, which may be explored independently.

Húsafell, Shortly before reaching Húsafell, the [F 550] highland road (►Kaldi-
Hraunfossar dalur) leads to ►Þingvellir; in good weather, it is passable with a regular saloon car. Húsafell makes a good base for walks in the surrounding area. Past Húsafell, the [518] follows the southern banks of the river until, a few kilometres later, a parking area announces the Hraunfossar waterfalls. Under the **Hallmundarhraun** lava flow, which formed around 800BC and is mentioned in the saga of Grettir the Strong, countless waterfalls gush forth along a stretch of around one kilometre/0.6 miles, to flow into the Hvitá. A little further upriver lies the **Barnafoss** waterfall, named »The Children's Waterfall« in memory of two children who drowned here.

✳
Reykholt The [518] eventually leads to the parish of Reykholt, which also has a school, in the **Reykholtsdalur** valley, one of the most important historic places in Iceland. This is where the most famous Icelandic poet and historian, **Snorri Sturluson** (1206 – 1241) lived and worked. With the *Heimskringla*, Sturluson composed a detailed historical analysis of his time. Even more important however is his skaldic manual, detailing the rules of the poetic art of the time and many Norse myths. Snorri Sturluson was not merely a poet and historian however, he also ranked among the most influential men of his time. He ruled over two goðorð, sat in the Alþing and was twice appointed

Hraunfossar: countless waterfalls feed the Hvitá

law speaker, at the time the highest office in the state. A power politician, Sturluson had good connections to the Norwegian royal dynasty and was probably involved in several intrigues, leading to his murder in Reykholt in 1241. Today, he is remembered with a statue in front of the school by Gustav Vigeland, a present from the Norwegian royal family. Behind the building lies the small round **Snorralaug** swimming pool, which dates back to the time of Snorri Sturluson and is fed by a hot spring. From there, a partially preserved underground passage leads to the dwelling. Snorri was probably buried in the cemetery next to the small wooden church, but the exact spot is not known. For the past few years, extensive archeological digs have been attempting to shed more light on medieval Reykholt. The **Snorrastofa cultural centre**, housed in the basement of the modern church, documents the life of Snorri Sturluson. Opening times: daily 10am – 6pm, www.snorrastofa.is

Djúpivogur

L 5

Region: East Iceland   **Population:** 400

The merchants of the Hanseatic League were among the first to trade here, taking advantage of the good natural harbour. Following on from them, the Danes came and made Djúpivogur one of the most important fishing ports in the eastern fjords.

▶ VISITING DJÚPIVOGUR

INFORMATION
Langabúð
Tel. 478 82 20

TRIPS TO PAPEY ISLAND
daily 1pm, duration approx. 4hrs.
Tel. 478 81 19

WHERE TO EAT
▶ Inexpensive to expensive
Restaurant in the Framtíð Hotel
Tel. 478 88 87

Lovely little restaurant in the old part of the house serving excellent Icelandic food with gourmet aspirations, a good wine list and cellar bar.

▶ Inexpensive
Langabúð
Tel. 478 82 20
The museum café serves coffee and cakes in a snug setting.

WHERE TO STAY
▶ Mid-range
Hótel Framtíð
Vogalandi 4
Tel. 478 88 87, fax 478 81 87
framtid@simnet.is

The hotel, named »Future«, was built in 1905 right on the harbour. A modern annexe does detract from the charm of the old house. Comfortable rooms in the new building, as well as rooms without a bathroom and sleeping-bag accommodation.

▶ Budget
Farfuglaheimili Berunes
Tel. 478 89 88
Simple and very cosy accommodation in a former farmhouse on the northern side of the Berufjörður, with views across the fjord. Also campsite and holiday cottages.

Djúpivogur lies on the relatively flat promontory of Búlandsnes, pushing out far to sea between the fjords of Hamarsfjörður and Berufjörður and petering out in numerous rocky islands. Inland, the regular, pyramid-shaped outline of the **Búlandstindur** (1,068m/ 3,504ft) draws the eye. The mountain is supposed to possess strong magical powers. Legend has it that after Iceland's conversion to Christianity, the old pagan statues and idols were cast into the depths from a rocky ledge on the eastern side at an altitude of 700m/2,300ft, called Goðaborg.

What to see in and around Djúpivogur

The long red house above the harbour is said to be one of the oldest trading houses in Iceland; with parts of it dating back to the year 1790, it served as the economic centre of Djúpivogur until the 1950s. Around the year 1850, another timber-framed house was erected, which stands in front of the Langabúð to this day. Today, the Langabúð's interior houses two collections: the works of the sculptor **Ríkarður Jónsson**, and memorabilia of the minister **Eysteinn Jónsson** among other Icelandic politicians. The attic is given over to an informative museum of regional history. Opening times: daily 10am–6pm.

Langabúð

Lying off the promontory of Búlandsnes alongside numerous other islands and skerries, Papey – measuring some two sq km/three quarters of a sq mile – was in all likelihood inhabited by Irish monks before the arrival of the Vikings. The name of the island could be a pointer, as the **Vikings** called the Irish monks »Papar«. The monks were followed on the island by farmers supplementing their income by collecting eggs and the down from eider ducks. Today the island

Papey

Puffins enjoying life on Papey

A boat, a house and swathes of fog against a spectacular backdrop – everyday life in Djúpivogur

is uninhabited and given over completely to the shrieking seabirds. In the water and on low rocks seals enjoy life. The house of the last island dweller, plus one of the smallest wooden churches in Iceland, dating from 1807, serve as reminders of the times when the island was still inhabited.

Teigarhorn The coast at the Teigarhorn farm, 3km/1.8 miles north of Djúpivogur, has been known for 300 years as a great site for attractive minerals and crystals; in particular, it is world-famous for its zeolite deposits. Today, the entire area is in private hands and its natural beauty **protected**. A collection of minerals for sale are on display at the farm, comprising finds exclusively from the area, mainly zeolites. Opening times: daily 9am – 9pm. Behind the building housing the mineral collection stands the old Teigarhorn dwelling, which was imported in 1880 by Niels Weyvadt, the head of the Ørum & Wulff trading company, as an assembly kit from Norway. His daughter Níkolína (1848 – 1921) learned to be a photographer in Copenhagen and studied mineralogy. Taking over the farmstead after the death of her father, she had a photographic studio built next to it where she worked successfully for many years. **Nikolina Weyvadt** is considered the first female photographer in Iceland; her work is held by the National Museum which also, in 1992, took over her residence in Teigarhorn, planning to extend it into a photography museum. Some reproductions of Níkolína's photographs can be seen in the Framtíð Hotel in Djúpivogur.

20km/12.5 miles northwest of Djúpivogur, a cul-de-sac branches off   Eyjólfsstaðir
and leads for some 2km/1.25 miles to the Eyjólfsstaðir farmstead in
the Fossárdalur. The **Fossá valley**, making its way to the fjord over
numerous basalt steps and waterfalls, is framed by mighty, terraced,
predominantly green mountain slopes. The ring road or the farm
can both serve as starting points for a hike, either along the river or,
more easily, on the jeep track leading uphill through the valley.

Eastern fjords

L/M 2-5

Region: East Iceland

**Around a dozen fjords are arranged along the coast of East Ice-
land, with the largest of them, the Reyðarfjörður, penetrating for
some 30km/18.5 miles inland. The eastern fjords are similar to
those in the west, just that everything here is on a slightly smaller
scale. The eastern fjords are also relatively old geologically and far
removed from the volcanically active zones of the island. Which is
why the typical rock here is the dark, often multilayered basalt
wrought by the Ice Age glaciers.**

The chain of fjords starts in the north with the relatively small Borgarfjörður and continues south to the Álftafjörður. On the good natural harbours along the coast a relative proliferation of settlements
have sprung up over time, the largest being **Neskaupstaður** and **Eskifjörður**. Until around 1900 they were all able to live comfortably
off herring fishing. Today, fishing and fish processing still form the
area's economic basis, but the golden times of the herring boom are
long over; abandoned farms and stagnating or dwindling numbers of
inhabitants bear witness to difficult realities.

Up to now, tourism has not taken on the role that was hoped for,   Hiking
which is why local people are trying to increase the choice of activities for visitors. A start was made with a few new cafés, giving a bit
of life to the very quiet villages. Waymarked trails and a generally im-
proved infrastructure are in place to lure more hikers into the region, who will find ideal conditions for short routes, but also for
longer expeditions through a spectacular landscape. There is now also a map showing all the waymarked trails.

Neskaupstaður

The largest town in East Iceland has held town status since 1929 and
does have a certain urban flair – at least compared to the other settlements along the fjord coast. The main road, running close to the

Bad weather in the eastern fjords might conjure up visions of the apocalypse

Eskifjörður

Eskifjörður, situated on the small, eponymous branch of the **Reyðarfjörður**, on the road to Reyðarfjörður, makes for a pretty sight. The colourful houses strung out along the town appear tiny in front of the impressive mountain backdrop. The town is somewhat hemmed in by the steep mountainside which in the winter often causes avalanche danger alerts. At a height of 985m/3,232ft, the **Holmatindur** is one of the most impressive mountains in the area, dividing the two fjords of Eskifjörður and Reyðarfjörður. Taking a stroll through Eskifjörður, some old houses still catch the eye between the new buildings. A monument by Ragnar Kjartansson on the main road honours the memory of the drowned mariners from Eskifjörður.

Maritime Museum The East Iceland Maritime Museum (Sjóminjasafn Austurlands; Strandgata 39b) is housed in the **Gamla Búð**, an old trading house dating back to 1816. In front of the museum visitors will find some old tools, a 200-year-old anchor from a sailing ship, cast-iron pots which would have been used for boiling cod-liver oil, and even a steamship propeller. On the ground floor, a faithfully reconstructed old grocery store may be viewed, as well as collections on whaling, shark hunting, and herring fishing. On the upper floor, the **heritage museum** shows a model of Eskifjörður town from the 1920s, all kinds of traditional working tools and equipment for the production of sweets. All in all, the museum gives a vivid idea of what life was like in the town during the time of the herring fisheries. Fittingly enough, the aroma wafting over from the fish-processing plant also provides a connection between the past and the present. Another part of the museum is a herring-processing plant from 1890, which can be visited in the eastern part of the town. Opening times: daily 1 – 5pm.

Further settlements

During the first half of the last century, Reyðarfjörður was the main trading centre for the farmers of the Fljótsdalshérað area, and during the Second World War, there was an **Allied base** here with over 3,000 soldiers. Today, Reyðarfjörður appears fairly sleepy. A war museum was established in 1995, to mark the 50th anniversary of the war ending. Without aspiring to provide an in-depth historical ana-

Reyðarfjörður

At the Reyðarfjörður

Lagarfljót Fed by the Vatnajökull, the Lagarfljót river forms a lake, some 25km/ 15.5 miles long and at its widest 2.5km/1.5 miles wide, south of Egilsstaðir. Some maps may list the lake as **Lögurinn**. At a depth of 112m/367ft and with a sediment layer up to 100m/328ft thick the bottom of the lake is the deepest point in Iceland. A muddy-grey colour due to the glacier water, the lake is the **Loch Ness of Iceland**, as its freezing waters are said to shelter the Lagarfljótsormurinn, a lake monster which guards a hoard of gold. The »Lagarfljót Worm«, also called **Laggi**, should now be a ripe old age indeed, as the first sightings – up to 20 so far – date back to the 13th century. Incidentally, Laggi is equally camera-shy as its relative in Loch Ness, which is why there is now a prize for the first photo of the monster. Some 11km/ just under 7 miles south of Egilsstaðir, the [931] turns off to lead around the entire lake (approx. 90 km/56 miles).

Hallormsstaðars- kógur Iceland's most extensive forest area on the eastern bank of the Lagarfljót at Hallormsstaður has been looked after and nurtured since 1899. 70% of the trees are birches, with the oldest 160 years old, but the most imposing among them only reach a height of 13m/42ft. As far back as 1903 the first trials began with the **planting of foreign trees**; since then 90 types of tree have been tested for their suitability to Icelandic life, of which only ten made the grade. The Atlavík campsite lies in the middle of the forest on the banks of the lake.

Hengifoss Shortly after crossing the bridge in the north of the Fljótsdalur, the waters of the Hengifoss plunge down 118m/387ft, which gives it the distinction of being the third-highest waterfall in Iceland. Below the Hengifoss, the **Litlanesfoss**, 30m/98ft high, features an unusually beautiful basin lined with basalt columns. From the car park at the western riverbank, a path leads uphill for roughly 2.5km/1.5 miles to the Hengifoss. Two kilometres/1.2 miles south of the waterfall, the [F 910] jeep track branches off to the 1,863m/6,112-ft **Snæfell** at the foot of the Vatnajökull (57km/35 miles).

Skriðuklaustur Originally, the farmstead in the Fljótsdalur was simply called Skriða (landslide), but following the foundation of an Augustinian monastery in the late 14th century, Klaustur (monastery) was added to the name of the place. It was the only monastery in East Iceland and also the last to be founded in Catholic times. In 1938, the poet **Gunnar Gunnarsson** (1889–1975) bought Skriðuklaustur and had a German architect design a stately home in the Bohemian style. Due to financial and health-related problems, Gunnarsson and his wife had moved to Reykjavík by 1948, where he lived until his death. He bequeathed Skriðuklaustur to the state, stipulating its use for cultural purposes. Today, his wish has been granted, and every year the Gunnar Gunnarsson Institute organizes several exhibitions in the prestigious house, beautifully located on the hillside. Opening times: daily 10am–6pm.

Golden Circle

D/E 5/6

Region: Southwest Iceland

Cultural and historic sites with breathtaking nature: the Golden Circle route takes in the region's touristic highlights east of Reykjavík, including Þingvellir, Geysir, Gullfoss and Skálholt.

The starting point for the Golden Circle route is usually ►Reykjavík. Taking the ring road from the Icelandic capital via Hveragerði soon leads to Selfoss. Here the circuit turns off northwards to the [35], leading past the Kerið explosion crater, stopping at the church of **Skálholt** – in medieval times the spiritual centre of the country – and eventually reaching the geysers in the **Haukadalur** and, a few kil-

 VISITING GOLDEN CIRCLE

INFORMATION

Hveragerði tourist office
Breiðamörk 2
Tel. 483 46 01, fax 483 46 04
www.southiceland.is

In the Geysir Center
Tel. 480 68 00, fax 480 68 01
geysir@geysircenter.is

WHERE TO EAT
►Reykjavík
►Þingvellir

WHERE TO STAY
► Mid-range
Fosshótel Ingólfur
Between Hveragerði and Selfoss
Tel. 483 52 22, fax 483 52 21
Mini apartments, all with whirlpool next to the terrace, and excellent cuisine. Attached to the restaurant is a riding arena, where Icelandic horse shows are put on every evening during the tourist season.

Geysir Center
Tel. 480 68 00, fax 480 68 01
www.geysircenter.com

With hotel, restaurant, pool, multimedia show, horses for hire and campsite, the Geysir Center offers tourists everything they need. There is also space for sleeping bags.

Hveragerði: Hótel Eldhestar
Tel. 480 48 00, fax 480 48 01
www.eldhestar.is
Small hotel with ten comfortable double rooms furnished in a rustic style. With all the riding excursions on offer, horse lovers will be particularly happy here.

Skálholt: Skálholtsskóli
Tel. 486 88 70, fax 486 89 90
skoli@skalholt.is
The modern school building of Skálholt offers 18 comfortable double rooms, with another 35 beds in a neighbouring building.

► Budget
Selfoss: Gesthus
Tel. 482 35 85, www.gesthus.is
Eleven bungalows with kitchen, bathroom and TV in Selfoss. Plus campsite.

ometres away, the **Gullfoss**, the Golden Waterfall. The return to Reykjavík passes the village of Laugarvatn, where visitors can find accommodation, and through ▶ Þingvellir National Park. Sightseeing coaches need about eight hours to complete the 250km/155-mile round trip. Visitors with their own car can build in additional side trips – for instance to the town of Selfoss or into the ▶ Þjórsárdalur – and detours such as returning to Reykjavík along the Þingvallavatn lake via Nesjavellir. Only a few sections of the Golden Circle have not yet been tarmacked, and the whole route is passable even in a small saloon car. The Golden Circle is kept free even in the wintertime.

To southern Iceland via the ring road

Hellisheiði   At the start of the Golden Circle, driving southeast from Reykjavík, the landscape seems to become more primal, raw and inhospitable by the minute. The dominant feature is black lava with minimal vegetation. Soon after the [39] turns off towards the Þorlákshöfn ferry harbour (▶ p. 169), the [1] ring road leads uphill to the Hellisheiði. On the western edge of this high plateau the ring road cuts through the very lava flow which in the year 1000 gushed out of an eruption fissure at the nearby **Hengill** massif, just at the time when not 30km/18.5 miles north of here, in Þingvellir, the medieval parliament resolved to introduce Christianity, which resulted in the lava flow being dubbed **Kristnitökuhraun**, »Christianization lava«. To the east, the Hellisheiði ends abruptly and the ring road wends its way down the steep Kambar slope.

Hveragerði   Situated right below the slope, Hveragerði is a spa and greenhouse town with some 2,000 inhabitants. There is no better place to witness the know-how of the Icelanders in outsmarting the vagaries of the Northern Atlantic climate using geothermal energy: local hot springs are used to heat innumerable **hothouses**, with even tropical fruit ripening under their glass roofs. While these serve to demonstrate what can be done, flower and vegetable cultivation are of more economic relevance. Iceland's hothouse gardeners – with their state-run horticultural college in Hveragerði – largely satisfy the country's demand for cucumbers, peppers and tomatoes. Some enterprises sell directly to the public. With a café under palm trees as well as a gigantic souvenir shop, the Eden greenhouse (Austurmörk 25) does not hide its ambitions to serve the tourist market.

Selfoss   Selfoss lies off the Golden Circle route, which turns off to the north before reaching the entrance to the town. With its nearly 5,000 inhabitants Selfoss is Iceland's largest inland town, despite having merged with the coastal villages of Eyrarbakki and Stokkseyri to form the municipality of **Árborg** during a local government reorganization in the late 1990s, which gave it access to the sea. The town's

The hothouse town of Hveragerði owes its livelihood to hot springs

history begins in the late 19th century, with the construction of the first suspension bridge over the Ölfusá. Selfoss owes another growth spurt to the founding of an agricultural cooperative in the 1930s, from which originated the core of today's most important employers and one of the biggest dairies in Northern Europe.

These three towns on the southern coast, with fewer than 2,500 inhabitants between them, live mainly by fishing. The biggest employer however is the Litla Hraun Icelandic state prison at the eastern edge of Eyrarbakki. Of the three towns Þorlákshöfn has the best harbour; at least once a day the car ferry from the Westman Islands docks here. Since the building of the bridge spanning the mouth of the Ölfusá, many fishermen from Eyrarbakki and Stokkseyri also land their catch here, saving themselves having to enter the small harbours of their towns, the stronger swell making them a trickier proposition. More information on the fishing business in the region can be found in Eyrarbakki's **maritime collection** (Túngata 59). Eyrarbakki might seem insignificant today, but the place can look back on a proud past as a commercial port for the southern coast of Iceland during colonial times. Built in 1756, the trading house of the Danish monopoly trader in the Eyrargata, called **Husið** for short, is now used as a heritage museum, showing the culture and history of the region (www.husid.com). Opening times of both museums: June – Aug daily 11am–5pm.

Þorlákshöfn, Eyrarbakki and Stokkseyri

A few kilometres north of Selfoss, the Golden Circle route crosses the Sog river on the [35]. Soon after, lying on the eastern side of the road, the Kerið explosion crater is a textbook maar (a broad volcanic crater). With a depth of 55m/180ft and a very regular shape, almost like an amphitheatre, it counts among the most beautiful of its kind

Kerið – crater at the roadside

in the country and has even been used as a **concert arena**. For that occasion, a pontoon was lowered into the crater lake to serve as a stage, and the acoustics proved to be excellent.

✳ Skálholt: in the land of the bishops

Stronghold of faith

The bridge at the Brúará river marks the transition to the region of **Biskupstungur**, the »Bishop's Tongue«, an area stretching like a tongue between the Brúará and Hvítá rivers and reaching inland to the highlands. The religious reference is due to the ancient episcopal see of Skálholt, whose large church stands isolated, towering above the surroundings and visible from afar. From 1056 until the Reformation reached southern Iceland in 1541, Skálholt was the spiritual – and eventually also the secular – centre of Iceland. For centuries, the associated elite school was the only one in the country that offered higher education. When, in 1106, a second bishop's seat was established at Hólar in northern Iceland, Skálholt remained the country's leading episcopal office.

> ### ! *Baedeker* TIP
>
> **Anthroposophic and ecological**
> By turning off at Borg, the [354] allows a 10km/6-mile detour via Sólheimar. This eco-village with 100 inhabitants and a dedicated special needs project has been run since the 1930s along the principles of anthroposophy (an educational, therapeutic and creative system established by Rudolf Steiner). Workshops sell crafts, candles and organic vegetables grown in their own hothouses. Guests also have access to the Græna kannan (Green Can) café and the Brekkukot guesthouse. For more information, call: Tel. 480 44 00; www.solheimar.is

Many **significant events** in Icelandic history and culture are closely linked with Skálholt. Thus, it was at its monastic school that the secret translation of the Bible was made; when printed at the end of the 1530s, this became the first book in the Icelandic language. And it was here that a good decade later the last Catholic bishop of Northern Europe lost his head: **Jón Arason**, who was actually bishop of Hólar, anticipated that the new faith would strengthen the influence of the Danish crown in Iceland and thus wanted to change the course of history with a counter reformation. In 1549, he subdued – more by the power of the sword than the Bible – the episcopacy of southern Iceland, which had been Protestant for some years. This proved a step too far: Lutherans faithful to the king arrested him, and in 1550 he was decapitated near the church of Skálholt together with two of his sons. The place where the bloody deed happened is today marked by a memorial stone.

In 1785, an earthquake damaged the old cathedral and the school to such an extent that the bishop and his retinue moved to Reykjavík, where soon a unified diocese for the whole country was established.

A place steeped in history: the church of Skálholt →

For a century, Skálholt was reduced to a simple parish church, although now it is once again the official seat of a suffragan bishop.

The modern style dominates

The first stone for today's church was laid in 1956 for the 900th anniversary of the foundation of the Skálholt diocese; it was finally completed in 1963. Excavations suggest that the church is probably the eleventh on this site. Although little is left from the old days, one gem was discovered when a crypt was excavated during the construction of the last church: a stone coffin dating back to the early 13th century containing the remains of the well-known saga personality, bishop **Páll Jónsson**, in full array. The sarcophagus is shown as part of a small exhibition. Otherwise, well-known 20th-century artists have contributed a lot to the style of the modern church. **Nína Tryggvadóttir** (1913–1968) created the dominating mosaic on the back chancel wall as an oversized altarpiece, while **Gerður Helgadóttir** designed the colourful stained-glass windows. In front of the church, two stone tablets by the sculptor **Páll Guðmundsson** show two famous men of the church, Gissur the White, who had the first church in Skálholt built, and Ísleifur Gissurarson, the first Icelandic bishop (1056).

✳ ✳ Gullfoss, the Golden Fall

Laugarás

To head in the direction of Gullfoss and Geysir, either go back to the [35] or take the slightly longer but more interesting route by changing to the [30] east of the mighty Hvítá, which is crossed at Laugarás. Thanks to hot springs, this village also has a flourishing business in **horticulture under glass**. Travellers with children should pay a visit to the small pet zoo at the Slakki farm. From the [30], another possible detour runs to the ▶ Þjórsárdalur, the valley of the Þjórsá; otherwise, after only a few kilometres, the road reaches Fluðir. From here, the Gullfoss is some 30km/18.5 miles away.

! Baedeker TIP

Whitewater rafting

It is obvious from the white spray of the Hvítá that its water is not in the business of flowing gently by, as one set of rapids follows another. Thus, the »White River« is also popular with rafters. An extensive programme of lessons and tours is offered by Arctic Rafting, Laugavegur 11, 101 Reykjavík, tel. 562 70 00, www.arcticrafting.com

With a double-cascade flowing across two tiers, at right angles to each other, the mass of water from the river Hvítá plunges down 70m/230ft into the ravine of **Gullfossgljúfur**. When, on sunny afternoons, a rainbow spans the Gullfoss or the evening sun lays a golden red halo over its spray, the significance of the name Golden Fall becomes abundantly clear. In an average summer, 130 cubic metres/over 34,300 US gal of water thunder down the fall per second, while record quantities of 2,000 cubic metres/over 528,300 US gal have been recorded.

Not always golden: the Gullfoss in its winter robes

The streams of visitors are led to a car park above the gorge where a **mini exhibition in the Sigríðarstofa visitor centre** has information on the waterfall and the surrounding landscape. Passing the parking area, the [35] carries on as the ►Kjölur Route through the highlands to northern Iceland.

✳ ✳ Haukadalur – »Valley of the Surging Waters«

Gullfoss marks the turning point of the Golden Circle route. Just under 10km/6.2 miles back west on the [35], Haukadalur represents **Iceland's most famous geothermally active area,** usually only referenced by the name of its most famous spring, **Geysir** (► 3D illustration p. 20). This proper name, derived from the Old West Norse word for »gush«, has become the generic term for gushing springs all around the world, whereas in Iceland they are called »goshver«; only the one in Haukadalur is actually called »Geysir«, or to be exact, **Stóri Geysir** – the Big Geyser. Reports on the time of the settlements don't mention it, even though **Ári Þorgilsson**, the most important chronicler of that era, lived for many years on the Haukadalur farm right next to it. Analyzing sinter deposits around the vent, geologists estimate Geysir's age to be at least 10,000 years. It is probable that the Stóri Geysir, when the first settlers arrived, was experiencing an extended period of calm, until woken by one of those earthquakes that frequently rocked southern Iceland at the end of the 13th century, and which repeatedly continued to influence it later on.

The Big Geyser

In its heyday the Big Geyser sent its column of water up to 60m/195ft high, accompanied by ghostly rumblings in the ground. As far as reliable descriptions are available, the intervals between the erup-

Woken from a deep sleep

tions varied over the years between 30 minutes and several weeks. In the 19th century, an earthquake stoked the Stóri Geysir to a phase with very violent eruptions, only to calm down and go to sleep entirely between 1916 and 1932. There have always been attempts to artificially stimulate the natural spectacle: for a short time, lowering the water level or adding large quantities of soft soap stimulated some activity – a trick used for tired geysers worldwide. The soap changes the water's surface tension, thus encouraging eruptions. However, the Icelandic Nature Conservation Council banned this **»aphrodisiac«** and any other aids in the Haukadalur in 1992. What humankind could not achieve was successfully brought about by an earthquake in June 2000: the Stóri Geysir woke up again and has been active since, if only with small eruptions that remain far behind its major displays of the past.

★ ★
Strokkur

There is no need to worry though – every visitor to Haukadalur will see the column of water from a geyser shooting towards the sky, courtesy of Strokkur. The »butter tub« might only achieve heights of

Reliable as Swiss clockwork: Strokkur – the »butter tub«

between 10 and 20m/33 and 65ft, but does so reliably every few minutes. What is fascinating about Strokkur's eruptions is the **water bell** which starts off every eruption, and from which the jet of water and steam shoots skyward. There are numerous other springs in the thermal field of the Haukadalur, of which some bubble away quietly, while others are just luke-warm puddles of water. Care should be taken anywhere though, as all the springs at Haukadalur have become more active – and, more importantly, hotter – since the last earthquake and many are visibly boiling. Warning signs are there for a reason, and putting a foot wrong can lead to seriously burnt toes.

Geysir Center

As Geysir and Strokkur count amongst the most visited sights in Iceland, it's no surprise to find an extensive service infrastructure in place: a hotel with cabins by the river, plus four luxury rooms, a campsite and a restaurant for hungry geyser spotters, as well as a large cafeteria and souvenir shop at the petrol station. Next to this, the multimedia Geysir Center serves up a presentation of **Iceland's geological phenomena**, which tends toward the loud and shrill school of popular science. Here visitors can even have themselves rattled by an earthquake. Opening times: daily 10am – 7pm.

Laugarvatn

Heading west on the [35], which later becomes the [37], the Golden Circle Route leads to the village of Laugarvatn on the lake of the same name. Along with its 150 inhabitants, this place is both an educational centre and tourist hotspot. It's really the proximity to Gullfoss, Geysir and Þingvellir that makes Laugarvatn attractive to tourists, with the place itself offering only one attraction: the **Gufubaðið** steam sauna, which stands above hot springs on the banks of the lake. Here the steam rises directly out of the soil. The hot springs at the lake at least ensured a place for Laugarvatn in the annals of Iceland with two events: after the introduction of Christianity in 1000 at nearby Þingvellir, some of the supposedly hardy men preferred to be baptized here in a warm spring instead of in the ice-cold Þingvallavatn, and when bishop Jón Arason and his sons were prepared for their last journey after their execution, the corpses were washed in this very spring.

Via Þingvellir to Reykjavik

The [365] leads from Laugarvatn to the Þingvallavatn. A short detour to the eastern flank of the Reyðarbarmur mountain ridge shows the simple country lifestyle some Icelanders still led at the beginning of the 20th century, as here the two lava caves of **Laugarvatnshellir** last served as permanent dwelling places for poor people in 1922. The road soon reaches the ▶Þingvellir National Park, giving views of the water of the Þingvallavatn, the largest natural lake in Iceland. The historical sites of Þingvellir lie on its western bank, reached by the [361] leading along the lake, or the [36] right through the park – both are charming drives. The [36] leads back to the point of departure ▶Reykjavík – thereby closing the circle.

Hafnarfjörður Map

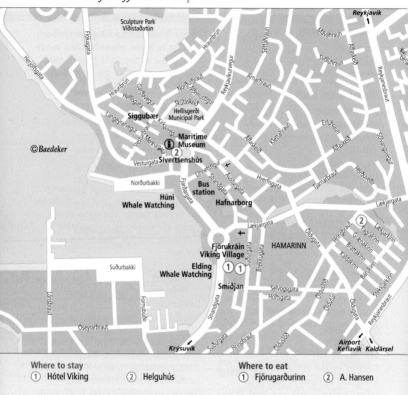

Where to stay
① Hótel Viking ② Helguhús

Where to eat
① Fjörugarðurinn ② A. Hansen

were used everywhere off Iceland's coasts for fishing, but have since been replaced by fibreglass boats.

Heritage Museum
Sívertsenshús ▶

One of the buildings belonging to the group of houses at the Vesturgata is the Sívertsenshús (no. 6), the oldest house in town, which shelters the section of the heritage museum dedicated to culture and history. It was built in 1803 for Bjarni Sívertsen, the »Father of Hafnarfjörður«, who in the late 18th century ran a small business empire engaged in trade, fishing and shipbuilding, thereby laying the foundations for the economic power of today's Hafnarfjörður. Much of the house's interior serves as a reminder of Sívertsen and his family, giving an insight into the life of the Icelandic upper class in the 19th century.

Opening times: June – Aug daily 1 – 5pm, outside the main season Sat/Sun only 1 – 5pm.

That life could be very different is shown by the second section of the heritage museum in the Siggubær workhouse, built in 1902 at the edge of the Hellisgerði lava park (Kirkjuvegur 10). Opening times: June – Aug Sat/Sun 1 – 5pm.

◄ Siggubær

🕐

The heritage museum has lately been using Smiðjan, the former blacksmith's shop on the harbour, right next to the Fjörukráin Viking village (Strandgata 50), for changing exhibitions. Opening times: May – Aug daily 1 – 5pm.

◄ Smiðjan

🕐

The place where Hafnarfjörður particularly lives up to its reputation as elves town is the small Hellisgerði town park, the **cave garden**, above the heritage and maritime museum. The name is taken from a grotto in the age-old lava, which makes the layout of the green park area with its hillocks and hollows as confusing as it is romantic. The very terrain stimulates the imagination, so it is not surprising that more invisibles live here than in any other part of town.

Hellisgerði town park

In 1983, the pharmacist couple Sverrir Magnússon and Ingibjörg Sigurjónsdóttir bequeathed their house in the town centre (Strandgata 34), together with a collection of 20th century Icelandic art, to the inhabitants of Hafnarfjörður. The building was integrated – in an architecturally fascinating way – into the construction of a new arts and cultural centre, which presents, under the name of Hafnarborg, works from their own collection as well as changing exhibitions – it is well worth having a look at the programme or paying a visit to the **museum café**. Opening times: daily except Tues 11 – 5pm, www.hafnarborg.is

Hafnarborg

🕐

More modern art can be seen in the Víðistaðatún sculpture park north of the town centre, where the campsite is. Most of the sculptures were made as part of an arts festival in 1991. The town is still active in promoting the arts, for instance by **providing artists' studios** on the Straumur farm, just west of the Straumsvík aluminium factory, instantly recognizable by its numerous gables.

Víðistaðatún sculpture park

✶✶ Hekla

F 6

Region: Highlands north of Mýrdalsjökull

Numerous legends surround one of the most famous volcanoes on earth; it has even been said to be the mouth of hell, the dwelling-place of lost souls. One thing is certain however: the Hekla is very active, and always »fired up«.

Its foundations were laid under the glaciers of the last Ice Age – approx. 20,000 years ago. Over the course of the following millennia, a volcanic fissure some 5km/3.1 miles in length has expanded to form an impressive **central volcano**, a ridge stretching from southwest to northeast with a current summit height of 1,491m/4,892ft at the Toppgígur crater. This is not guaranteed to remain the same however, as during one eruption in 1947 the mountain grew by nearly 40m/131ft, and the Hekla is always ready for a new eruption. Typical for the Hekla are fissure eruptions stretching along different sections of its ridge, like the one which occurred in February 2000, at nearly 7km/4.3 miles in length.

»Fire Mountain« and »Hell's Mouth«

Dragon's back Turning off the ring road 7km/4.3 miles northwest of Hella on the [26] and heading north, visitors will notice that the further inland they penetrate, the more strongly the scenery is dominated by the Hekla. From the south, it is the »Fire Mountain«'s narrow front end that first becomes visible, but to see the Hekla's true dimensions revealed, visitors need to view its flanks. Whilst the mountain is often likened to a boat floating bottom up, it has more similarities to the spine of a huge reptile, a dragon maybe, as it is not reluctant to spew fire: using **tephrochronology**, dating layers of volcanic ash, proved that the Hekla has erupted over 100 times now, in five major cycles. In between there have been breaks lasting centuries, but always end-

February 2000: the Hekla spews fire

ing in a particularly violent eruption. Thus, the biggest volcanic eruption that Iceland experienced after the last Ice Age, in the 10th century BC, is likely to have marked the beginning of one of Hekla's eruptive periods. The ash from that eruption – scientists have projected its volume to be 9 billion cubic metres/nearly 2.4 trillion US gal – can be detected in the soil of some 80 % of the surface of Iceland, all the way from the western fjords to the extreme east of the country.

The last eruption cycle, continuing to this day, was triggered in 1104 by the eruption that extinguished nearly all life in the ► Þjórsárdalur under a thick layer of pumice ash. All in all, since 1104 the Hekla has blown around 7 billion cubic metres/nearly 1.9 trillion US gal of ash into the skies – enough to fill some 115 million ship containers – and spewn around 8 billion cubic metres/over 2 trillion US gal of lava from its craters and fissures. Shorter active phases within the large cycles also usually begin with an explosive **initial eruption**, followed by prolonged lava flows. The eruption in late March 1947 is classified by scientists as such. Without warning the mountain blew an ash cloud into the atmosphere that took less than half an hour to reach a height of some 30,000m/nearly 100,000ft, and over the following days rained down over Scandinavia all the way to Finland. In 1970, the ash from a smaller eruption proved fatal to thousands of sheep in northern Iceland, as it deposited toxic compounds onto their pastures. The eruptions of 1980/1981, 1991, and the most recent on 27 February 2000, brought almost solely lava to the surface, which spread itself over uninhabited areas of the mountain.

Active cycle

Early European travellers often described the Hekla as the gateway to hell, from whence the cries of the lost souls could be heard. Old Icelandic literature however does not mention Hekla as a gateway to hell – this is the fruit of the imaginations of early, religiously-motivated visitors to Iceland. Legends and scientific facts on the Hekla are presented by the volcanological edutainment centre at Leirubakki farm. The centre uses a multimedia concept incorporating the **simulation of an eruption**, including an artificial earthquake. The architecturally extravagant building consists of walls made from lava blocks and shows the subject of the exhibition, reflected in large windows, at different times of the day and year. The exhibition is part of the Leirubakki tourist centre on the [26].

Hekla Exhibition Centre

Visitors can get closest to the Hekla on the Landmannaleið track [F 225] running north of the volcano. Two turnings lead off from the [F 225] to the foot of the volcano, from where the Hekla can be climbed on a waymarked route. All this effort is rewarded by a fantastic view of the **volcanic landscape** spreading out below. It should be kept in mind however that the wind on the Hekla sometimes reaches gale force and mist severely reduces visibility on the lava fields.

Climbing the Hekla

▶ VISITING HEKLA

INFORMATION

Hvolsvöllur
Austurvegi 4
Tel. 487 80 43
www.hvolsvollur.is

Hella
Suðurlandsvegi 1
Tel. 487 51 65, tourinfo@rang.is

WHERE TO EAT/ WHERE TO STAY

▶ **Budget**
Hella: Hekluhestar
Austvadsholt
Tel. 487 65 98
Fax 487 66 02
hekluhestar@islandia.is
Guesthouse with 18 beds (plus sleeping bag accommodation) in a house built in 1990 in the traditional Icelandic style. Varied activities on offer include riding tours and trips to the Hekla. Open all year round.

Hvolsvöllur: Hótel Hvolsvöllur
Hliðarvegur 7, tel. 487 80 50
Small hotel with 28 rooms, some en suite. Pleasant breakfast room in the conservatory. Sauna, jacuzzi, bar and restaurant inside the main house. Various trips may be organized from here.

Leirubakki
Tel. 487 65 91
www.leirubakki.is
Equine holiday farm on the [26], with comfortably equipped cabins, plus sleeping bag accommodation for up to 50 people. Also a good restaurant, hot pots, sauna and Viking bath, covered riding arena, horses for hire and various organized trips.

As a general rule, hikers should check the current conditions on the mountain with the Leirubakki tourist centre (see above).

Hella and Hvolsvöllur

Alongside the tourist hub of Leirubakki (see above), other starting points for exploring the Hekla region are the villages of Hella and Hvolsvöllur. Counting some 600 inhabitants, the village of Hella only started developing from the 1920s onwards around the bridge that had been built at this site over the **Ytri Rangá**. The accommodation and restaurants on offer here only tempt the odd tour group to schedule a short stop in Hella.

Hvolsvöllur Saga Centre

Marginally bigger, Hvolsvöllur suffers a similar fate, hard though it tries to interest tourists with a saga centre. The exhibition, with many text-heavy panels and displays but few exhibits, is only really worth visiting in bad weather. More fun are the trips organized by the saga centre to the sites of the famous *Njál's Saga*, which can be identified everywhere around Hvolsvöllur. Opening times: June – Aug daily 9am – 6pm, Sat/Sun only from 10pm.

The historic settlement of Keldur near Hvolsvöllur is well worth a look around. One of the houses belonging to the farmstead, the 12th-century **Keldnaskálinn**, is considered the oldest surviving building in Iceland. Another was built around a spring, hence the name Keldur – spring. More recent excavations uncovered an **escape tunnel** dating back to the 12th century, which led from the farmstead to the river. This tunnel is mentioned in the Njál's Saga. Keldur can be found near the western approach to the Fjallabaksleið Syðri [F 210] dirt road, accessible via the [264], which turns off inland 5km/ just over 3 miles west of Hvolsvöllur and leads to the Ragnávellir valley.

★
Keldur historic farmstead

At the Keldur farmstead, the **Fjallabaksleið Syðri** [F 210] turns off in an easterly direction. The road winds its way through spectacular mountain scenery, offering superb visibility, past three glaciers, the large **Mýrdalsjökull** and its smaller neighbours **Torfajökull** and **Tindfjallajökull**. With suitable vehicles, this can be used as a route through southern Iceland as an alternative to the [1] ring road. The road does actually have this function in official emergency plans in case the Katla volcano below the Mýrdalsjökull should erupt and flood the foreland, including the ring road, all the way to the coast with one of its feared glacier runs. The [F 210] does require the crossing of several watercourses and fields of quicksand and should only be attempted with well-equipped jeeps, preferably in convoy.

> ! **Baedeker** TIP
>
> ### On the West Men Islands
>
> The shape of the ►Vestmannaeyjar can easily be seen toward the south on a clear day. If you have five minutes turn off 10km/6mi east of Hvolsvöllur to Bakki Airfield: Flugfélag Vestmannaeyja flies to the islands every hour. Duration of the flight: five minutes! (Reservations necessary: tel. 4813255).

Going east on the ring road

Driving further east along the coast from Hvolsvöllur, the Eyjafjöll massif, formed from volcanic rock and some 1,666 m/5,465ft high, marks the end of the more densely populated southwest of Iceland. The summit region is topped by a mighty icecap covering some 100 sq km/39 sq miles, the Eyjafjallajökull, and hides below it a massive volcanic crater that was last active in the early 1820s, triggering dangerous glacier runs.

Eyjafjöll

At the southwestern corner of the Eyjafjöll, at the spot where the access road to ►Þórsmörk turns off the ring road, two **unusual waterfalls**, each very different from the other, mark the transition from the mountains down into the flat foreland. The Seljalandsfoss is visible from afar, and at night even illuminated, and it is possible to »go behind its back« – with whoever you like – while a few hundred

Seljalandsfoss and Gljúfurárfoss

Veiled beauty: it's easy to go behind the back of the Seljalandsfoss

metres further north at the edge of the Hamragarðar campsite the Gljúfurárfoss furtively slips into a moss-covered crack in the rock and cannot be reached without getting one's feet wet.

Seljavallalaug

One valley, the Seljavellir, pushes particularly far into the southern flank of the Eyjafjöll. This is a worthwhile detour, as amid the imposing mountain panorama a quaint little swimming pool, the Seljavallalaug, looks rather inviting. The water stems from a warm spring further up in the mountains, where there was a geothermic pool as early as the 1920s. Where the ring road goes around the Eyjafjöll in the south, back in the mists of time the sea broke against the steep cliff, clearly discernible in many places, and gouged some caves into the rock. These were used as shelters in the early days of the settlement, and to this day serve as stables or sheds. Good examples such as the **Rútshellir** and the stable caves of **Drangshlið** can be seen on the southern slopes of the Drangshlídarfjall, a small mountain spur situated shortly before Skógar.

✳
Skógar

The regional museum of Skógar counts among the most interesting in Iceland and is the life work of one man: **Þórður Tómasson** not only brought – and furnished – old turf houses, a school and a church to Skógar, he also left the museum countless items of daily life. Next to the museum, the nearby **Skógafoss** waterfall is the town's biggest attraction. The deluge of water plunges down 60m/over 195ft across a width of 25m/82ft. According to legend the settler Þrasi hid a box

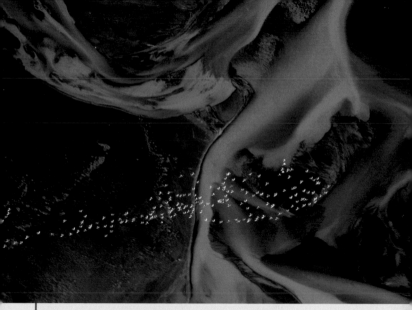

Pretty as a picture: the Skógasandur on the southern coast of Iceland

full of gold in a cave behind the waterfall, which today has protected status. The Skóga river, with its source at the Fimmvörðuháls highland pass, forms a lot more waterfalls further upriver, some of them fairly big.

Höfn

Region: East Iceland   **Population:** 1,750

For English-speaking visitors, there is little clue in the name as to the significance of the town; but Höfn means harbour in English, and the only two harbours on the southern coast of Iceland can be found here and at far-away Þorlákshöfn.

For visitors the harbour is of less interest than the location of the town: Höfn makes a good base for exploring the region south of the ►Vatnajökull.

What to see in Höfn

Höfn í Hornafirði, to give the town its full name, is not exactly a highlight on the tourist circuit. It's mainly the proximity to the Vatnajökull which (temporarily) attracts travellers, who tend to overnight here – and then move on. Nevertheless, Höfn does play host to three cultural institutions that are worth seeing.

Gamlabúð heritage museum

Upon entering the town, to the left Höfn's oldest building catches the eye – a building with an unusual past. A merchant called **Ottó Tuliníus** had it erected in 1864 as Gamlabúð trading house – not here however, but in a place called Papós on the banks of neighbouring Skarðsfjörður. Papós did not enjoy a long future as a trading post however; by 1897 there was only one merchant living there – the aforementioned Ottó Tuliníus. Tuliníus took down his house in Papós and rebuilt it on the harbour of Höfn at the **Hornafjörður**. In 1978, the house once again found itself on the wrong spot. Having been dismantled and put up again at its current location in Hafnarbraut, filled with period furniture and objects from the region, it is now open to interested visitors as a museum of local history. Opening times: June – Aug daily 1 – 9pm.

Glacier show

In the same street (Hafnarbraut 30), but situated in the centre of town, words and images, films and slides, paintings and other artworks, plus historical and contemporary tools and material on glacier research, give visitors an insight into the **icy world of the Vatnajökull**. Opening times: June – Aug 10am – 9pm.

The harbour of the little town of Höfn is the only one along the southern coast of Iceland. Trying to land somewhere else might not be such a good idea

▶ VISITING HÖFN

INFORMATION
Hafnarbraut 25
Tel. 478 15 00, www.east.is

WHERE TO EAT
► **Moderate**
Veitingstaðurinn Víkin
Víkurbraut 2
Tel. 478 23 00
A choice of traditional Icelandic
dishes or pizzas.

WHERE TO STAY
► **Mid-range**
Arnanes
Nesjum
6km/3.7 miles west of Höfn
Tel. 478 15 50

Fax 478 18 19
www.arnanes.is
Guesthouse near the ring road, with
16 rooms in five small cottages, some
en suite. There is also a restaurant and
art gallery.

► **Budget**
Nýibær Farfuglaheimili
Hafnarbraut 8
Tel. 478 17 36
Fax 478 1965
nyibaer@simnet.is
Youth hostel with friendly service in
the town, 33 beds in 2 to 6-bed
rooms. A lot of wood in the rooms
makes for a cosy atmosphere.

In the basement of the Pakkhúsið (Krosseyjarvegur, right on the har-   **Pakkhúsið**
bour), the heritage museum shows its maritime collection: boats and
exhibits from the field of shipping. More interesting is the **Hanraðin
Hafnarfirði** shop on the top floor, offering crafts, Icelandic jumpers
and jewellery, with the rustic atmosphere of this former warehouse
attic inspiring a good browse.

Húsavík

H 2

Region: Northeast Iceland   **Population:** 2,400

**There can be few better places to spot whales than Húsavík. Which
is why the small town proudly wears the self-proclaimed title of
»whale watching capital of Europe«.**

Húsavík lies in a gently curved bay with a beach of dark sand, part of
the larger Skjálfandi Bay. Every year the small town attracts 80,000
visitors, a third of whom come in order to take part in a **whale
watching safari**. However, just approaching the town reveals a
strong smell of fish in the air, an unmistakable sign that this place
too cannot live purely from tourism and still has to partially rely on
fishing and fish processing.

What to see in Húsavík

✷✷
Whale watching

The biggest attraction in Húsavík is the whale watching safaris that in the summer run several times a day. **North Sailing**, founded in 1995 by a local family, was the first Icelandic company to offer whale watching tours. Two years later, the Whale Centre was opened, presenting sound scientific research on whales in an accessible way. Since the tours began the probability of spotting whales has stood at 99 % – a rate that is achieved nowhere else in Europe. In the summer, whales and dolphins find ideal conditions in Skjálfandi Bay, thanks to, among other things, the depth of water on the western side, the rivers flowing into the bay, its sheltered location protected by high mountains and the minor tidal variations. So far, **twelve different kinds of whale** have been spotted, amongst them humpbacks, with their impressive size, sperm whales and fin whales. Very rarely blue whales can also be seen.

 VISITING HÚSAVÍK

INFORMATION

Húsavíkurstofa
Garðarsbraut 7
640 Húsavík
Tel. 464 43 00
www.markthing.is

WHALE WATCHING EXCURSIONS

North Sailing offer whale watching and other boat trips in restored oak boats and an Icelandic coastal sailboat, tel. 464 23 50, www.nordursigling.is. Departures 10am, 1.30, 5 and 8.15pm, plus, if there is enough demand, 9am and 12.30pm. The Gentle Giants tour operator offers whale watching safaris several times daily (9.45am, 1.15, 4.45 and 8.15pm), tel. 464 15 00, www.gentlegiants.is.

WHERE TO EAT

▶ **Moderate**
Salka
Garðarsbraut 6
Tel. 464 25 51
Cosily furnished wooden house from the late 19th century, serving mainly fish dishes such as seafood salad.

WHERE TO STAY

▶ **Mid-range**
Fosshótel Húsavík
Ketilsbraut 22
Tel. 464 12 20
Fax 464 21 61
www.fosshotel.is
Mid-range hotel right in the centre of town, all rooms en suite and TV, some with views across the bay. Good hotel restaurant with fair prices.

Baedeker recommendation

▶ **Budget**
Kaldbakskot
Tel. 464 15 04
Fax 464 15 03
www.cottages.is
A dozen camping huts of varying sizes south of Húsavík. Comfortably furnished, with kitchen and terrace. Superb location with sea views and a short stroll to the water's edge.

The harbour at dusk: night falls in Húsavík

Housed in a former abattoir, the museum (Hvalamiðstöðin, Hafnar- **Whale museum**
stétt) gives extensive information on the giant sea dwellers. Much
space is given over to presenting the various species of whales as well
as their development. There is also information on whaling, beached
whales and whale watching. Nine whale skeletons form a »whale
walk«. Opening times: June – Aug 9am – 7pm, May and Sept 10am –
5pm, www.icewhale.is

Art is all well and good, but the risqué is obviously a bigger draw: **Phallological**
when the museum was located in Reykjavík, it was **one of the most- Museum**
visited in the whole of Iceland**, and its move to Húsavík probably
hasn't changed that much. The museum (Héðinsbraut 3a) shows
over 100 **mammal penises**, with the largest belonging to the whales.
So far there is no human member in the collection though descriptions of the museum rarely fail to mention that several have been
promised in testaments. Alongside the originals, which are presented
sometimes dried, sometimes stuffed or preserved in alcohol, phallic
objects of utilitarian or artistic value may be viewed and purchased.
Opening times: May – Sept daily 10am – 6pm, www.phallus.is.

All angles covered: two Icelandic horses on the lookout at the coast near Húsavík

Safnahúsið The regional museum (Stóragarði 17) houses several sections and collections, such as the interesting **regional folk museum**, the **maritime museum**, the **art museum**, which shows mainly works by local artists, and a natural history collection. Opening times: in the summer daily 10am – 6pm.

Erected between 1997 and 1999 from driftwood, the buildings on the **harbour promenade**, amongst them the »Gamli Baukur« fish restaurant glow in the sunlight in wonderfully warm hues. The terrace with a view of the harbour is the ideal spot for an afternoon coffee. The substantial lunchtime sea food buffet offered by **»Gamli Baukur«** is worth trying. Visitors looking to indulge in some nostalgia will very much enjoy the ship lanterns, compasses and steering wheels of the nautical collection.

Hvammstangi

E 3

Region: Northwest Iceland   **Population:** 600

This quiet village off the ring road has a nice mountain viewpoint, a gallery with high-quality crafts and a large selection of woollen goods. A drive around the Vatsnes peninsula offers many opportunities to spot lazing seals.

What to see in Hvammstangi

Iceland's biggest **woollenware factory** is located in Hvammstangi; its outlet, »Ísprjón« (Höfðabraut 34), not only offers a large selection of Icelandic jumpers, but also many other woollen goods for sale. Strolling through the village, the **goldsmiths' workshop** of Einar H Esrason (Eyrarland 1), who doesn't mind visitors watching him at work, is also worth a visit. The »Gallerí Bardúsa« (Brekkugata) has **crafts** of a high quality for sale, with part of the building additionally serving as a museum consisting mainly of an old grocery shop. Above Hvammstangi, the bizarre rock formation of **Káraborg** (476m/1,562ft) offers a good view over the village and surrounding mountains. The track up to the summit starts in Helguhvammur; on foot the climb takes about 2 hours.

High-quality souvenirs

What to see around Hvammstangi

The regional museum, some 22km/14 miles south of Hvammstangi, mainly documents the shark-fishing carried out in Húnaflói Bay in the 19th and up to the 20th century. The most important exhibit is the open *Ófeigur* **shark-fishing boat**, built entirely from driftwood and rowed by eight to ten men. Also on view is a »Baðstofa«, the communal living and sleeping room of a traditional Icelandic farm. Opening times: June–Aug daily 10am–6pm.

Reykir

Still cultivated today, the Bjarg farm in Miðfjörður, south of Hvammstangi on the [704], is the birthplace of **Grettir the Strong**, who entered Iceland's history books as the country's most famous outlaw. Probably born around the year 1000, he spent his childhood

Bjarg

▶ VISITING HVAMMSTANGI

on the farm, but even when he was an outlaw, he kept returning to his mother Ásdís. Grettir was eventually beaten to death on Drangey, an island in the Skagafjörður. His murderers brought Ásdís his head, which she in all probability buried on the farm. On the way to the farm stands a monument with reliefs by **Halldór Pétursson**, showing scenes from the Grettir saga.

Vatsnes Peninsula

The roughly 80km/50-mile trip around the Vatsnes Peninsula takes the [711] along the predominantly flat coast. In many places, such as in the bay of Hindisvík on the northern tip, or at Ósar,, lazy seals lie in the sun. At **Ósar**, in the east of the peninsula, rubble has been piled up to form a wall, which allows visitors to get a closer view of them. As the seals have enjoyed protected status for decades, they don't really let any curious visitors get in the way of a lazy life. **Hvítserkur** (»White Shirt«) is a 15m/49ft-high rock bathed by the swell on the eastern side of Vatsnes at Húnafjörður. The rock takes its name from the colour of the excrement of the main birds breeding here, the cormorants and kittiwakes. Of course, the Hvítserkur is also at the centre of a story involving trolls. This time one of them is supposed to have thrown stones at the monastery of Þingeyri, only to have been surprised, as is wont to happen, by the sun, and since then has had to stand here petrified and suffer the screeches of the breeding birds. Just before the ring road, consider a detour via the [717] to **Borgarviki**, where basalt columns up to 15m/49ft high, arranged in a circle, are reminiscent of a castle.

Lighthouse on the Vatsnes Peninsula

◀ ✱ # Jökulsárgljúfur National Park

J 2

Region: Northeast Iceland

Over the course of the millennia, the grey floodwaters of the Jökulsá in the Jökulsárgljúfur National Park have dug into the basalt, creating a deep canyon, which, with the Dettifoss plunging into it, receives the waterfall with the highest volume of water in Europe. The Grand Canyon and the Niagara Falls might be much larger, but the Icelandic version of those natural wonders is hardly less impressive. Another scenic highlight of the national park is the horseshoe-shaped Ásbyrgi Gorge.

In 1973, the gorges of the Jökulsá á Fjöllum river and the Ásbyrgi Gorge were protected by the establishment of the Jökulsárgljúfur National Park, covering 120 sq km/46 sq miles. To the east, the borders of the national park follow the course of the river from the Dettifoss to the [85], while the western border runs in a relatively straight line from the Eilífur in the south to the [85] in the north. At 25km/15.5 miles in length, 500m/1,640ft wide and with a depth of up to 120m/nearly 400ft, the Jökulsárgljúfur (the gorge of the Jökulsá) is the mightiest **erosion gorge** in Iceland. Its river is one of the longest in the country at a length of 206km/128 miles, and also carries one of the highest volumes of water. With its two-pronged source at the

▶ ## VISITING JÖKULSÁRGLJÚFUR

INFORMATION

At the campsite in Ásbyrgi
Tel. 465 21 95
www.ust.is
National park administration:
Tel. 465 23 59

WHERE TO EAT

▶ **Moderate**
Skúlagarður
Kelduhverfi
Tel. 465 22 80
Guðrún Helga Sigurðardóttir and Andrés Júlíus Ólafsson create a homely atmosphere in this guesthouse and restaurant 12km/7.5 miles west of the national park.

WHERE TO STAY

▶ **Budget**
Campsite Ásbyrgi
Tel. 465 23 91
Pretty area at the entrance to the gorge, with good sanitary facilities.

Campsite Vesturdalur/Hljóðaklettar
Basic facilities in a very scenic location.

Grímstunga i Fjallahreppi
Tel. 464 42 94
Small house in a quiet location, shortly after the [864] turns off the [1], 27km/17 miles south of the Dettifoss.

Vatnajökull glacier, the Jökulsá becomes a single river south of Herðubreiðarlindir. With little gradient initially, at the edge of the highlands the current becomes stronger, and near the Dettifoss the
waters, by now dark-grey through the sediment they carry, plunge
into the depths via several waterfalls. The rock walls shelter a thriv-
ing and – by Icelandic standards – **lush vegetation**, and in places the
trees reach considerable heights. The largest forest areas, consisting
of birches, willows and rowan trees, lie near Ásbyrgi, otherwise shrub
forest and heather dominate the scenery.

What to see in the national park

The Ásbyrgi Gorge is approx. 3.5km/just over 2 miles long, one kilo-
metre/0.6 miles wide and 100m/328ft deep. The »Eyjan« wedge protruding into the gorge from the north lends it the shape of a horseshoe. It comes as no surprise then that according to legend it was
created by a **hoofprint of Odin's eight-legged steed Sleipnir**. Scientists also spent a long time wondering how this imposing rock formation with its vertical walls might have come into being. The solu-
tion to the mystery could lie in two waterfalls that once sat very close
to each other but were eventually joined through erosion of the crest
lines, leaving only the wedge in the middle of the gorge. The course
of the riverbed also later changed, as today it flows some 3km/1.9
miles further east.

★ ★
Ásbyrgi

From the campsite, a hiking trail leads onto the island in the gorge
and then on to its southern end. It is only from up here that the
horseshoe shape of the Ásbyrgi Gorge becomes clear. The rock pro-
jection also allows a good view of the sandy flats stretching north all
the way to the sea (trail length 5km/3.1 miles, approx. 1.5hrs). Several other hiking trails start from the parking area inside the gorge;
one simple walk leads to the Botnstjörn lake and then on to a viewpoint. Somewhat more challenging is the trail from the campsite
through the **Tófugjá Gorge**, as the only way up to the plateau from
the valley floor is by means of a rope. Afterwards the trail continues
east to the Jökulsá Gorge and around the wooded Áshöfði back to
the starting point (approx. 2hrs).

Roughly in the middle of the national park lies Hljóðaklettar. The
starting point for the following walks are the parking area or the
campsite, both easily reached on a track. The **circular hike to the
»Echo Rocks«** (Hljóðaklettar) takes about an hour, leading through
an imposing volcanic landscape with bizarrely eroded remains of volcanoes, strange basalt formations, »petrified trolls« and a large cave.
Another short walk leads from the parking area to »Karl og Karling«
(Man and Wife), supposedly two petrified trolls standing on a gravel
bank by the Jökulsá river.

Hljóðaklettar

← *Bizarre rock formations in the Jökulsá Canyon*

Natural mosaic: a basalt pillar in Jökulsárglúfur National Park

★ ★
Dettifoss

The Dettifoss might only measure 45m/148ft in height, but as the vast quantities of grey water plunge over the edge, some 100m/328ft wide, into the depths below in a foam of spray, it is one of the most impressive waterfalls in Europe. Above the Dettifoss lies the **Selfoss**, with a height of 10m/33ft, and below the **Hafragilsfoss**, at 27m/88ft; all three falls are connected by a hiking trail. In this area, the Jökulsá river has eaten particularly deeply into the dark basalt, forming a spectacular gorge. From the Dettifoss waterfall a waymarked trail leads along the western side of the gorge, time and again offering spectacular views to the campsite at Ásbyrgi. The complete hike takes two days and is relatively simple apart from the narrow Hafragil canyon and the Tófugjá Gorge at Ásbyrgi. Access to the Dettifoss from both north and south is via the [864] – dusty but fine to drive. The [862], on the western side of the gorge, is also fine from the north to the Dettifoss, but after that point it turns into a track only suitable for off-road vehicles.

Kaldidalur

E 5

Region: West Iceland

At just 40km/25 miles, the Kaldidalur [F 550] is the shortest road traversing the highlands. As there are no deep rivers to cross and in good weather the track can be negotiated with a regular saloon car, it is also called »highlands for beginners«.

The Kaldidalur route is the shortest link between ►Þingvellir and the north and west of Iceland – which is why it has been used since the time of the settlements to ride to the Alþing. Drivers coming from the south follow the [52], the **Uxahryggjavegur**, from Þingvellir for

23km/14 miles north to Brunnar, where the [F 550] track turns off. East of the road the striking 1,060m/3,477-ft **Skjaldbreiður** shield volcano catches the eye. Onwards through the Kaldidalur, the cold valley lying between the glaciers of **Ok and Þórisjökull** does indeed do merit its name. After that the road goes uphill, leading eventually to the head of the pass, Langihryggur (727m/2,385ft). A little to the north lies Skúlaskeið, of which the saga reports that it was here the lawbreaker Skúli, condemned to die at the Alþing, escaped his pursuers after fleeing Þingvellir. He owed his life to his fast horse Sörli, which at the end of the flight in Húsafell collapsed and died from exhaustion. Grímur Thomsen tells the story of this flight in his poem *Skúlaskeið*. From the top of the pass the road eventually leads down into the **valley of the Hvitá**, and the barren highlands, devoid of vegetation, change into the small birch forests at Húsafell.

 **KALDIDALUR**

WHERE TO STAY
► **Budget**
Feraþjónustan Húsafelli
Tel. 435 15 50, fax 435 15 51
www.husafell.is
Five double-rooms in the Old Farm guesthouse (during summer), sleeping-bag accommodation in cabins and a campsite in the birch forest of Húsafell at the northern end of the Kaldidalur. Open all-year round. Horse riding, swimming pool, hiking and golf available.

Kirkjubæjarklaustur

G/H 6

Region: Südisland   **Population:** 150

Nuns still play an important role here, although there have not been any resident in Kirkjubæjarklaustur for a long time. An odd monument in the middle of the village, rocks and lakes – which are said to guard strange secrets – and even the only restaurant here, act as reminders of the nuns of old.

Whilst Kirkjubæjarklaustur might only count 150 inhabitants, it is the largest settlement for miles around. Formerly called just Kirkjubær, for a long time it was a rich farm. This formed the core of to-day's village, which locals simply call »Klaustur« (convent). Klaustur can look back on a long history, as according to the ***Book of Settlement*** there were Irish hermits living here before the Norse Vikings arrived. It is said that when the hermits left, they cast a spell on the place to fall on any heathens there. After the Irish, **Ketill the Foolish** settled in Kirkjubær, owing his nickname to the fact that he had turned his back on the Norse gods to become a Christian. According to one legend, the unbaptized Hildir Eysteinsson is said to have tried

⊙ VISITING KIRKJUBÆJARKLAUSTUR

INFORMATION
Kirkjuhvoll
Tel. 487 46 20, fax 487 48 42
info@klaustur.is

WHERE TO EAT

► **Moderate**
Systrakaffi
Klausturvegur 13, tel. 487 48 48
This restaurant right in the village
centre is always busy. Homely atmosphere and good food, for instance the
fish soup.

WHERE TO STAY

► **Mid-range**
Hörgsland á Síðu
Tel./fax 487 66 55

www.horgsland.is
13 new, very well equipped holiday
cottages sleeping 6 people each. 5km/
just over 3 miles east of Klaustur in an
attractive location on a green hillside.

► **Budget**
Farfuglaheimili Hvoll
Tel. 487 47 85, fax 487 48 90
nupsstadarskogur@simnet.is
Youth hostel 24km/15 miles east of
Kirkjubæjarklaustur, 2km/1.2 miles off
the ring road towards the coast. Large
former farmhouse with 70 beds,
mainly in doubles and three-bed
rooms, with daily tours to Núps-
staðarskógur.

later to settle in Kirkjubær; however, when he reached the edge of
the village, he dropped down dead. The next important event was
the founding of a convent by the Benedictine order which remained
active up to the Reformation. That convent is also at the centre of
several legends. Thus, the graves of two nuns **burned at the stake**
are supposed to be at Systrastapi, a rock formation west of Klaustur.
One is said to have pledged her soul to Satan and shared her bed
with men, the other to have blasphemed against the pope. Incidentally, the reputation of the latter was rehabilitated following the Reformation, as the flowers on her grave were in bloom, whilst the
grave of the promiscuous nun stayed barren. As there was a monastery fairly nearby at Þykkvibær at the time, with mutual visits probably a daily occurrence, these stories may well contain a kernel of
truth.

What to see in Kirkjubæjarklaustur

Kirkjugólf Just outside the village, on the [203], the so-called »church floor«
can be found: a few square metres of perfectly paved ground right in
the middle of a meadow. These are the ends of basalt columns, pol-
ished smooth by water and ice.

Walk to the
Systrafoss and
Systravatn
This hike starts at the campsite and leads on the main road through
the village, past the odd **monument of the two nuns** carrying a huge
stone on their heads. At the end of the village lies the Systrafoss, the

»Waterfall of the Nuns«. A short steep path leads to the edge of the high plateau, with a good view of Klaustur and the green pseudo crater south of the ring road at Landbrot. The path then carries on along the edge past Systravatn, the **»Nuns' Bathing Lake«**, and into the valley to the »church floor«. From here it is not far to another waterfall, the Stjórnarfoss.

Around Kirkjubæjarklaustur

The odd formation of the Dverghamrar, some 12km/7.5 miles east of Klaustur, consists of several basalt columns and was probably created around the end of the last Ice Age, when the tide was still nibbling away at the coast. Since time immemorial the superstition has persisted that this is the place where supernatural beings come out into the light of day. Not far away from here, and visible from the ring road, is a pretty waterfall, the **Foss á Síðu**. A little bit further on in the direction of Núpsstaður, the road crosses the **Brunahraun** lava flow.

Dverghamrar

The farm of Núpsstaður was made famous by the post rider Hannes Jónsson (1880–1968), who for over 50 years led travellers safely through the dangerous labyrinth of rivers of the Skeidarársandur. His grave is located behind the small 17th-century church which was completely refurbished in 1972. This is the smallest **grass sod church**

✱
Núpsstaður

The car isn't bad, but it is the turf farm buildings that make Núpsstaður special

in Iceland, only fitting 30 visitors who can hardly stand up straight inside. At a height of 767m/2,516ft, the striking **Lómagnúpur** mountain has one of the highest steep-faced walls in Iceland. All in all, the landscape around Núpsstaður counts amongst the **most beautiful and most extreme** that Iceland has to offer: bizarre lava mountains, sometimes dark and hostile, in other places covered by a thick green carpet, huge congealed lava flows, dozens of glacier tongues flowing down to the valley from the Vatnajökull, and desert-like sandar plains crossed by countless rivers, all creating a grandiose and dramatic scenario.

To the Lakagígar crater row

Fjaðrárgljúfur

Five kilometres/just over three miles south of Klaustur, the [F 206] turns off the ring road to lead more than 42km/26 miles north to the Lakagígar crater row. After about 3km/1.8 miles a track branches off, leading after one more kilometre/just over half a mile to a parking area at the entrance to the Fjaðrárgljúfur Gorge. Up to this point the road is still passable by regular saloon car, whilst the stretch to Lakagígar is a mere **off-road track** requiring vehicles with a high clearance. Some 2km/1.25 miles long and 100m/330ft deep, the Fjaðrárgljúfur gorge consists of tuff stone, lava and igneous rock intrusions. This deeply-carved gorge was formed by the river and processes of erosion over the course of two million years. A path leading uphill from the car park on the eastern edge of the gorge gives many good views of the river as it snakes its way down below.

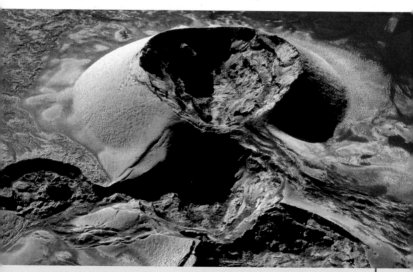

As menacing as they look: the Laki craters

From Fjaðrárgljúfur, the track to Lakagígar leads steadily uphill, through a landscape which is initially green but becomes ever more barren and inhospitable. Along the way lies the Fagrifoss, the pretty waterfall where the **Geirlandsá** river plunges into the depths. In 1783, the Lakagígar crater row on the high plateau of Síðumannaa-fréttur became the **scene of the biggest volcanic eruption in recorded history**. On 8 June, in the so-called fissure land between Mýrdalsjökull and Vatnajökull a 25km/15-mile chasm of fire opened up. With more than 100 craters it produced an overall mass of 14 billion cubic metres/3,700 billion US gal of lava. At the time, the jets of lava, several hundred metres high, could be seen for miles around and a huge gas and ash cloud hung over the area. The lava flow poured in two streams onto the plain, where it widened and carried on flowing in the beds of the Skaftá and Hverfisfljót rivers. When the lava finally stopped eight months later, the biggest lava flow since time immemorial had buried over 300 sq km/115 sq miles of countryside. However, the biggest catastrophe only happened after the end of the actual eruptions, as the ash and sulphur clouds covered large parts of Iceland with highly toxic dust. As a consequence, nearly all the horses and sheep died, and harvests fell dramatically. In the following years, around a quarter of the population fell victim to the biggest **famine** that Iceland has ever seen. Today, large parts of the impressive crater landscape of Lakagígar are covered in moss. The best view of the crater row can be had from the summit of the 818m/2,684-ft Laki mountain.

✷ Lakagígar

> **! Baedeker TIP**
>
> **Detour to the Lakagígar craters**
> Even visitors travelling without an off-road vehicle can easily reach the most important destinations in the highlands via high-clearance buses. Between June and August daily tours leave Skaftafell (departure 8am) and Klaustur (departure 9am) to Lakagígar, leaving 3.5hrs for exploring (Austurleið, tel. 545 17 17, www.austurleid.is).

✷ Kjölur · Kjalvegur

E/F 3-5

Region: Western highlands

The Kjölur Route [35] – also called Kjalvegur – is considered to be one of the easier ways to cross the highlands: by Icelandic standards the track is in good shape and all fords are bridged, so that the Kjölur is manageable with a regular saloon car. At the same time, the track's washboard character can make the drive in a saloon car a tortuous experience. A jeep, whilst not essential, makes the drive a lot more comfortable.

The Kjalvegur [35] starts in the south at the Gullfoss. The last opportunity to fill up with petrol is at the geothermal area of Haukardalur. Visitors coming from the north should fill up in Varmhalíð or Blönduós, although there is the possibility of an **emergency tankful at Hveravellir** in the middle of the highlands. The total length of the stretch from the Gullfoss to the ring road in the north is about 180km/110 miles.

Back in the time of the settlements, the north-south link between the Langjökull and Hofsjökull glaciers was of major importance. It was only in 1780, with the **death of the Reynistaðir brothers**, two farmers who were trying to cross the highlands on the Kjölur, that the passage was consigned to oblivion. A curse that according to local folklore was visited upon the farmers brought a quiet life to the Kjalvegur. Today, this stretch is again much frequented, by highlands standards, and the curse nearly forgotten.

> ## ! Baedeker TIP
>
> ### Only half
>
> Travellers crossing the highlands but also wanting to go around Iceland on the ring road are presented with a problem: it is difficult to go around something that one is traversing at the same time! The drive from the Gullfoss on the [35] to Hveravellir and – ideally after one or two overnight stays locally – back on the same road, has the advantage of offering an experience of the highlands without having to forgo the classic circumnavigation of Iceland in full. Turning back in Hveravellir is made easier by the fact that the Kjölur Route north of the geothermal area has little to offer.

However, when gale force winds make breathing difficult, swirling dust restricts visibility, and an icy cold penetrates the limbs, visitors will get an idea of the kind of curse that afflicted the two brothers.

From the Gullfoss to Hveravellir

Detour to the Hagavatn Let's start this trip with a detour only suitable for off-road vehicles: 10km/6 miles north of the Gullfoss, the [335] turns off west, and after 15km/9 miles of typically desolate Icelandic highlands, brings drivers to the small Hagafell refuge at the foot of the **Jarlhettur mountain range**. Beyond a ford that is not without its challenges, the track leads steeply uphill to the glacier lake of Hagavatn. It is better to leave the car at the refuge and attempt the climb beyond the ford on foot.

Bláfell, Hvítárvatn Back on the [35] main route, after a few kilometres the track leads uphill to the **Bláfellsháls**, the high pass west of the Bláfell mountain, situated at an altitude of around 700m/2,300ft. Below the pass, the view opens up of the lowlands lying far below, dominated by the glaciers of Langjökull in the west and Hofsjökull in the east. Two kilometres/1.2 miles beyond the bridge over the Hvítá, a track (jeeps only!) branches off to the left, leading along the Hvítárvatn lake to the oldest lodge of the Ferðafélag Ísland Touring Association in an area called **Hvítárnes**. After 12km/7.5 miles, the track rejoins the [35].

▶ VISITING KJÖLUR

BUS CONNECTIONS

Daily from Reykjavík via the Kjölur to Akureyri and back, with stops in Hvítárnes and Hveravellir. Bus companies: SBA-Norðurleið (tel. 550 07 70, www.sba.is) and BSÍ (tel. 591 10 20, www.bsi.is).

WHERE TO STAY/ WHERE TO EAT

▶ Budget

Áfangafell
Cottage at the Blöndulón reservoir
Tel. 854 54 12
Sleeping-bag accommodation in shared rooms, hot showers.

Hveravellir
Two lodges/campsite
Tel. 854 11 93, 452 46 85

www.hveravellir.is
One of the two lodges is reserved for groups, the other has a large dormitory. Coffees and the occasional hot snack can be had in the main lodge. The campsite is stony and the sanitary facilities scant, but the hot pot makes up for this.

Kerlingarfjöll
Managed cottages
Tel. 852 42 23
www.kerlingafjoll.is
Sleeping-bag accommodation in the large dormitory as well as smaller cottages sleeping up to twelve. Hot pot and camping. Dinners need to be booked in advance, otherwise snacks only.

A detour leads from the Kjölur to the geothermal area of Kerlingarfjöll

Kerlingarfjöll   At kilometre mark 62 (counting from Gullfoss), the [F 347] turns off east towards the summer ski and geothermal area of Kerlingarfjöll. Striking rhyolite mountains and several steam springs in the **Hvera-dalur**, the »Valley of the Hot Springs«, make the 16km/10-mile drive (only possible by jeep) worthwhile.

Kjalhraun   Back on the [35], the Kjalvegur runs along a lava field by the name of Kjalhraun, which was created after the glaciers of the last Ice Age receded. A cul-de-sac leads some 7km/4.3 miles into this wasteland to the **Beinahóll**. It was here, on »Bone Hill«, that the mortal remains were found of those sheep and horses that in 1780 had been herded through the Kjalhraun by the two farmers. Where exactly the two men died is not known. After this tragedy, the Kjölur route was shunned for a long time, and later its course moved further east. A **memorial stone** on the Beinahóll commemorates the brothers' fate.

✳
Hveravellir   At the northern edge of the Kjalhraun the sound of bubbling and hissing, the unmistakable smell of sulphur, and the retreating clouds of steam vapour announce the geothermal area of Hveravellir. Getting closer to the **»Plain of the Hot Springs«**, the first impression is rather sobering: not only is the environment barren and desolate, but the two huts of Hveravellir with a couple of parked cars outside, a »campsite« on rocky ground and probably also a strong wind – its strength meticulously recorded by the nearby weather station –

Bubbling earth in Hveravellir, the »Plain of the Hot Springs«

! | *Baedeker* TIP

Caves, craters and outlaws

Past the lava cave (Eyvindarhellir) of Fjalla Eyvindur, a legendary 18th-century outlaw who spent years in isolation here with his wife Halla, past a lava fissure, a natural pen in which Eyvindur Jónsson, to give him his full name, kept sheep, a hiking trail leads from Hveravellir into the Kjalhraun to the crater of the Strýtur shield volcano (duration one way: approx. 2hrs). This is a hike through a lava desert with highly interesting vegetation. The return is either done on the same trail or via the Þjófadalir lodge to the west. For more information and maps, contact the lodge staff in Hveravellir (tel. 452 42 00) or visit the following website: www.hveravellir.is.

don't exactly seem inviting. However, a **stroll through the geothermal field** with its bubbling springs and hissing miniature volcanoes, as well as a fantastic hot pot that is hard to leave once in, make Hveravellir appear in a different light.

Going north on the Kjölur from Hveravellir, beyond the bridge over the Seyðisá, the desert-like conditions gradually give way to a tundra landscape called Auðkúlurheiði. Parts of the Auðkúlurheiði have been flooded by the dammed lake of Blöndulón, which feeds the **Blönduvirkjun hydroelectric plant**. The highland crossing ends with the drive down into the valley of the Blanda, which welcomes visitors after 180km/110 miles of desert and scree with occasional lush greenery. After this the [35] turns into the [732], leading to the ring road.

Auðkúlurheiði, Blöndulón

✳ ✳ Landmannalaugar

F/G 6

Region: Highlands north of Mýrdalsjökull

Famous for its rhyolite mountains and hot springs, Landmannalaugar lies at the centre of a unique hiking area and is the start and finish point of one of the most popular trekking tours in Iceland, the Laugarvegur. Landmannalaugar, including its surroundings, enjoys special protection as the Fjallabak nature reserve.

The »Baths of the Men of Land«

Landmannalaugar's popularity is understandable, with its brook being heated by hot springs, allowing visitors to lie in it for hours and look up into the sky, by day or night. Back in the times of the sagas, the men from the region who herded cattle called the area northwest of Hella »Land«. Therefore, Landmannalaugar translates as »the Baths of the Men of Land«. The banks of the warm brook are lined with green marshland. On one side, a black wall of glass-like obsidian lava pushes up, as high as a house – the **Laugahraun**. On the other, the vista opens up across the wide bed of the **Jökulgilskvísl**, all in light shades of yellow and ochre. Further on, the eye sweeps across a bleak but fascinating mountain landscape in all the colours of the rainbow – rhyolite, an acidic, extrusive rock, is famous for its colours and nowhere else in Iceland does it cover such a large area.

Climbing Bláhnúkur

Climbing Bláhnúkur is best attempted when the skies are clear. The route begins only a few metres past the campsite, and involves a climb of 350m/1,150ft. At the summit, a panoramic dial helps visitors get their bearings, all the way to the Vatnajökull. The way down – passing the hot vapour springs of the **Brennisteinsalda** and cutting across the Laugahraun back to the campsite – can be done in four to five hours, but leaves impressions that will last a lifetime. When the

Contrasts: algae in the hot springs of Landmannalaugar ...

mountains are hidden by clouds, the hike into the gorge **Grænagil**, which divides the foot of the blue-green Bláhnúkur from the jet-black Laugahraun, might not be quite the real thing, but at least gives a good idea. Hikers can pick up a walking map of the area around Landmannalaugar FÍ hut.

✳ ✳ Laugavegur – the four-day-trek

Iceland's most famous long-distance hiking trail covers just under 50km/31 miles from Landmannalaugar to ► Þórsmörk. It is usually walked from north to south with three overnight stops. En route there are only smaller brooks to ford, as all larger ones are spanned by pedestrian bridges. The four to six-hour stages are prescribed by the **FÍ mountain huts**, as overnighting is only possible in these or – for hikers who have brought their own tent – at dedicated camping areas nearby; wild camping along the way is not allowed. Spaces in the huts have to be booked in advance; for summer dates this is best done in the spring (tel. 568 25 33, www.fi.is). In season, there is always somebody looking after the lodges, but there is no food provision, so hikers need to bring their own supplies.

It is on the first day that the track is most demanding, with the ascent of the Landmannalaugar – a good 600m/1,970ft – to the mountain hut, which lies at an altitude of nearly 1,100m/3,610ft at the

A potpourri of colours

… and perpetual ice at the Hrafntinnusker

Hrafntinnusker. But there is plenty of variety too, such as the Laugahraun with its obsidian lava, the sulphur springs of Brennisteinsalda, colourful rhyolite mountains and the Stórihver hot spring. On the second day, the route leads mainly downhill, although there are sections which can have snow even in the peak of summer. At the end of the second day, there is a choice between two huts: one at the **Álftavatn** – the »Swan Lake« – and, a good hour further on, at the **Hvannagíl**. On the third day, the track leads through more flat terrain, a few kilometres of which run parallel to the Fjallabaksleið Syðri [F 210] highland track. From the stage destination, the Botnar hut in Emstrur, take a stroll to the largest river of the region, the Markarfljót. Here its grey waters, which come from Torfajökull and Mýrdalsjökull amongst others, squeeze through the narrow canyon of **Markarfljótsgljúfur**. On the last day of the hike the landscape becomes progressively greener as the route nears the end point of Þórsmörk with its national forest. There are several lodges and campsites available here, as well as a bus service back to civilization.

! **Baedeker TIP**

Laugavegur tours

Ferðafélag Ísland (Iceland Touring Association) offers exciting Laugavegur tours with experienced guides. Accommodation is in the association's own huts. Bus from Reykjavik to Landmannalaugar, bus back from Þórsmörk. Info: Tel. 568-2533; www.fi.is

Ófærufoss: sadly, the basalt bridge across the last tier of the fall has collapsed

✳ Eldgjá – the Fire Fissure

Going south from Landmannalaugar on the Fjallabaksleið Nyrðri [F 208], some 30km/18.5 miles southeast of Landmannalaugar the track crosses the Eldgjá »fire fissure«. Nearly 40km/25 miles long, up to 600m/1,970ft wide and in parts 200m/650ft deep, this is currently the **largest eruption fissure on earth** and a textbook example of the fissure volcanism of the region. At least one eruption is known for certain to have happened after the settlement of the country. A cul-de-sac running 2km/1.2 miles leads from the F 208 to the fire fissure. Shortly before a parking area at the end of the road, the »unconquerable« **Ófæra** has to be forded. From the car park, it takes about 30 minutes by footpath to the Ófærufoss.

? DID YOU KNOW ...?

■ ... that in the excellent Icelandic-Swedish feature film *The Shadow of the Raven* (1988) – an historic adventure film about the bloody feud between three families in the Iceland of 1077 – the basalt bridge over the Ófærufoss, now collapsed, »carries« a lot of significance?

Up to 1993, the multi-tiered Ófærufoss waterfall was one of the country's most-photographed sites and would appear in every one of the older coffee table books on Iceland. The lower fall was spanned by a natural **basalt bridge** which visitors could even walk on. However, as the first tourists arrived in the spring of 1994, after a harsh winter, it had disappeared! Whether frost blew up the iconic landmark or blocks of ice plunging down the fall with the first meltwaters had taken the bridge with them, is not known. The destruction of the bridge meant the waterfall lost its special charm – it is still pretty, but no longer exceptional.

Ófærufoss

✳ # Melrakkaslétta

J/K 1/2

Region: Northeast Iceland

Only a few tourists make the detour to the far north of Iceland. Visitors who can take the loneliness of a primal landscape will be enthralled by the deserted beaches covered in driftwood and the company of the screeching seabirds.

The circumnavigation of the Melrakkaslétta peninsula, the **Plain of the Arctic Foxes**, is done on the [85] or the [867]. The route, some 110km/68 miles long, leads mainly along the coast through an extremely sparsely populated, ancient landscape, to the northernmost point of Iceland. The west of the peninsula is dry, and the sparse greenery is often broken by dust and scree. Sprinkled with small lakes and moors, the east appears a little more welcoming.

and blackfly. As they don't sting, the midges are relatively harmless unless they stray into the eyes, ears or mouth, and of the blackflies, it is only the females that are out for blood. And another bit of good news: the two midge generations hatch in June and August each year, so that there are significantly fewer of them about in July. One thing to bear in mind is that without these swarms of midges the Mývatn would not have such a rich bird life, and the trout too enjoy the insects.

Conservation and protection of the natural environment

The Mývatn lake and the Laxá river have enjoyed protected status since 1974, which means wild camping and putting up for the night just anywhere, off-road driving, boat traffic, and entering the breeding grounds on the northwestern banks from mid-May to mid-July are all prohibited. Despite this, the Mývatn area still suffers from a number of environmental problems, mainly through erosion and the extraction of kieselguhr. Erosion is particularly problematic on the eastern side of the lake, threatening to silt up the **Dimmuborgir** a few years ago. The extraction of kieselguhr, a siliceous material used as a filter aid, requires mud to be sucked from the bottom of the lake, increasing the water's depth and thereby changing the fauna on the bottom of the lake, which in turn affects birdlife.

 VISITING MÝVATN

INFORMATION
In Reykjahlíð supermarket

WHERE TO EAT

► **Moderate**
Reykjahlíð: Gamli Bærinn
Tel. 464 41 70
Cosy pub with a nostalgic touch opposite the Reynihlíð Hotel. A good-value choice is fish soup or fish and chips. Guests are also allowed to play the piano!

Skútustaðir:
Restaurant in the Gígur Hotel
Tel. 464 44 55
For trout with a lake view, look no further than the Gígur Hotel in Skútustaðir. The view from the restaurant sweeps across the lake and the pseudo craters. Visitors in the mood for a gourmet experience should splash out on the three-course meal.

WHERE TO STAY

► **Mid-range**
Reykjahlíð: Hótel Reykjahlíð
Tel. 464 41 42
Small hotel right on the lake, with some rooms and the breakfast room offering good views.

Reykjahlíð: Fossótel Laugar
Tel. 464 63 00, www.fosshotel.is
Summer hotel in a quiet location, an ideal base for day trips to Húsavik, Mývatn, Goðafoss and Akureyri.

► **Budget**
Reykjahlíð: Hlíð
Tel. 464 41 03
A little outside Reykjahlíð, and enjoying a sea view due to its elevated location. Some 50 good-value sleeping-bag accommodation places in a large house, plus cabins of varying sizes and a campsite.

The flat, heavily indented banks of the Mývatn with their rich nutritional value offer ideal conditions for many birds to breed. The ducks are particularly famous with bird-lovers, as of the 15 different species of duck to be found in Iceland, all except the eider duck breed around the lake. Apart from the seabirds, nearly the entire range of Icelandic species is present on the Mývatn. One speciality is the **Barrow's Goldeneye**, an immigrant from America that breeds nowhere else in Europe. Bird stocks have consistently declined over the past decades however; among the suspected reasons are increasing traffic and tourism, minks that have become feral, and disturbances caused by the kieselguhr extraction.

Flora and fauna

The Mývatn area lies exactly on the border of the Eurasian and American tectonic plates, which are drifting apart. The resulting gap is continually filled up by rising lava, so the landscape is shaped by various kinds of volcanic activity, with, at its centre, the **Leirhnjúkur**. A hundred thousand years ago, the mountain was still a volcanic cone producing large quantities of lava and ash; at some stage however, it gently collapsed, giving it the rather flat appearance it has today. There is however, at a depth of some 3km/1.8 miles, still an **active magma chamber** which is liable to expand and break open. This lessens the pressure in the chamber, resulting in the earth's surface sinking again. This change can repeat every few months over many years. Over the past centuries there have been two major eruptions in the Mývatn area. The so-called **Fire of Mývatn** started in 1724 with a massive eruption, resulting in the creation of the **Víti crater**, and continued with earthquakes and eruption on the **Krafla**. In 1729, lava flowed all the way to the Mývatn, destroying parts of Reykjahlíð. The lava flow, with hardly any vegetation on it even today, is still clearly visible. During the **Krafla fires** in 1975, the volcano of the same name came to life, causing numerous eruptions up to 1985. The effects of this active phase may still be seen in Leirhnjúkur today.

Geology and volcanism

> **!** *Baedeker* TIP
>
> **Mývatn Marathon**
>
> Since 2002, the Mývatn Marathon has been taking place around the lake at the end of June. To register and for more information, contact: Sel Hotel Mývatn, tel. 464 41 64, myvatn@myvatn.is

What to see around the Mývatn

Visitors coming in from the west on the ring road soon reach Skútustaðir, after Reykjahlíð the biggest tourist centre at the Mývatn. In spite of this, Skútustaðir has kept its character of a tiny, sleepy settlement of old. Worth seeing here are the **pseudo craters**, which can only be found in Iceland and show up particularly well at Skútustaðir. They were formed by rivers of lava flowing across wet ground such as flat lakes or fenland. Heat made the water below the lava

★
Skútustaðir

At the Krafla power plant, the heat of the earth is harnessed for energy production …

evaporate in an explosion-like way, sometimes blasting craters of up to 300m/985ft in diameter into the landscape. This explains why pseudo craters, as opposed to »real« volcanoes, have no chimney. The campsite at Skútustaðir is the starting point for a short walking trail through the **crater landscape**, largely covered by grass.

✳ **Dimmuborgir** At Geiteyjarströnd, roughly in the middle of the eastern banks, a cul-de-sac branches off towards Dimmuborgir. This area might only measure approximately one square kilometre/a third of a square mile, but it is full of the most bizarre **lava formations**. The »dark castles« consist of towers, bridges, caves and overhangs, some of which look like petrified trolls. Not much imagination is required to read all kinds of stone figures into the jagged rock. A little over 2,000 years ago there was a dammed lava lake at this place. When the water below the lava evaporated and the steam made its way up to the surface, the lava solidified into a bizarre **variety of shapes**. At some point the dam broke and the still liquid lava ran down to the Mývatn, leaving the already solidified towers behind.

Reykjahlið This village on the northeastern banks of the lake is the tourist hub of the Mývatn area, with hotels, guesthouses and campsites. During the **Mývatn fire in 1729** the inhabitants of Reykjahlið narrowly escaped diaster, as the lava flow destroyed their homes, but spared the church on the hill where they had taken refuge. Today, the lava flow can still be made out clearly near the village.

... while it escapes untapped at the solfatara field of Hverarönd

Once the ring road leaves the Mývatn to go east, after a few kilometres it reaches the head of the pass at **Námaskarð**, and shortly after, at the foot of the Námafjall mountain, unfolds the most impressive solfatara field in Iceland: Hverarönd. This natural spectacle's assault on the senses starts at the parking area at Hverir. The barren plain and the mountainside glow in strong shades of yellow, orange and brown, a vista reminiscent of photos from Mars. Everywhere white plumes of steam escape from cracks, some of which force their way onto the surface with a loud hissing and spitting. Hot **mud pots** bubble and boil away, with a pervasive smell of rotten eggs. From the parking area, a steep path leads onto the 485m/1,591-ft Námafjall, offering a panoramic tour through this unreal landscape. The path leads part of the way along the ridge, and eventually ends on the top of the pass at the ring road.

Shortly after passing Námafjall, the [863] track branches off from the ring road and leads to the **Krafla power station**, the Viti crater and the Leirhnjúkur lava field.

★
Námafjall

> ❗ *Baedeker* TIP
>
> **Total relaxation ...**
>
> ... and a real alternative to the Blue Lagoon are the new Mývatn Nature Baths between Reykjahlið and Námaskarð. The water in the generously-sized open-air pool is milky-blue and blissfully warm, with a superb view over the lake for good measure. Whether in the light of the midnight sun or the pale glow of the northern lights, a dip in the new Blue Lagoon is always a treat. Opening times: summer daily 9am – midnight, winter daily noon – 10pm. For more information: tel. 464 44 11, www.jardbodin.is

ENERGY FOR FREE

Iceland wants to become the first state in the world to be independent of fossil fuels. The conditions to achieve this are better here than almost anywhere on earth. Nature is kind to the island nation in the North Atlantic. Power plants harness the force of huge glacier rivers, and the geothermal potential is plain to see. Today, 70% of the country's energy needs are already met by these alternative, renewable forms of energy.

Iceland is rich in natural sources of energy. At several dozen sites on the island, pressurized hot water surges up to the surface, sometimes shooting forth in fountains of water as high as a house. The reason for this is the location: the island is situated exactly where the American and the Eurasian tectonic plates join on the **Mid-Atlantic Ridge**. These plates drift apart, causing Iceland to become over 2cm/ 0.8 inches larger each year. This also means that the earth's crust is particularly thin and fissured here.

Nature's gift

The Icelanders have used these gifts of nature for centuries. A hot bath has always been taken for granted for Norse men and women. However, it was only in the 1930s that Icelandic engineers started to exploit geothermal energy in a planned way, bringing the water via pipelines into the capital. And it was only the oil crisis of the 1970s that really pushed alter-native energies forward. Today, **Nesjavellir**, some 30km/18 miles east of the capital, is the largest geothermal plant in the country. The surrounding hills are a patchwork of green mosses and blue-green lichens. The closer the proximity to Nesjavellir, the stronger the smell of rotten eggs: this is hydrogen sulphide, rising with the hot steam from the bowels of the earth. Past the last ridge of hills, the visitor looks down into a valley leading to the large basin of the Þingvallavatn, the largest lake in Iceland. At the foot of the hills, the excess steam from the **geothermal plant** rises towards the sky. It might look like polluting fumes, but this is pure water vapour! Apart from that, there is not a lot to see here, except two large buildings resembling oversized shoe-boxes, which are filled with pipes, pumps and generators.

The boreholes going down 1,000 to 2,000m/3,280 to 6,560ft into the depths are only a few centimetres in

Pipeline at the Krafla power plant: a straight line is not necessarily the quickest link between two points

diameter at the bottom, but more impressive at the top end where they measure about one metre/3.3ft. They are sealed, and massive pipes transport the steam onwards, which then shoots out under enormous pressure at temperatures of 200 to nearly 400°C/about 390 to 750°F. In order to harness the steam, the pressure is lowered to 30 bars. The excess evaporates, which explains the huge **cloud of steam** always hanging over the valley. Moisture is then extracted from the usable water, resulting in hot water and hot air, both with a temperature of about 190°C/375°F. The pressurized hot air powers turbines, producing electricity. Untreated, the hot water is not usable as it contains many minerals, most notably sulphur which would attack and destroy the pipes. Thus, using **heat exchangers**, the water from the depths transfers its heat on to fresh pure water – which is then brought to Reykjavík by long-distance heating pipes.

The power of water

The second major natural energy source of the island is its glacier rivers. Tourist magnets such as the Gullfoss gush through gorges and over waterfalls with enormous force. However, the government is increasingly putting dams in their way. For a

while now, the country has been attracting energy-intensive sectors of industry from all over the world – **aluminium smelters** in particular. Thus, the seemingly endless energy reserves of the country are being utilized and even, indirectly, turned into exports. Thanks to the cheap electricity, it makes economic sense to

Geothermal energy and hydropower form the two pillars of Icelandic energy policy.

ship the raw material of bauxite from Australia or Canada to Iceland in order to smelt it down here and then sell it to the world again – as aluminium. However, not all Icelanders are in favour of this. At the moment, the US Alcoa group is building a huge aluminium smelter, with the Icelandic government setting up a large hydropower plant to go with it. The **Kárahnjúkar Project** envisages nine dams holding back three glacier rivers in the east of the island. Environmentalists see this as a threat to the wilderness around Europe's largest glacier, the Vatnajökull. However, their protests have proved to be fruitless.

Travellers interested in taking a look inside the plant should head for the **Visitor Centre**, which offers a lot of information on the construction of this facility and how it is run.

Viti crater, Leirhnjúkur

With its diameter of 300m/984ft, the Viti crater was created during a mighty explosion at the beginning of the Mývatn fire in 1724. Over 100 years after this eruption, a mud pot bubbled in the crater, where today there is a green lake at its bottom. From the car park a path leads to the crater's edge and then runs along the ridge. After the creation of the Viti crater the **Leirhnjúkur fissure** opened up further west, producing large quantities of magma. The parking area is the starting point for a walk of approximately an hour across the gloomy, steaming lava field.

Grenjaðarstaður folk museum

On the way from the Mývatn to Húsavik, consider a short detour off the [87] to the Grenjaðarstaður folk museum in the Aðaldalur, presenting a large grass sod farm with a collection of historical exhibits. The farmstead dates from the 19th century and was inhabited into the middle of the last century. Opening times: June – Aug daily 10am – 6pm.

✷ Reykjanes

C/D 6

Region: Southwest Iceland

Reykjanes is an Iceland in miniature, with just the glaciers missing. Signs of volcanism – lava areas, old craters, geothermic fields – are everywhere. The porous lava soil is hardly able to hold the copious rainfall, and most water quickly seeps away into the depths. There are no rivers worth mentioning, only a peculiar lake, Kleifarvatn, with no major inlets or runoffs.

The proper name for the Reykjanes peninsula – pushing far out into the North Atlantic in the southwest of Iceland, its shape resembling a rhino – is really **Suðurnes**. However, it is more commonly named after the furthest point – Reykjanes. The rhino's horn pointing north with Iceland's international airport Keflavík has its own (if seldom used) name: **Miðnes**.

Paradise for birdlovers

The peninsula is fringed by steep cliffs, smooth, black sandy beaches and ecologically valuable rocky mud flats. These coasts are inhabited by countless seabirds, including all kinds of guillemots, razorbills and fulmars as well as gulls. Of the two largest bird cliffs, the one at **Hafnaberg** south of Hafnir is easier to get to and offers better views than the larger **Krýsuvíkurberg** on the southern coast. At a height of 77m/252ft, and situated some 14km/just under 9 miles off the southwesterly point of the peninsula, **Eldey rock island**, the dormant remains of a volcano, is home to one of the largest gannet colonies in the northern hemisphere. Until the last of its kind was shot in 1844 on Eldey, **great auks** were living there too. Eldey is now a conservation area and not freely accessible to the public. However, the gannets also show up on the southwestern point of Reykjanes on the Valahnúkur (►p. 225).

The sun says goodbye to the Reykjanes Peninsula

The waters around Reykjanes are a favourite haunt of dolphins and whales, which with a little luck may even be spotted from the banks. For a better chance of seeing them, consider a whale watching tour. Between April and October, the *Moby Dick* sets sail at least once a day from Keflavík or, in suitable weather, from Sandgerði or Grindavík (Dolphin & Whalespotting, tel. 421 77 77 or toll-free 800 87 77, www.dolphin.is; transfer service from Reykjavík with the option to take a dip in the Blue Lagoon). — Whale watching

The name Reykjanes, **»Smoke Peninsula«**, leads visitors to suspect the existence of geothermal springs. Indeed, steam emerges from the ground in a lot of places, sometimes more or less naturally as in the solfatara field of Krysuvík, sometimes from boreholes as at the Svartsengi power plant, with its »effluents«, cooled down to swimming temperature, filling the Blue Lagoon, Iceland's most famous thermal spa. Geologically, Reykjanes is considered the surface continuation of the Mid-Atlantic Ridge, the restless boundary between the continental plates of America and Eurasia. In principle, in the southeast of the peninsula visitors stand on European soil, and in the northwest on American. South of Hafnir, the **»Bridge between the Continents«** spans a crack in a lava field – a clever idea to visualize the continental drift. — Intersection of the continental plates

Keflavík and Njarðvík – the twin towns

Starting from Reykjavík, the Reykjanes peninsula can be explored in a varied round trip. Follow the [41] road west from Reykjavík, to arrive after a good 40km/25 miles at the town of Keflavík. Practically now one entity, seamlessly grown together, the towns of Keflavík and Njarðvík – the latter consisting of larger Ytri Njarðvík, dominated by the harbour, and the smaller, more rural Innri Njarðvík – enjoy a protected position on **Stakksfjörður**, a side bay of the large Faxaflói. Along with Hafnir, the twin towns form the greater community of **Reykjanesbær**, boasting not one but three important ports, namely

and motors from fishing and seafaring, amongst them one of the open boats that used to be rowed for fishing. Opening times: in summer daily 1 – 5pm.

On the [425] into the south of Reykjanes

Hafnir – the adjunct

With its 120 inhabitants, Hafnir is the small adjunct of the larger Reykjanesbær municipality, situated at a distance of 10km/6.2 miles from the two other »districts«, Keflavik and Njarðvík, in a lonely location on the western coast. Before motorized fishing cutters and trawlers, Ósar Bay, north of Hafnir, was an important base for the fishing industry and a busy stretch of coast. Even the Hanseatic League had a representation for a while on the northern banks of the bay. The downward spiral was triggered by a storm flood destroying the Danish trading post of Básendar in January 1799.

In its seawater tanks the Sædyrasafnið in Hafnir (Kirkjuvogur 13) shows what lives in Icelandic waters. In the »**touch pool**«, visitors can touch crabs and other crustaceans, sea stars and sea anemones, as well as a few flatfish – particularly attractive to children.

An artificial bird cliff gives an insight into the birdlife of Iceland. Opening times: June–Aug daily 2–5.30pm, Sept–May daily noon–4pm.

Hafnaberg

South of Hafnir, soon after the fish farm of Kalmannstjörn, the coast pushes up the bird cliffs of Hafnaberg like a protective shield against the waves of the Atlantic. Whilst these cliffs might not be as high and spectacular as the ones at Krysuvíkurberg on the southern coast, the birds are easier to watch here. In this section, the [425] runs a bit further inland, so visitors should schedule in an hour for a walk along the waymarked trails from the parking area to the cliffs. South of the cliffs, at the **Stóra Sandvík** – »Great Sandy Bay« in English – the coast becomes flat and sandy again. In good weather, the locals practise proper beach life, except it is nearly always too cold for swimming. The flat beach lakes in the dunes are good spots for bird-watching.

Bridge between the Continents

Level with the Stóra Sandvík, east of the [425], an 18m/59-ft long steel-and-wood bridge spans the Alfagjá, the continental gorge, described by local tourism managers as »one of the major wonders of the world«. While this is a bit of an exaggeration, the cut, a good 6m/20ft deep, is undoubtedly worth seeing, particularly as it is embedded in a **dramatic lava landscape**. The gorge was formed, as were others in the surrounding area, as a consequence of continental drift. Here, the continental plates of Eurasia and North America drift apart by up to 2cm/0.7 inches per year, according to geologists' measurements. The bridge is named after the first European who stepped onto American soil in the 11th century: Leifur heppni, Leif the Lucky, better known as **Leifur Eiríksson** (► p. 60). What many a tourist might at first glance consider a folly with no discernible function, holds such significance for Icelanders that its inauguration on 3 July 2002 was attended by the head of the government no less, alongside the foreign and transport ministers who made their way from Reykjavík to step onto the bridge.

While the [425] turns off east, a cul-de-sac leads to the most south-   Valahnúkur
westerly point of Reykjanes. The last kilometres should be driven carefully, without leaving the car, as the road crosses a colony of belligerent Arctic terns (once you reach the coast there is no need to fear their attacks). At the end of the track, rising above the banks, the Valahnúkur is clearly recognizable as **part of a volcano crater**.

The lighthouse of Valahnúkur is protected by belligerent Arctic terns

Towards the sea it shows vertical cliffs, towards land a steep but eminently climbable slope. A lighthouse used to warn seafarers from its peak, but in 1887 an earthquake destroyed the tower. Its successor has been pointing skywards from Bæjarfell hill just inland since 1908. The rugged coast gives excellent views on to the sea, and from here it is easy to observe the seabirds, usually gannets, nesting in their thousands on the off-shore rock island of Eldey.

Gunnuhver

Looking back inland, columns of steam reveal the existence of a high-temperature area. Part of the latent energy is harnessed to boil seawater for the extraction of salt. The factory lies near the main road, while a cross link to the road leading west passes a relatively unspoilt field of hot springs surrounding the legendary Gunnuhver, **Gudrun geyser**. This is supposedly the place to which the spirit of an argumentative woman was banished.

Grindavík

Towards Grindavík, the road crosses some more inhospitable lava fields, eventually reaching the green outskirts of the port town, and as so often happens in Iceland, as soon as there is a blade of grass, a golf course appears! Grindavík is an important base for the fishing industry, with large processing facilities. The great fishing and fish-processing tradition here is documented by the Icelandic **Saltfish Museum** at Hafnargata 12a. Opening times: daily 11am–6pm, www.saltfisksetur.is.

Driving through Grindavík gives food for thought: in the modern town centre alongside the church, supermarket and sports centre with swimming pool, seemingly historical walls catch the eye. The ostensibly ancient is in fact modern art: this sun temple was built between 1995 and 1997 by the esoterically inspired multimedia artist and »earth house architect« **Tryggvi Hansen** (born 1956).

✷ ✷ Blue Lagoon · Svartsengi power plant

Svartsengi

Five kilometres north of Grindavík, visitors might think they've found themselves on a **science fiction film set**: shiny steel towers, modernist concrete architecture, hissing steam, and thick reddish-brown pipelines, the whole thing framed by black lava and whitish-blue expanses of water. The Svartsengi power plant is however very much of this world, even if its technology has a futuristic touch. It provides the entire west of Reykjanes with energy and heat, and while it's by no means inconspicuous, it is certainly environmentally friendly. From boreholes nearly 2,000m/6,561ft deep, a mixture of water and steam, with a temperature of 242°C/467°F, shoots up. The fact that it is not just steam, as might be expected at this temperature, is due to the pressure down below, which significantly increases the water's boiling point. The **mix of water and steam** coming out of the ground is saline and full of minerals, as the porous lava soil allows salt water from the surrounding Atlantic to seep into the subsoil

Without its power plants Iceland would be much poorer visually

of Reykjanes. This makes the hot liquid unsuitable for electricity turbines and long distance heating pipes; it is however, by a process of heat exchange, heating clear spring water. Condensed and cooled to approx. 70°C/158°F, at the end of the process at least a million litres/nearly 265,000 US gal of perfectly clean »wastewater« per hour flows into the surrounding lava.

The power plant also runs the **Eldborg visitor centre**, with its very well presented Gjáin exhibition, informative on both the technology harnessed to use the geothermal potential, and on the geological composition of the soil (opening times: daily 10am–5pm, in the winter to 4pm, www.bluelagoon.com.)

◀ visitor centre

⏱

Until well into the 1980s hardly anybody took a second glance at the shimmering blue lake forming in the cooled-down lava. The lake owes its colour to a special mix of silicic acid, minerals and algae covering the jagged lava lake floor as a smooth, dense layer of sediments – as if it were lined with a synthetic material.

✷ ✷
**Bláa Lónið –
Blue Lagoon**

It was young people who first discovered the lake for late-night parties and to splash around in. Workers from the nearby power plant would also sometimes use their breaks for a dip. When one of them noticed an improvement in the psoriasis that had been plaguing him for a long time, the situation promptly changed, and the »wild« swimming lake was turned into an orderly bathing establishment named **Bláa Lónið**, the Blue Lagoon, with a treatment section for

The Blue Lagoon: a warm bath amid the lava

psoriasis patients. In 1999 the original lagoon had to make way for the expansion of the power plant. A little bit further west a new, rigorously planned spa complex was set up, with lava grottoes and islands, as well as small sections of beach, steam baths in a lava cave, a white-tiled luxury bath, various spa facilities, a service centre with changing rooms, souvenir shop and tourist information, catering and a conference centre. In 2007, the whole complex was extended again and modernized. A wastewater lake created by chance has become one of the most popular tourist attractions in Iceland. Whether under the summer sun or in a snowstorm, a soak in the Blue Lagoon is always an experience, and a healthy one at that: the **curative powers of the water** for psoriasis have by now been scientifically confirmed, and the mineral-rich mud has long been for sale in a broad range of skincare products under the **»Blue Lagoon«** label. Opening times: mid-May – Aug daily 9am – 9pm; Sept – mid-May daily 10am – 8pm; daily bus shuttle from Keflavík airport and the capital Reykjavík; for more information: tel. 420 88 21, www.bluelagoon.com.

! *Baedeker* TIP

Beauty delivered to your door
The entire range of Blue Lagoon skincare products is on offer in a boutique on the Blue Lagoon, as well as at a duty-free store in Keflavík airport. Visitors can also order the products online from the comfort of their own homes: www.bluelagoon.com (look for »Shop Online«). By now even some pharmacies abroad stock them, although they are expensive everywhere.

Via Krysuvík back to Reykjavík

From Grindavík, the rough and not yet tarmacked [427] winds its way east along a wild coastline and through lonely lava fields. Way-marked trails lead into the surrounding mountains and to the coast where the cliffs of the **Krysuvíkurbjarg**, nearly 7km/4.3 miles long and up to 70m/230ft high, are a special attraction. Near the parking area, where the hiking trail to the cliffs starts, the road passes the small **Krysuvíkurkirkja**, the remains of an estate of some importance in the Middle Ages. Old documents show that there was a church here as early as 1100. The current one was built in 1857, but used as a residence for decades in between until it was reconsecrated in 1964. The name Krysuvík is also used for the geothermal steam, sul-phur and mud springs around the area. Also of volcanic origin is the **Grænavatn**, a turquoise crater lake, barely 1km/0.6 miles north of where the [427] joins the [42], which is in a significantly better state. **Seltún**, the best-known geothermal field in Krysuvík, lies another 1.5km/0.9 miles further north and is easily accessible via paths and platforms.

Krysuvik

Krysuvík is an enclave of the town of ► Hafnarfjörður, reached by taking the [42] leading north. The same road going east crosses a section of the coast which is deserted today, where only the **Stranda-kirkja**, or »good-luck church«, steeped in legends, is a reminder of happier times. On the way north, the 10 sq km/3.8-sq mile Kleifar-vatn mountain lake soon presents a real conundrum: the lake has hardly any inlets and no visible outlets, yet the water level rises and falls at regular intervals. After an **earthquake in 2000** it was even feared that somebody had pulled a plug deep down below, as the water level fell rapidly, only to stabilize again after a few months. The road running along the banks of the lonely lake is a scenic route.

Kleifarvatn

Level with the aluminium smelter of Straumsvík the [42] joins the main road connecting Reykjavík with Keflavík airport. The alumi-nium works represents Iceland's largest industrial firm, set up in the late 1960s. Since the end of 2000 the company has been part of the Canadian aluminium and packaging group Alcan. In Straumsvík about 500 people produce some 170,000 tons/187,400 short tons of aluminium per year for Alcan Iceland.

Straumsvik

The electricity needed for the production is provided by the hydro-electric plants on the **Þjórsár** at such a good price that it is worth transporting the raw material, alumina, from the Alcan mines in northern Australia halfway around the globe to Iceland, and to sub-sequently ship the end products to the markets in North America and Europe. Visitors to the area can't miss the red and white striped silos, next to the long factory workshops, where the alumina is stored.

★ ★ # Reykjavík

Region: Southwest Iceland   **Population:** 118,000

In every respect, Reykjavík is the dominant city in the country. Nearly two thirds of all Icelanders live in the metropolitan area – and the numbers are increasing. The most important cultural and educational institutions are housed here, along with the leading media organizations, the largest banks and companies and the cor-ridors of political powers. Reykjavík is very much the centre of a centralized state.

In actual fact, the metropolitan area consists of not just one, but seven autonomous municipalities. These blend into each other in such a way that the borders between them are hardly visible to an outsider. Also, nearly half of the population of the city of Reykjavík proper lives in suburbs such as Árbær, Breiðholt, Hraunbær or Grafarvogur, which are further away from the centre than the separate neighbouring towns of Kópavogur or Seltjarnarnes. And while other regions of the country have to deal with a shrinking population, the capital region is always growing. It took the population of Reykjavík up to the mid-19th century to hit the 1,000 mark and until the early 1990s to cross 100,000; today, around 120,000 people live here.

While at first glance Reykjavík seems modern and – thanks to the multicoloured roofs – very colourful, it also has something quite American about it. This is the Reykjavík that shows itself mostly in the large shopping malls such as **Kringlan**, the centre of the New City. Visitors looking for the true character of Iceland will be disappointed by these temples to consumerism, by the spreading concrete architecture and the broad main roads tailored to the needs of cars, and often don't spend enough time in the city to discover its charm. The Reykjavík that knows how to please shows its face in the **Old Town** and the **shopping streets of the city centre**, with their small shops, trendy boutiques, cosy cafés and noisy pubs, in the traditional residential areas with their little houses clad in corrugated iron, or at the Tjörnin, the lake where some four dozen types of bird may be spotted.

Discovering the city's charm

Greatness came late – some city history

It would have been hard to predict from Reykjavík's history that it would achieve the importance it has today. The city can however look back on **Ingólfur Arnarson**, Iceland's first permanent settler,

← *A beacon of light: the Hallgrímskirkja towers over Reykjavík*

▶ VISITING REYKJAVÍK

INFORMATION

Adalstræti 2
tel. 519 15 50
www.visitreykjavik.is

TRANSPORT

The yellow city-centre buses run on 20 lines between 7am – midnight, in the daytime every 20 minutes, in the evenings and at weekends every half hour. The main interchange points are Lækjartorg in the historical centre, Hlemmur, Grensás, Mjódd and Ártún. A town map showing the bus routes can be picked up from the tourist office. Single tickets cost about 250 Icelandic króna, and transfer tickets are called »skiptimiði«. Two hours before every international departure, an airport bus leaves from Hotel Loftleiðir for Keflavík airport. The overland buses run by the BSÍ company depart near the Hringbraut; tickets may be bought between 7.30am and 10pm.

REYKJAVÍK TOURIST CARD

The Tourist Card gives free entrance to all seven thermal spas and nearly all museums and galleries, free internet access, various shop and restaurant discounts and unlimited travel on Reykjavík's buses. The card can be bought at the tourist office, bus station, Hotel Loftleiðir and in the youth hostel (24 hrs for 1200 ISK, 48 hrs 1700 ISK, 72 hrs 2200 ISK).

GOING OUT

Reykjavík has become a hot spot of good cheer in the far north. On summer weekends in particular, there are high jinks into the small hours, lubricated by rivers of alcohol. Which locality is the »in« place can be judged from the length of the queue at the door. Don't be too disheartened however, as the turnover is usually fairly high, with the locals preferring to drift from pub to pub. Don't expect much to be happening before midnight though; Icelanders start the party at home, drinking one or three beers before coming out – not such a bad idea given the price of a beer in the pubs.

① *Gaukur á Stöng*
Tryggvagata 22
Tel. 551 15 56
There's a good atmosphere here every evening – and has been for the past 20 years. A classic across three storeys with restaurant and live music and space for up to 700 guests.

② *Grand Rock*
Smiðjustígur 6
Tel. 551 55 22
In the daytime a good spot for a round of chess, in the evening live music with many well-known Icelandic bands. Those with deep pockets will appreciate the large selection of whiskies.

③ *Kaffibarinn*
Bergstaðastræti 1
Tel. 551 15 88
This is where the cult movie *101 Reykjavík* was filmed, which might explain why it is always so full. Or it might be to do with the good music that the DJs put on at the weekends. In any case, the Kaffibarinn is a good place for Icelandic celebrities.

④ *Kringlukráin*
Kringlan
Tel. 568 08 78
This is where theatregoers meet before and after performances for a

snack or drink in a cosy pub atmosphere. Live music at the weekends.

⑤ *NASA*
Austurvöllur 101
Tel. 511 13 13
The largest club in Iceland, playing the hottest music – incredibly »in«.

WHERE TO EAT
► Expensive
① *Perlan*
Öskjuhlið, tel. 562 02 00
International gourmet cuisine in a spectacular setting. The view across the city changes constantly, as in one hour the revolving restaurant in the glass dome – above the huge silver, gleaming hot water tanks – completes its turn. One floor below the restaurant, the café has a terrace with panoramic views.

► Moderate
② *Apótek*
Austurstræti 16
Tel. 575 79 00
This restaurant used to be a pharmacy, which is why diners receive a »prescription« instead of a menu. The mix of nostalgia and a modern interior works very well, and the chefs work behind glass to create a fine selection ranging from sushi via tapas to Icelandic dishes.

③ *Humarhúsið*
Amtmannsstígur 1
Tel. 561 33 03
Lobster is the speciality in this stylishly furnished establishment – as a soup it is pretty good value even. Other fish specialities are served too however.

④ *Þrír Frakkar*
Baldursgata 14
Tel. 552 39 39

Cosy restaurant in the Old Town specializing in fish. Highly praised chef Úlfar Eysteinsson likes to give traditional Icelandic recipes a contemporary makeover.

Baedeker recommendation

► Budget
⑤ *Lækjarbrekka*
Bankastræti 2
Tel. 551 44 30
Old wooden house in the centre with extremely cosy, slightly old-fashioned furnishings. Excellent cuisine, mainly lamb and fish dishes. Daily tourist menu and homemade cakes.

► Inexpensive
⑥ *First Vegetarian*
Laugavegur 20b
Tel. 552 84 10
Inexpensive, frequently changing, vegetarian meals, often with an Indian flavour. Good selection of cakes.

⑦ *Mokka*
Skólavördustígur 3a
Tel. 552 11 74
Reykjavík's oldest café, which has been looking after its regulars since 1958. Popular meeting place for artists and intellectuals.

⑧ *Shalimar*
Austurstræti 4
Tel. 551 02 92
Good selection of Indian and Pakistani dishes, inexpensive lunch and dinner specials.

⑨ *Súfistinn Bókakaffi*
Laugavegur 18
Tel. 552 37 40
Visitors will not only get a good cup of coffee above Reykjavík's largest

bookshop, they can also browse the books and magazines to their heart's content.

ACCOMMODATION

▶ Luxury

① Hótel Borg
Pósthússtræti 11
Tel. 551 14 40, fax 551 14 20
www.hotelborg.is
Four-star hotel, built in 1930 in the Art Déco style and restored in 2007. Offering modern rooms, individually styled. Awarded Best Hotel in Iceland in 2003.

② Hótel Holt
Bergstaðarstræti 37
Tel. 552 57 00, fax 562 30 25
www.holt.is
In a quiet and central location, this member of Relais & Chateaux is no great beauty from the outside. However, the interior more than compensates: the corridors, 30 rooms and 12 suites house the largest private art collection in Iceland. Some 300 paintings and sculptures by Icelandic artists ensure a unique ambience.

▶ Mid-range

③ Fosshótel Baron
Baronsstígur 2 – 4
Tel. 562 32 04
Fax 552 44 25
www.fosshotel.is
Modern, centrally-located hotel, both family-friendly and suitable for busi-

ness travellers and long-term stays. An additional draw is Iceland's first hot pot restaurant!

▶ Budget

④ Baldursbrá Guesthouse
Laufásvegur 41
Tel. 552 66 46
Fax 562 66 47
baldursbra@centrum.is
This guesthouse offers an experience of pure cosiness. Eight large, welcoming rooms in a central location, with a hearty breakfast buffet. In the garden a hot pot awaits guests.

⑤ Reykjavík Farfuglaheimili
Sundlaugavegur 34
Tel. 553 81 10
Fax 588 92 01
info@hostel.is
Modern youth hostel near the public swimming pool. The campsite is right next door too.

who settled in 874 at **»Smoky Bay«** – which is the English translation of the name »Reykjavík«. Two carved tree trunks that Arnarson had thrown into the sea just before he first landed on the coast of southern Iceland, were washed ashore here. For Ingólfur, this was a sign from the gods to take up residence at this place; today, the coat-of-arms of the city of Reykjavík shows the two trunks in the sea's waves. Archaeologists reckon that Ingólfur's farmstead used to stand round about where the Aðalstræti joins the Túngata, only a few metres from today's town hall and the parliament. However, the farm did not play an important role in the settlement phase and the period of the sagas, but rather always stood in the shadow of Bessastaðir on the Álftanes peninsula. More important in the end was Viðey Island, the site of an influential Augustine monastery from the 13th century to the Reformation.

A good two centuries after the monastery was razed by marauding Danish troops, 18th-century Viðey moved back to the centre of Icelandic politics. This was where **Skúli Magnússon** (1711 – 1794) had his Viðeyarstofa residence built, today the oldest stone house in town. Change came with Skúli in 1749, the year that he was appointed governor, the highest administrative civil servant of the colony. Skúli was the first Icelander to hold this position and as such was able to stand up to the interests of the Danish monopoly traders for nearly one-and-a-half decades. During this time, he started the development of independent economic structures in the country, which was starving, exploited and completely dependent on its colonial masters. Inspired by the fresh wind of the Enlightenment, he established a company to invest in a programme of industry and infrastructure for Iceland. Where today the Aðalstræti runs through the

Rise from the 18th century onwards

Bright façades against the grey days: Reykjavík shows its colours

Old Town, Skúli had apartments and companies for wool and fish processing as well as for shipbuilding – the roots of the metropolis. When the monopoly traders took over Skúli's life work in 1764 and disempowered him, the seeds of Reykjavík's rise were already planted, even if the big breakthrough had not yet come. When the Danish king officially founded the town of Reykjavík by royal decree in 1786, its inhabitants were counted and found to total 167.

Reykjavík becomes the centre of power
In 1784, the bishop of Iceland moved his seminary to Reykjavík from Skálholt, which had been largely destroyed by earthquakes. With the consecration of the cathedral in 1796, the town officially became the bishop's see for the island. In 1819, secular power joined the spiritual, as the governor turned the prison at the Lækjartorg, finished in 1771, into his personal and official residence. After 1874, as Iceland gained more of its own institutions and administrative tools with every step towards independence, these too established themselves in Reykjavík; for instance in 1885 the national bank was formed, and in 1911, the university founded, with the merger of several higher education colleges. The biggest push however came with the start of **self-governance of the country** in 1904. The city was by now growing quickly and continuously, the nearly 7,000 inhabitants (Greater Reykjavík some 9,500) representing 12 % of the entire Icelandic population. From 1909 onwards, water and gas provision was secured, and between 1913 and 1917 the port was built. In 1921, a power plant at the Elliðaár began feeding homes with electricity, and from 1928, geothermally heated water was put to use; by the end of the 1930s, the hot-water provision covered the entire country. No other town in Iceland benefited so much from the economic boom that the British and later the American troops brought to the country during the Second World War. From this, Reykjavík developed into the undisputed economic and administrative centre of Iceland, and the population figures, still rising today, attest to the continuing appeal of the metropolis.

Culture in Reykjavík

The summer lull
Most visitors miss out on the variety of culture, which in Reykjavík is vastly superior to many European cities of a similar size, as during the main summer holiday season the performing arts largely take a break. The season of the major **theatres** and the **opera** – Reykjavík boasts ten stages at seven venues – as well as the Icelandic Symphony Orchestra, run from October to May. Some actors do use this free time to stage historical material from the times of the sagas, or scenes from folk culture in a tourist-friendly format. *Light Nights* is a well-established production of this kind in English, and another is staged in the Skemmtihus chamber theatre at the Laufásvegur; the Tourist Information knows the current programmes and performance times.

The Gay Pride Festival: it's not just the façades that are colourful in Reykjavík

Since 1970, in even-numbered years cultural life has stayed vibrant up to the beginning of the travel season, thanks to the »**Listahátíð í Reykjavík**« biannual arts festival with its broad-ranging programme of good national and international events (www.artfest.is). In early/ mid-June however, this festival too nears its end. After the first weekend in August, with the following Monday a holiday which nearly all city-dwellers celebrate somewhere in the countryside, leaving Reykjavík quiet and sleepy like no other day, the city wakes up again. On the two subsequent weekends, the carnival atmosphere of the gay and lesbian procession **Gay Pride Reykjavík**, and the long, colourful Menningarnott culture night following the **Reykjavík Marathon**, set the pulse of the city racing again.

Reykjavík – City of the Seven Spas

Is there one thing that the visitor absolutely has to do in Reykjavík? While the museums are undoubtedly interesting and worth seeing, in global terms they are second rate. The position of the city, with a mountain panorama on one side and the sea on the other, is impressive but not unique. Some tourism PRs might characterize the nightlife as a global hotspot, but in reality it is probably rather the whiff of the exotic than a real comparison with Berlin, London or New

Reykjavík Map

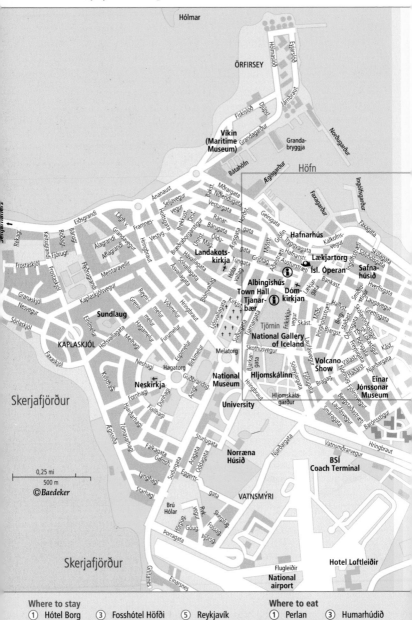

Where to stay
1. Hótel Borg
2. Hótel Holt
3. Fosshótel Höfði
4. Baldursbrá
5. Reykjavík Farfuglaheimili

Where to eat
1. Perlan
2. Apótek
3. Humarhúdið
4. Þrír Frakkar

© Baedeker

0,1 mi
200 m

Viðeyjarsund

Faxagata
Geirsgata
Tryggvagata
Hafnarhús
Hafnarstræti
Grjótag.
Austurstræti
Aðalstr.
Kirkjustræti
Suðurgata
Tjarnargata
Albingishús
Dóm-
kirkjan
Town
Hall
Iðnó
Tjörnin
Vonarstræti
Lækjartorg
Hverfisgata
Ísl. Óperan
Bankastræti
Amtst.
Bókhl.
Skálholtsstíg
Þingholtsstr.
Safnahúsið
Lindargata
Hverfisgata
Laugav.
Grettisg.
Frakkast.
Njálsgata
Bergþórug.
National
Gallery
of Iceland
Volcano Show
Frikirkjuvegur
Skálhst.
Skothús-
vegur
Sóleyjargata
Fjölugata
Laufásvegur
Njarðar-
gata
Bragar.
Barónsstígur
Snorrabraut
Einar
Jónssonar Museum
Hallgrím
kirkja

Hljomskálinn
Hljomskálagarður

Sólfar
Rauðarárvík
Sæbraut
Höfði
Borgartún
Samtún
Höfðatún
Sóltún
Katrínartún
Kringlumýrarbraut
Hrauntegur
Kirkjuteigur
Sil-
furt.
Hofteigur
Laugateigur
Sigtún
Laugardalslau
Laugardalur
Engjavegur

Natural History
Museum
Hlemmur
Bus Terminal
Sundlaug
Skipholt
RAUÐARÁRHOLT
Nóatún
Mjölnisholt
Brautarholt
Skipholt
Ásmundarsafn
Engjateigur
Suðurlandsbraut

Hall-
grímskirkja
Kjarvalsstaðir
Miklatún
Háteigsvegur
Kringlumýrarbraut

Kringlan
Shopping Center
Miklabraut
Fellsmúli

ÖSKJUHLÍÐ
Perlan
Öskjuhlíð
Keflavík, Hafnarfjörður
Akranes, Borgarnes, Selfoss, Vestmannaeyjar
Árbæjarsafn, Hverager

⑤ Lækjarbrekka ⑦ Mokka ⑨ Súfistinn Bókakaffi
⑥ First Vegetarian ⑧ Shalimar

Entertainment
① Gaukur á Stöng ② Grand Rock ④ Kringlukráin
③ Kaffibarínn ⑤ NASA

York that makes it attractive. One thing however is truly unique: **Reykjavík's spa life**. Don't leave the city without visiting one of the many pools. Surveys of foreign visitors who enjoyed a bathing experience here show their attractiveness: 98 % would definitely go bathing again if they came back to Reykjavík.

Warm bath on the Arctic Circle

Elsewhere, any treasurer of a city with 100,000 inhabitants would need several relaxing baths a day if they had to finance the running of seven thermal spas all year round, only one of them with a roof. However, in Reykjavík this is no problem despite the proximity to the Arctic Circle. Heating costs are hardly worth mentioning, particularly when weighed against the nearly 2 million visitors per year – far more than the baths of a much bigger city might attract. And the seven spas in Reykjavík are complemented by another half a dozen in the suburbs. In terms of size and facilities most reach standards only offered elsewhere by more expensive recreational baths; in Reykjavík, by contrast, a visit to the swimming pool is an **inexpensive pleasure** compared to other living costs. And as the open-air pools have fairly long opening hours even in winter, there is a good chance to take a bath after dark under the Northern Lights.

Alongside normal swimming pools with water temperatures rarely below 29 °C/84°F, most baths also have steam saunas, whirlpools, warm water pools and hot pots, or **heiti potturinn**. Stepping into these mini pools, with steam temperatures of 37 – 42 °C/98 – 107 °F, has a similarly relaxing effect to a sauna.

Beginners should however be sure to start by testing the »coldest« of the pots, as for bodies not used to it, water temperatures over 40 °C/104°F can seem scaldingly hot. Also, don't spend any longer than 15 minutes in the hot pots, and cool off afterwards in an outdoor or normal swimming pool. And lastly, don't schedule in too much for the evening – hot pots are tiring!

Go swimming, live longer!

The population statistics show the results of the Icelandic passion for swimming: health experts are convinced that Icelanders' life expectancy, high by international comparison, is partly due to the country's spa culture. Thermal spas are credited with **curative powers** for degenerative diseases, such as arthritis, as well as for modern stress-related illnesses. However, the whirlpools and hot pots don't just promote health but also communication: the cosily warm pools are a meeting place for the people of the city to chat about daily life or politics, to gossip about neighbours or celebrities, and are also where it is easiest for visitors to get chatting to the locals or other guests. **Laugardalslaug**, the main swimming pool of the city next to the campsite in the Laugardalur (Sundlaugarvegur), offers an open-air competition pool with 50-meter lanes as well as six hot pots, plus a sauna and steam bath area. Close to the centre, in the west of the city, is Sundlaug Vesturbæjar (Hofsvallagata), while the baths of Kópavogur and Seltjarnarnes are also easily accessible. For further details of all the baths in terms of facilities, opening times and bus connections in English, check www.visitreykjavik.is for »Tours and activities« and click on »Thermal Pools and Spas«.

✶ The Old Town between the Harbour and Tjörnin

The streets, lanes and squares in the centre between the harbour to the north and the Tjörnin lake on the southern side are the oldest part of Reykjavík. Visitors will notice this most clearly west of the Ingólfstorg in the so-called Grjótaðorp, a block of streets with small crooked lanes and houses from the early days of the town in the late 18th and early 19th centuries. The building at **Aðalstræti 10** is considered the oldest house. It was built in 1752 for one of the small enterprises with which Skúli Magnússon stimulated Iceland's economy.

Grjótaðorp

Skúli, in this sense the real founder of the city of Reykjavík, stands as a monument at the corner of Aðalstræti and Kirkjustræti. Practically at his feet, extensive archaeological ground surveys were made during preparations for the construction of a new hotel, which revealed the foundations of the first buildings in Reykjavík.

The fact that in this quarter which lies so far west, the most important shopping street is called **Austurstræti**, i.e. East Street, is due to

the historical development of the city: when the name was chosen in the mid-19th century, it was leading eastwards out of town! There is also a counterpart going in the other direction: leading west, the Vesturgata is a road lined with small shops selling arts and crafts.

The quarter between the harbour and Tjörnin stays extremely lively until late at night. Here, visitors will find several institutions of the café, pub and restaurant scene, such as the **»Gaukur á Stöng«** at Tryggvagata 22, where in the early 1980s legal beer cocktails mixing light beer and vodka were created, sounding the death knell of the

Shopping and nightlife in the Old Town

Highlights *Reykjavík*

Old Town
A stroll through the streets and small lanes between the harbour and Tjörnin is a walk through the heart of Reykjavík.
► page 241

Municipal Art Museum
Museum spread over three sites. Icelandic art from Erró via Kjarval to Sveinsson.
► page 244/255/259

National Art Gallery
For those that want to see more (Icelandic) art. Landscape and nature paintings are well represented.
► page 248

National Museum
A journey through the history and culture of the country.
► page 254

Árbæjarsafn open-air museum
Historical buildings and demonstrations of traditional trades – an excellent and authentic museum.
► page 255

Nightlife
Reykjavík is famous for its bars, pubs and clubs. In Iceland's capital, nightowls have come to the right place!
► page 232/241

decades-old prohibition on beer. With their outdoor tables on summer days, bistro cafés such as the »Paris« and the »Thorvaldsen« at the Austurvöllur, the »Café Victor« at the Ingólfstorg or the »Kaffi Reykjavík« right around the corner from the Vesturgata, even manage to exude a near-Mediterranean vibe which clashes somewhat with the woollens shops at the Ingólfstorg or along the Hafnarstræti. One of the most conspicuous houses in the area, the Falcon House on the northern side of the Ingólfstorg, is shared by the Café Victor and one of these shops. Carved falcons on the roof crest are a reminder of its role in colonial times, when coveted gyrfalcons from the whole country were collected here before being shipped off as presents from the Danish kings to delight European aristocracy.

More action at night than during business hours

The cafés, along with several restaurants of the Old Town, change character in the evening and turn into bars. At least at weekends, nearly all offer **entertainment** as well, with either a DJ getting people moving on the dance floor or live musicians performing on a little stage somewhere. The largest of those where better-known names of the national music scene perform, belongs to the »Gaukur á Stöng« (www.gaukurinn.is). Visitors not wanting to spend their weekend evenings queuing outside trendy venues or paying inflated entry fees and alcohol prices, can choose open-air entertainment: bikers and young skaters meet at the **Ingólfstorg**, and in the streets cars cruise through the night in an endless convoy – the Icelanders' name for this activity is »rúnturinn« – with at the wheel a fair few Icelanders old enough to have a driving licence, but not to step inside a pub let alone drink alcohol.

From Thursday to Sunday, there is more going on late at night on the streets of the Old Town – as well as at the Laugavegur – than during business hours. Visitors wanting to get the full experience need a lot of stamina though, as the evening seldom starts before 11pm. One famous **nightlife attraction** has now lost its shine however: as there has effectively been no enforced closing time since 2002, the **Lækjartorg** no longer suddenly fills with noisy revellers continuing the party, as it did when all establishments had to close on the stroke of three o'clock. Despite this, the square is still full of activity all night long, as it is here that people order the last hot dogs, pancakes or waffles from fast-food stalls, before catching a taxi or nightbus home.

! **Baedeker TIP**

Forever electro

Proof that Björk and Sigur Rós do not have a monopoly on Icelandic music are the band Gus Gus, now firmly established in the pop business with their strange sounds that defy description. Bubbling electronica, pounding dance rhythms and unconventional vocal lines are Gus Gus' trademarks. Just have a listen to the debut album *Polydistortion*, its successor *This Is Normal* or the most recent studio album *Forever.*

Until 1915, larger ships could only moor off Reykjavík; people and **City harbour** goods had to be brought ashore or landed by tender boats that anchored on the banks level with today's Hafnarstræti. The area lying

Back in action, unfortunately: the Icelandic whaling fleet in Reykjavík harbour

in front of it today was only created by the expansion of the port between 1913 and 1917. Meanwhile, the modern container and freight port of **Sundahöfn** a few kilometres further east, has considerably reduced the role of the more central Reykjavíkurhöfn, which has however kept the fish trawlers and coastguard boats. A long quay right in front of the city centre on Geirsgata is reserved for small and mid-size cruisers, while the really big ones have to go into deeper Sundahöfn. The old steam engine standing on the quay is a favourite climbing frame for children. Having been used during the construction of the harbour for transporting material, to this day it has remained Iceland's only train.

Kolaportið

Right opposite the »Crusaders' Quay« at weekends the gate to the underground car park in the **Tollhusið** (Customs House) is opened for the Kolaportið weekly market and flea market, with its colourful mix of food and junk on display: cucumbers and peppers grown in private greenhouses, potatoes and home-baked pancakes from a farm in southern Iceland, dried or fresh fish from a fishing village on the Reykjanes Peninsula, as well as sweets and all kinds of bric-a-brac, antiques and second-hand goods, mobile phone accessories and neckties.

Víkin (Maritime Museum) ⏱

A former fish factory in the northwest of the old harbour uses fishing to tell the story of Icelandic seafaring. The 1970s cod war also gets a mention (opening times: July–Sept Tues–Sun 11am–5pm, otherwise only Sat and Sun 1–5pm; internet: www.sjominjasafn.is).

Municipal Art Museum: Hafnarhús ⏱

The most recent and certainly the most attractive branch of the Municipal Art Museum (Listasafn Reykjavíkur), which shows its treasures at two more addresses in the city (Kjarvalsstaðir ▶p. 255 and Ásmundarsafn ▶p. 259), fills the Hafnarhús at Tryggvagata 17. Modern architecture, inspired by minimalism, has turned the office and warehouse of the harbour administration building from the 1930s into a **temple of the arts**. Steel and concrete are the dominant materials, and six exhibitions rooms across two floors arranged around an open courtyard make for a compact museum. Alongside changing exhibitions, works are shown from a collection of about 3,000 pieces, which the **pop-art artist Erró** (* 1932) – easily the most renowned contemporary Icelandic artist – bequeathed to the city in 1989 (opening times: daily 10am–5pm; website: www.listasafnreykjavikur.is).

Austurvöllur

The Austurvöllur seems more like a small park than one of the central squares of a capital. In nice weather, the grassy areas become a sunbathing lawn, and above everything, right in the middle on a high plinth stands **Jón Sigurðsson** (1811–1879), the 19th-century leader of the Icelandic independence movement and thus the father of the country's independence (▶history p. 48). The monument is a work by Einar Jónsson (1874–1954). Sigurðsson stands looking at

Sun-seekers having a coffee liven up the Austurvöllur

the Alþingishús, which he didn't actually see during his lifetime as it was only inaugurated in 1881, two years after his death. The **parliament building** is a simple, even modest affair with a grey basalt-block façade. Above the entrance, the coat-of-arms of the Danish king Christian IX can be seen, who at the time was Iceland's head of state. Before Iceland's parliament – the Alþing – reconvened in 1845 in Reykjavík, it had sat exclusively in ►Þingvellir, but had dissolved half a century earlier and slipped into complete obscurity. Up to moving into the new building, the Menntaskólinn í Reykjavík, the old high school a few hundred metres further east at Bókhlöðustíg 7, served as the meeting place. Well into the 19th century, this was the only school in the country which would award a qualification for university entrance, which mostly led students to Copenhagen. Thus, many of the country's well-known personalities feature on the list of former pupils, amongst them two Nobel Prize winners. Born on the Faroe Islands, **Niels Finsen** (1860 – 1904) was awarded the Nobel Prize for Medicine in 1903 for his work on light therapy for tuberculosis patients, and **Halldór Laxness** (1902 – 1998; ► p. 61) was awarded the Nobel Prize for Literature in 1955.

◄ Alþingishús

◄ Menntaskólinn í Reykjavík

Between Alþingishús and Menntaskólinn, the modest cathedral – the Dómkirkjan – occupies the southeastern corner of the Austurvöllur. It was built between 1788 and 1796 as the seat for the bishop of Iceland who had just moved from Skálholt to Reykjavík. At the time, the church didn't need to be big, as the town had fewer than 200 inhabitants. A real gem inside is the baptismal font, carved in 1839

Dómkirkjan

from Carrara marble by **Bertel Thorvaldsen** (1770–1844) – »created in Rome and given to Iceland, his fatherland, in faith«, as a Latin inscription explains. Thorvaldsen, in his time one of the most important classical sculptors in Europe, worked in Rome for a long period and normally figures in the history of art as a Dane. Icelanders like to claim him as one of their own though, as his father came from the island. This is also the reason why a few more of his works can be seen in the city, amongst them a self-portrait from 1839 in the green spaces on the southern part of the Tjörnin, beyond the Skothúsvegur.

Hotel Borg
Appearing bigger and more pompous than both parliament and cathedral, the Hotel Borg on the eastern side of the Austurvöllur is a house entirely inspired by Art Déco and built to designs by **Guðjón Samúelsson** (1887–1950). Since the day of its opening in 1930, the Borg has been Iceland's only real luxury hotel, with a long list of illustrious guests from the ranks of the aristocracy, politics and showbusiness, including the Danish king Christian X, Marlene Dietrich and Kevin Costner.

Tjörnin – a Paradise for Birds in the City Centre

Oasis of nature
Just a few steps south of the parliament and cathedral, visitors find themselves standing at the water's edge again: the Tjörnin city lake makes a natural boundary to the Old Town and forms an unusual **oasis of nature**: over 80 species of bird have been sighted here, nearly 50 of them regularly. In cold winters, when parts of the Tjörnin become an ice-skating rink, warm water is used to keep one piece on the Old Town side free of ice for the birds.

When the city fathers wanted to have a new **town hall** in the city centre, given the lack of other land to build on, their only choice was to pinch a corner of the Tjörnin. In 1992, the two-winged building with its striking, semi-circular roofs was put into service. The trademark feature is the southern façade looking onto the lake: mighty concrete pillars shelter a glass frontage reaching from the roof to the water level. Originally controversial because of its dimen-

> ! **Baedeker TIP**
>
> **On the trail of elves**
> Whilst the Icelanders have both feet firmly in the 21st century, they still have an enormous amount of trouble with gnomes, light-fairies, elves and trolls, who can get very annoyed when, for instance, roads are built through their invisible residences. Which is why in 1995 an elf school finally opened – the first and only one in the world! Since then, every Friday at 4pm historian Magnús Skarphédinsson has been initiating people, including tourists, into the universe of the elves (Álfaskólinn, Síðumúli 31, 108 Reykjavík, tel. 834 40 14, mhs@vortex.is).

A hotel like no other in Iceland: the Borg →

sions and building costs, the new town hall has long since become an accepted and central **part of the cityscape**. Inside, tourists find a municipal information office, rarely overrun with people, as well as a pretty and inexpensive cafeteria.

National Gallery of Iceland

On the eastern banks of the Tjörnin, a church clad in grey corrugated iron might catch the eye, but the museum right next to it is Listasafn Íslands, the National Gallery of Iceland (Fríkirkjuvegur 7). Here, the architectural combination of a former ice storehouse – where blocks of ice sawed from the Tjörnin were kept cool for the summer – with a light-filled new construction works well. Changing exhibitions by national and international artists regularly fill the rooms, while in the summer months the museum fulfils its duties to visitors by showing selected works by Icelandic artists from the collection, always including the classical pieces of **landscape and nature painting** which dominated the art of the country up to the 1940s. A pioneer of Icelandic painting and the country's first full-time artist was **Ásgrimur Jónsson** (1876 – 1958), who studied in the early 20th century at the Royal Academy of Art in Copenhagen and had his first exhibition in his home country in 1903. Jónsson is well represented in the National Gallery. Opening times: Tues – Sun 11am – 5pm.

Not all at once now... the National Gallery

Laugavegur and Bankastræti

Forming an extension of the Austurstræti, the Laugavegur and its Bankastræti continuation represent the most important shopping streets in the city. Thanks to the geothermal springs under the cobbles providing underfloor heating, they stay free of snow and ice even in the winter. This is where long-established jewellers, boutiques of international fashion chains and national designers, souvenir shops, book and music shops, restaurants and some **trendy hangouts** are clustered together.

Looking for art, crafts or simply a souvenir a little out of the ordinary? Where the Bankastræti becomes the Laugavegur, turn off onto the Skólavörðustígur leading up to the Hallgrímskirkja. On both sides there are many galleries and shops selling art, crafts and handicrafts, with souvenir hunters flocking in particular to the shop of the **Handknitting Association of Iceland** at Handprónasambandið, no. 19. Shoppers needing to take a breather during the »climb« should head for Reykjavík's oldest café at no. 3: the »Mokka Kaffi« is an institution, pervaded by a 1960s charm.

Arts and crafts

> **!** *Baedeker* TIP
>
> ### ÁTVR – Booze Central
>
> Legendary amongst tourists, they are not allowed to publicize themselves and their discreet exteriors are somewhat reminiscent of the chic of Soviet-bloc retail. Often visitors don't even realise they've reached their destination until they are standing more or less in front of them. These are the sales outlets of the state-owned alcohol and tobacco monopoly ÁTVR. Vínbúðin in Austurstræti 10 a is one of six liquor stores in Reykjavík and has an excellent selection. Visitors who appreciate the finest and more unusual tipples will be pleasantly surprised. Open: Mon – Fri 11am – 6pm, Sat 11am – 2pm.

Moving from the Old Town via the Lækjargata to the Bankastræti, a complex of 19th-century houses catches the eye, one of them providing an appropriate setting for the **Restaurant Lækjarbrekka**, a culinary institution in Reykjavík. The conspicuous building with its jet black paint and gleaming white windows was built in 1832 as a private home for a Danish trader, but was converted and put to different uses several times. For some years a growing Reykjavík was provided from here with bread, rolls and cake by the bakery dynasty of Bernhöft, and today the whole area is still called **Bernhöftstorf** in memory of it. On fine days, the café tables sheltered from the wind on the small square between the houses are a popular pit stop with tourists.

At the corner of Lækjargata and Bankastræti, the Stjórnarráðshúsið functions as **the official residence of the prime minister**. The first residents to move in here in 1771 however were not highly regarded nor did they come here voluntarily: the building served as a prison until 1820, when a governor had it converted into an official resi-

Stjórnar-ráðshúsið

dence. Since then it has always served this function for the most powerful in the country. The two statues in the front garden show **Hannes Hafstein**, who in 1904 became the first Minister for Iceland in the Danish cabinet to actually be Icelandic and reside in Reykjavík, and **Danish king Christian IX**, who in 1874 was the first Danish monarch ever to visit this part of his empire. With him he had a constitution for his subjects that promised them partial autonomy and paved the way for independence realized 70 years later. A few steps further north, from the Arnarhóll hill a belligerent-looking Ingólfur Arnarson, leaning on the dragon prow of his ship, is looking out for new shores. This monument to Iceland's first permanent settler, like the two outside the Stjórnarráðshúsið, was executed by Einar Jónsson.

★★
Safnahúsið cultural centre

Behind the monument to Ingólfur, the striking Þjóðmenningarhúsið building, also called Safnahúsið, catches the eye with its classical features (Hverfisgata 15). Built in the early 20th century to house various collections, for several years it sheltered nearly all its country's treasures – whether cultural or related to natural sciences – and then served for a long time as the National Library. The »books« exhibited here today are considered the most valuable art treasures in Iceland: the **originals of the medieval Saga manuscripts**. Opening times: daily 11am – 5pm, www.thjodmenning.is.

National Theatre

The next house on Hverfisgata is the National Theatre, built in the late 1920s. The Art Déco influenced façade is a precursor of those basalt formations cast in concrete which **Guðjón Samúelsson** was to give full expression to on the Hallgrímskirkja.

The Living Art Museum

Visitors taking a stroll here should head back from the Hverfisgata onto the Laugavegur, to join one of the side streets, the Vatnsstígur. In late 2002 the Living Art Museum, **Nylistasafnið**, moved into its new premises here, often showing avant-garde exhibitions with works by the latest crop of Icelandic artists (Vatnsstígur 3; programme information online under: www.nylo.is).

Natural History Museum

Right at the eastern end of the Laugavegur, next to the main Hlemmur bus station, the Natural History Museum (Hlemmur 5) documents and explains the flora, fauna and geology of the island, with stuffed specimens of all the country's animals, in particular the birds, often displayed in their natural habitat. The museum possesses both a skeleton and a stuffed **specimen of the great auk**, a species that once used to be widespread in northern climes. Unfortunately, the flightless bird was tasty and meaty, which made it a staple food source of the North Atlantic. On 3 June 1844, bird hunters on the rock island of Eldey off ▶Reykjanes killed the last specimens left in the world. The museum is run by the Icelandic Institute of Natural History and actively involved in research. Opening times: Tues, Thurs, Sat, Sun 1 – 5pm.

From Tjörnin to the Hallgrímskirkja

Together with the Tjörnin to the west and the Laugavegur to the north, the hill of Skólavörðuholt towers above the historic city centre, with at its top the striking **Hallgrímskirkja**, the most conspicuous landmark in town. The rows of houses stretching up the hill above the lake are among the classier residential areas in Reykjavík. Many diplomatic representations – amongst them the British embassy at Laufásvegur 31 and the US embassy at no. 21 – can be found here, and Iceland's president has his official residence near the banks of the lake too.

Just beyond the National Gallery, visitors can discover art in a context that seems unusual at first glance: the Hotel Holt (Bergstaðastræti 37). Seen from the outside, the hotel might display all the brutalist charm of prefab architecture, but inside it is a high-class hotel with equally classy cuisine, highly rated by gourmets. In its restaurant, bar, foyer and corridors, the Holt displays one of the best private art collections in the country, among them many **landscape paintings and portrait sketches by Jóhannes S Kjarval**.

Hotel Holt

Between the National Gallery and the Hotel Holt, visitors pass the Volcano Show put together by nature filmmaker Villi Knudsen. This **institution of tourist entertainment** was set up by his father Ósval-

✱
Volcano Show

America on his mind: Leifur Eiríksson pays no attention to the Hallgrímskirkja

dur. Over the past decades wherever a jet of lava has shot skywards in Iceland, a Knudsen has quickly appeared with his camera, often circling the eruption site in a small plane. The mini cinema centre at Hellusund 6a shows the constantly updated edits of the material they have collected (showings in English 3 x daily, in summer 5 x , duration approx. 2 hrs; tel. 551 32 30).

Hallgrímskirkja ✳

Visitors can't miss the Hallgrímskirkja, visible from all over the city and from far around. In 1986, after a good 40 years in construction, the church was finally consecrated. Reaching into the sky at the very top of the Skólavörðuhólt, the Hallgrímskirkja, with its striking profile and constantly blinking warning lights, is somewhat reminiscent of a space shuttle on its launch pad, even though Iceland's state architect **Guðjón Samúelsson** was thinking more of the basalt pillars of the volcanic regions when he drew up the plans. With its slim pillars, the light-filled interior draws on gothic architecture, but as a modern interpretation rather than a copy. The central nave of the concrete church has extraordinary acoustics, a fitting theatre for the 5,275 pipes of the German-made 72-stop organ. In summer, there are lunchtime organ concerts on Thurs and Sat, as well as Sun evenings. The church's second attraction is the **viewing platform** in the nearly 75m/250-ft church tower, accessible by elevator (access: daily 10am – 6pm, in winter closed Mon). In front of the Hallgrímskirkja, look out for **Leifur Eiríksson**, the man who discovered America, cast in bronze on a granite plinth. Created by the American sculptor A S Calder, the statue arrived in Iceland in 1930 as a present from the US to celebrate 1,000 years since the foundation of the Alþing.

> ! *Baedeker* TIP
>
> **Reykjavík – city of winter sports**
>
> Within a radius of 25 km/15 miles around Reykjavík, there are three skiing areas to choose from: Skálafell at the eastern edge of the Esja Massif as well as Bláföll and Hamragil, both only a few kilometres off the ring road towards southern Iceland. When skiing is possible, buses link the BSÍ bus station (Vatnsmyrarvegur) with all three. For more information, contact Tourist Information.

Einar Jónsson Museum

Right next to the Hallgrímskirkja, an unusually severe-looking concrete building catches the eye too; this is the Listasafn Einars Jónssonar (Njarðargata), a museum and artists' residence designed by its long-term occupant Einar Jónsson (1874 – 1954), Iceland's first sculptor of note. The work was completed in 1923. Whilst Einar Jónsson portrayed several famous personalities, as shown by the statues in front of the Stjórnarráðshúsið and on the Austurvöllur, he only really achieved his breakthrough in 1901 with a sculpture of the outlaw *Útlagar*. Later, his work was increasingly informed by mythological and religious symbols; he felt very close to the Symbolists of his time. A good idea of Jónsson's work can be gained in the **sculp-**

ture gardens behind the museum. Opening times museum: June – mid-Sept Tues to Sun 2 – 5pm, mid-Sept. – May only Sat/Sun 2 – 5pm, closed Dec/Jan; sculpture gardens: daily 11am – 4pm, www. skulptur.is.

From Tjörnin into the University Quarter

In the first years of the 20th century, a row of villas was built for the »better classes« of the time above the western banks of the town pond. Today, these houses with their colourful corrugated iron façades along the Tjarnagata form a picturesque contrast to the Modernist grey concrete of the town hall. Running parallel a bit further up, the **Suðurgata** borders the old main cemetery of the city, not only the last resting place of many famous Icelanders, but also an idyllic spot with good views across the Tjörnin all the way to the Skólavörðuholt with the striking Hallgrímskirkja on top. At the roundabout, where the Suðurgata meets the Hringbraut, the city's most important east-west link, a despairing man looks over the traffic, a child on his arm, a lifeless woman across his shoulder, a dog at his feet: this is ***Útlagar***, the sculpture by Einar Jónsson showing the outcast with his family after he had been declared an outlaw by the legal authorities of Old Iceland. Should he ever make it across the road, he will reach the extensive university quarter with the National Museum right opposite.

In Einar Jónsson's sculpture garden

National Museum

Þjóðminjasafnið Íslands, the National Museum (Suðurgata 41), coordinates and registers all archaeological activities in the country, collects and preserves the finds and is responsible nationally for the restoration and preservation of nearly four dozen historic buildings, amongst them the old grass sod farms and churches. The archive holds **tens of thousands of exhibits** from Viking times, the early settlements and later folk culture; however, only a part of it is on display in the museum. The collection is presented following the latest museum techniques, and a generously-sized café as well as a museum shop fill the ground floor. Opening times: daily 10am–5pm, in winter closed Mon, www.natmus.is.

National Library

The modern, bulky building on the other side of the Suðurgata is full of books – over a million volumes by now. Its fortress-like architecture has earned it the nickname of »**Book Castle**«. Opened in late 1994, the National Library (Þjódarbókhladan) brought together under one roof the former state library and the university library.

Institute Árni Magnússon

Back on the other side of the Suðurgata lies the university's main building; dating from the late 1930s, it represents another major design by Guðjón Samúelsson. Today, some 6,000 students are enrolled in nine faculties at the Háskóli Íslands, formed in 1911 with the merger of the medicine, law and theological colleges. The adjacent Árnagarður building houses the Institute Stofnun Árna Magnússonar, named after Árni Magnússon, who in the 17th century brought together most of the remaining **originals of the Icelandic sagas**, preserving them for posterity. Many of these are today in the possession of the Institute; a selection is exhibited in the Safnahusið cultural centre (► p. 250).

Museum of Telecommunications

Heading up the Sturlugata from the Árni Magnússon Institute to the Suðurgata, opposite the T-junction stands the former building of the »Reykjavík Radio« shipping broadcast station, called **Loftskeytastöð**. For over half a century after its completion in 1918, it was from here that contact was maintained with Icelandic ships on the seas of the world. Today, its rooms house a display by the Fjarskiptasafnið of the Icelandic Landssíminn telephone company documenting telecommunications from its beginnings all the way into the mobile phone age. It is interesting to see how Iceland's geographic isolation was overcome: it was only in 1906 that a telegraph cable under the sea reached Seyðisfjörður in eastern Iceland from Scotland; after that, telephone and telegraph lines began to be put down in the country itself. By the 1960s, all populated

? DID YOU KNOW …?

■ … that until 1986 the sparsely populated valleys of Iceland shared »communal lines«: all the farms in one valley were connected by one telephone cable, so that everybody was able to listen to the conversations of their neighbour.

areas were connected up. Today, Icelanders rank among the world's most dedicated users of all forms of modern communication; for example, no other country has a higher rate of mobile phones per capita. Opening times: Tues, Thurs and Sun 11am–5pm.

In Reykjavík's younger east

Still within walking distance of the city, nestling in the green spaces of the Miklatún lies the Kjarvalsstaðir (Flókagata) exhibition building, completed in 1973 as a further branch of the Listasafn Reykjavíkur Municipal Art Museum. The building is dedicated to **Jóhannes S Kjarval** (1885 – 1972), to this day Iceland's most prominent painter. Works from his oeuvre regularly fill one of the rooms. As Kjarval bequeathed his personal collection of paintings, drawings and sketches, as well as pieces from his artistic life – nearly 5,000 items – to the city of Reykjavík in 1968, the art museum is spoilt for choice. Kjarval lived in the capital from 1922 onwards, at least for the winters, while in the summer he would travel around Iceland looking for suitable subjects. The artist's fame and the admiration he inspires today still rest most of all on his images of the **people and landscapes of his native country**, which made him the painter of Iceland's nascent national identity in the first half of the 20th century. Opening times: daily 10am – 5pm, www.listasafnr eykjavikur.is.

★
Municipal Art Museum: Kjarvalsstaðir

> ❗ *Baedeker* TIP
>
> ### Warm and welcoming North Atlantic
>
> Reykjavík can afford to heat the water of a small bay: Ylströndin Nauthólsvík is the name of the idyllic beach scene below the hot water tanks on Öskjuhlíð. The heaped up sand creates a real beach feeling, and while the sea hardly ever reaches temperatures of more than 12 °C/54°F, the water temperature in the bay doesn't sink much below 20 °C/68°F (at high tide maybe a bit cooler, at low tide warmer). A hot pot on the banks reaches a good 30 °C/86°F, another at the service center over 35 °C/95°F. Opening times: mid-May – mid-Sept. daily 10am – 8pm.

Visitors driving eastpast the Kjarvalsstaðir on the major Miklabraut road linking west and east, will soon spot lying to the right the **Kringlan Shopping Center**, the centre of the so-called New City. Kringlan is one of those luxury malls that can be found in many large cities all over the world. Visitors who enjoy this kind of thing will find good shopping and eating opportunities here in around 140 shops and restaurants.

In the east of Reykjavík, on the northern banks of the Elliðaár river above the small Arbæjarstífla dam, houses catch the eye that definitely don't match the modern architecture of the suburbs of Reykjavík: here grass sods, wooden planks tarred black and corrugated iron are the construction materials of choice. Today, nearly two dozen buildings from the 19th and early 20th centuries stand in the Árbæjarsafn open-air folk museum. Most were taken down from

★ ★
Árbæjarsafn open-air museum

The domestic life of bygone days comes alive at the Árbæjarsafn open-air museum

Reykjavík's Old Town and rebuilt again here; only the small grass sod church came from northern Iceland in 1959. It forms a pretty ensemble with the Árbær farmstead, built in several stages between 1880 and 1920 and the only building which has always stood on this site. A new exhibit on childhood and toys was opened in 2008. In many houses visitors can watch demonstrations of **traditional trades and old-fashioned household chores,** or shop like in grandmother's day in the store near the entrance, with all the employees here doing their jobs in traditional costumes. The museum café in the Dillonshusið serves home-baked goods and at weekends usually a sumptuous buffet with coffee, for which Icelanders also like to come to the museum. Opening times: June – Aug Tues – Fri 10am – 5pm, Sat/Sun to 6pm, www.arbaejarsafn.is.

Laugardalur sports and leisure park

Another green oasis of relaxation and sport fills the Laugardalur. Its warm springs, the Þvottalaugarnar, once bubbled profusely and were used in the early days of Reykjavík as public washing places. It was also from here that in 1928 the first hot water flowed through a pipeline into town. A reminder of those times is the monument of the washerwoman by **Ásmundur Sveinsson** in the middle of the park. Four attractions come together in the Laugardalur: in the Grasagarður Reykjavíkur, the Botanic Gardens, some 4,000 species of plant grow, including all of Iceland's indigenous varieties. Families with children like to head next door for the Húsdyragardurinn petting zoo, containing all the mammals, wild or domesticated, that can be found in Iceland, as well as the small **Fjölskyldugarðurinn family leisure park**, with all sorts of entertainment, rides and playing equipment for children. Slightly older children and teenagers prefer the Laugardalslaug, the largest open-air pool in town, featuring a huge slide, at the northern edge of the park, which also houses all the important sports facilities of Reykjavík, including Iceland's national stadium.

A few metres west of the sports facilities, large sculptures grouped around an unusual building indicate the third branch of the Listasafn Reykjavíkur Municipal Art Museum, the Ásmundarsafn (Sigtún 5). What Jóhannes S Kjarval represents for painting, **Ásmundur Sveinsson** (1893–1982) represents for sculpture, and he also bequeathed the city of Reykjavík many of his works: a good 370 sculptures as well as the studio he planned and built himself in the 1940s with residence and exhibition hall – an extravagant building taking up forms of Arabic-Egyptian architecture. This is where nearly all the main works can be seen, at least as replicas, among them his famous sculptures of women from the 1930s, such as the *Woman Churning Butter* or the *Water Carrier*, but also some of his more abstract later works. Opening times: May–Sept daily 10am–4pm, Oct–April daily 1–4pm, www.listasafnreykjavikur.is.

✷ Municipal Art Museum: Ásmundarsafn

☺

Going north from Laugardalur it is a short walk to the Sundahöfn container port, where a boat leaves for Viðey Island from the pier several times a day. In the Middle Ages an important Augustine monastery stood on the 1.7 sq km/0.6 sq-mile islet, while later important personalities resided on the island, among them »the father of Reykjavík« **Skúli Magnússon**, who is buried in the local church. Used as a restaurant today, the Villa Viðeyarstofa just above the island's pier was built for Magnússon in 1755 using designs by Nicolai Eigtved, most famous as the architect of the Amalienborg Palace royal residence in Copenhagen. In the cemetery next to the church, the writer **Gunnar Gunnarson** lies buried with his wife.

Viðey has good hiking trails and paths for a leisurely stroll, and its nature is surprisingly undisturbed considering the proximity to the big city. In the western part a circular trail leads past secluded basalt pillars: this is a 1991 work of Land Art by Richard Serra called *Afangar*. Parts of Viðey are a bird conservation area, with access restricted during the breeding season. Further bird paradises can be found on the other islands off Reykjavík, small Akurey north of Seltjarnarnes and Lundey northeast of Viðey in particular, both with large populations of puffins.

Viðey

The industrial area at the edge of the Sundahöfn is forever pushing further west, already stretching onto the headland of Laugarnes. However, its western banks have managed to hang on to an artistic refuge: the Sigurjóns Ólafsson Safn (Laugarnestangi 70) honours the

Museum Sigurjón Ólafsson

life and work of Sigurjón Ólafsson (1908 – 1982), an **exponent of spontaneous abstract sculpture**, well-known in Scandinavia mainly, but also in the US. Sigurjón was also one of the most important Icelandic portrait sculptors, often working with wood and other materials that he would find by the sea. It is no coincidence that the museum, which used to be his studio, is right on the water. Thanks to this location, the small museum café always offers great views, while the summer concerts, which are traditionally put on in the museum on Tuesday evenings, are a treat for both eyes and ears.Opening times: June – Aug Tues – Sun, otherwise Sat/Sun 2 – 5pm; closed Dec/Jan, www.lso.is.

Höfði
In one of his most famous works, Sigurjón Ólafsson in 1971 gave an abstract rendition of the pillars of the high seat that showed Ingólfur Arnarson the way into the Smoky Bay. The sculpture stands not far from the shore about halfway between Sundahöfn and the city centre right next to the Höfði, the house where guests of the Icelandic government are put up. This two-storey wooden house was built in 1909 for a French consul. On 11 and 12 October 1986 it suddenly found itself in the international spotlight when **Ronald Reagan, US President** at the time, and his Soviet counterpart, the **General Secretary of the Communist Party of the Soviet Union, Mikhail Gorbachev**, chose Reykjavík for their first summit, holding their talks here. What initially seemed like a failure, with hindsight marks the begin-

Sólfar: Viking boat or spacecraft?

ning of the end of the Cold War, thereby changing the world. It was here, amid the drizzling rain and stormy squalls that the ice between the two biggest world powers began to melt.

The platform upon which the large, gleaming stainless steel sculpture *Sólfar* by **Jón Gunnar Árnasson** (1931 – 1989) looks ready to launch into the sky, has become a popular viewpoint on the coastal promenade. Even though the shape of the sculpture resembles a Viking boat, for the artist it represented more a spaceship for a voyage to the sun.

Sólfar

Outside Reykjavík, a little north of Mosfellsbær, the [36] turns off towards ►Þingvellir. A few kilometres past the junction, in the Mosfellsdalur, the subsequent **Nobel Prize winner Halldór Laxness** (►Famous People p. 61) spent his youth on the Laxnes farm, nowadays a farm for riding holidays. Even though he had achieved fame and fortune, Laxness had the rather modest-looking Gljúfrasteinn residence built close by and lived there up to his death in 1998. In September 2004, a museum dedicated to arguably the most famous Icelander of the 20th century opened here. Opening times: Tues – Sun 10am – 5pm.

Laxness farmstead

⊙

Sauðárkrókur

F 3

Region: Northwest Iceland   **Population:** 2,600

The entire region of Skagafjörður, with Sauðárkrókur as the largest town and administrative centre, has always made its living from agriculture and is well-known for its horses, which can be seen grazing on the pastures everywhere. Nearly every farm here keeps and breeds Icelandic horses, with many offering holidays on horseback. Nearby lie some of the most popular sights in Iceland, including the Glaumbær open-air museum, the Víðimýri church and the former bishopric of Hólar.

Sauðárkrókur lies at the end of the broad Skagafjörður fjord; heading inland, the valley of the same name is initially broad, only becoming narrower many kilometres further upcountry, before splitting into three smaller valleys. The entire valley and the gently rising slopes might be a lush green, but there are hardly any shrubs or trees. The **Hofsjökull** in the highlands feeds two rivers, the Austari-Jökulsá and the Vestari-Jökulsá, which join together to form the mighty Héraðsvötn river. Before the river flows into the fjord, it splits into many branches, forming a delta 15km/9 miles in width, with fine dark, sandy beaches.

▶ VISITING SAUÐÁRKRÓKUR

INFORMATION

Sauðárkrókur
In the Fosshótel Áning
Sæmundarhlíð
Tel. 453 67 17

Hólar
In the agricultural college
Tel. 455 63 00
www.holar.is

TRIPS – TRANSPORT

Boat trips to Drangey island
from Sauðárkrókur, Hofsós or Reykir
Tel. 453 63 10

Highland drives
From Varmahlíð via the [752] and the
[F 752] through the Vesturárdalur,
access to the Sprengisandur (only by
jeep). From Varmahlíð, driving west
for 25km/15 miles the Kjölur Route
turns off the ring road. The first
stretch of the road is paved, and in
favourable conditions the whole road
is negotiable by normal saloon car.

LEISURE AND SPORTS

Rafting
The two glacier rivers Jökulsá Vestari
and Jökulsá Austari, with their source
south of Sauðárkrókur, lend themselves superbly to rafting tours (Activity Tours, Sæmundagata 1, tel. 453
50 66).

WHERE TO EAT

▶ Moderate
Sauðárkrókur:
Ólafshús
Aðalgata 15
Tel. 453 64 54
It's hard to miss the blue house on the
main road. A restaurant with a long
tradition, serving everything from
pizza to lobster.

Sauðárkrókur: Kaffi Krókur
Aðalgata 16, tel. 453 62 99
The rival to the Ólafshús sits right
across the road. Good value in the
daytime – salads, pasta and soups –
but markedly more expensive in the
evening. Live music at weekends.

ACCOMMODATION

Baedeker recommendation

▶ Luxury
Sauðárkrókur: Hótel Tindastóll
Lindargata 3
Tel. 453 50 02
Understatement is the trademark of the
Hótel Tindastóll in Sauðárkrókur. Only
from the outside however, as the »inner
qualities« are probably unrivalled in Iceland. The old timber-framed house, where
the first hotel in Iceland was opened in
1884, has just ten double rooms. They are
all furnished in a different way, skilfully
integrating the comforts of a high-end hotel
without destroying the antique-retro charm
of the house.

▶ Mid-range
Sauðárkrókur: Fosshótel Áning
Sæmundarhlíð
Tel. 453 67 17, www.fosshotel.is
Summer hotel in a boarding school
with 65 comfortable rooms with
shower. In a quiet, central location.

▶ Budget
Hólar
Tel. 455 63 00
Holiday cottages and apartments,
accommodation in the former school
on mattresses or in double rooms.
Restaurant serving inexpensive snacks
and good Icelandic cuisine.

What to see in Sauðárkrókur

The Skagfirðingabraut main street runs straight as a die through Sauðárkrókur, but the choice of shops, pubs and restaurants is not exactly extensive, leaving the local youth not much in the way of evening entertainment, other than driving their cars up and down the main street. They turn at the petrol station and at the Villa Nova, which makes the place seem busy; however, it is always the same cars passing. Apart from the few colourful wooden houses along the main street, such as the **Hótel Tindastóll** or the red **Villa Nova**, which served as a hotel for a long time, Sauðárkrókur has a modern appearance. At the harbour, fish is dried on wooden racks, and more often than not fish heads strung up on cords rattle in the wind. Good views across the town can be had from the local Molduxi mountain and the 989m/3,245-ft Tindastóll, where it is said that wishing stones can be found.

The heritage museum (Aðalgata 16b) shows all kinds of household items and musical instruments as well as an exhibition on Sauðárkrókur in the first half of the 20th century. Opening times: daily 2–6pm.

Minjahús Sauðarkróks

Around Sauðárkrókur

In the fjord lie the islands of Drangey and Málmey, with the 180m/590-ft tuff rock of Drangey being the **emblem and landmark of the Skagafjörður**. The island used to be the residence of Grettir Ásmundarson (»Grettir the Strong«), the legendary Icelandic outlaw who was killed on Drangey in 1031. Today, in the early summer up to a million seabirds breed on the bird rock. For centuries, the island was a plentiful larder, where in one season up to 200,000 birds were caught and 24,000 eggs collected. For 50 years the **Earl of Drangey**, real name Jón Eiriksson, would collect eggs, while secured only by a rope, until he decided to take tourists onto the island on his boat and to tell them tales from his life. South of Drangey a single rock juts out of the water, called Kerlingin – »the Old Woman«. The rock is supposedly one of two trolls who led their cow across the fjord but were taken by surprise and petrified when the sun rose. The second troll, called Karlinn – »the Old Man« – and standing north of the island, was released from his tedious existence by an earthquake in 1755.

Drangey and Málmey

Reykir is the last farmstead on the western shores of the bay, north of Sauðárkrókur at the foot of the Tindastóll mountain. Below the farm lies the flat **Reykjadiskur Peninsula**, where saga hero Grettir the Strong is said to have come ashore. A hot spring on the beach, south of the headland, bears the name of Grettislaug – »Grettir's Bath« – and has recently been recently restored as a place to bathe.

Reykir

Lonely farm near Varmhalíð, south of Sauðárkrókur

✳ Glaumbær Open-air Museum

Two to a bed

The buildings of this unique farmstead – 15km/9 miles south of Sauðárkrókur – were erected in the 18th and 19th centuries in the turf construction style. Along with its neighbouring church, Glaumbær is one of the most popular sights in Iceland. What is special about this farm is that all the furniture still dates from the 18th and 19th centuries too. The buildings of Glaumbær consist of thin slats of wood covered with thick layers of turf and roofed with thick sod for heat insulation. The frontages of the houses are clad with wood, pointing to the fact that the farm must have been a rich one. Because of their static qualities, turf houses could only be built relatively small, so the old Icelandic farms consisted of a **group of individual buildings**, with those most often used linked by a central corridor. With a length of 20m/65ft, this corridor is unusually long in Glaumbær, linking nine individual houses. Two interior doors, in addition to the entrance door, protect the living rooms from the cold. Only the forge and the storage rooms have a separate entrance. The two guest rooms are located just past the entrance door, which is why it never really got properly warm there. Following on from the guest rooms, the kitchen also served as a smoking room for the **Hangikjöt** (smoked lamb meat), in addition to a few rooms used for storing provisions. Situated at the end of the corridor is the **baðstofa**, the largest room and living space of the farm where the farmer, his family and the labourers would work, eat and sleep. The baðstofa of Glaumbær has eleven beds, but as in those days there were often two to a bed, the farm was home to up to 22 people. Opening times: daily 9am – 6pm.

Standing in the cemetery of the neighbouring church is a small sculpture by Àsmundur Sveinsson showing Guðriður Þórbjarnardóttir with her son Snorri Þófinson, who was the first European to be born in America and the first American to die in Europe. Having in all likelihood had the first church in Glaumbær erected, he lies buried in the cemetery.

Sculpture by Àsmundur Sveinsson

There has been a simple country church in Víðimýri, a few kilometres south of Glaumbær, since as early as the 12th century, and many important pastors, such as **Guðmundur Arason**, who later became bishop in Hólar, (1203–1237) have worked here. Today's church was erected in 1834 from driftwood from the coast of the Skagi peninsula and turf from the Víðimýri area. The church is one of the most beautiful and authentic examples of the traditional style of architecture; there are only six of this type of church left in Iceland. Most of the interior is original, with only the turf having been renewed in the meantime. The **altarpiece**, dating from 1616, was imported from Denmark. The small interior space is kept simple and almost entirely without decoration, so that even the beams and slats of the roof construction are visible. The narrow benches on the northern side used to be occupied by the women while the men had the southern side to themselves. The rich folk were allowed to sit at the front, while the poor had to sit at the back.

Church of Víðimýri

! Baedeker TIP

Icelandic horses for all

Whether a short hack, day ride or an entire holiday on horseback, the area around Sauðárkrókur has a lot to offer horse lovers. For example, one option is to cross the highlands on the Kjölur Route in six days or, again in six days, ride to the Mývatn via the Sprengisandur highland track. When the sheep and horses are brought down from their summer pastures in September guests are welcome, and also in March to explore the wintry Iceland. An operator with lots of experience is Hestasport Varmahlíð, tel. 453 83 83, www.riding.is.

Hólar í Hjaltadalur

For seven centuries, little Hólar was the capital of northern Iceland, an **important bishopric and centre of education**. For a long time, wealth and power accumulated here, and by the first half of the 16th century every fourth farm in northern Iceland belonged to Hólar –

The grass sod farm of Nýibær: protected against the vagaries of wind and weather

over 350 in all. In addition, 36 bishops resided in Hólar, 23 of them Catholic and 13 Lutheran. Some of the best-known were Jón Ögmundsson (»the Holy«, 1106–1121), Guðmundur Arason (»the Good«, died after 1340), Jón Arason (1524–1550) and Guðmundur Þorláksson (1571–1627). After a long hiatus, Hólar – situated 25km/15 miles east of Sauðárkrókur – has been a bishop's see again since 1986.

Cathedral The dominant building here is the cathedral; made of red sandstone and dedicated in 1763, today it has been restored to its original splendour. The protected grass sod building **Nýibær**, near the cathedral, dates from 1854 and was inhabited up to the mid-20th century. A marked one-hour history trail leads around the town; the historical background of the 14 stations en route is explained by a brochure available from the tourist office.

Hofsós

The small village of Hofsós on the eastern banks of the fjord extends on both sides of the Hofsá river and is one of the oldest trading places in the country. Due to the favourable position of the harbour, there was brisk trade here as early as the 16th century. Today, the community of Hofsós lives mainly off fishing and services, with the good museums bringing in tourism.

The emigration centre of Hofsós, housed in several buildings in an **Vesturfarasetrið** attractive location on the water, illuminates the conditions in Iceland which between 1870 and 1914 led to a **mass emigration to America**. Visitors also learn a lot about the circumstances that the emigrants found in their new home country. Another role of the emigration centre is to support Americans of Icelandic heritage in tracing their ancestry. Opening times: mid-June mid-Sept Tues–Sun 11am–6pm, www.hofsos.is.

South of Hofsós, the estate of **Gröf** used to be one of the most important farms in the Skagafjörður area and is the birthplace of the writer of Passion Hymns, **Hallgrímur Pétursson**, who gave his name to the Hallgrímskirkja church in Reykjavík. Worth seeing is the small 17th-century grass sod church, which is one of the oldest churches in Iceland. The basalt columns on the beach south of Hofsós are also worth a short detour.

> ! **Baedeker** TIP
>
> **After a visit to the museum...**
> ...the ideal place for a cup of coffee is the sunny terrace of the Veitingastofan Sólvik, right next to the Vesturfarasetrið, with a view across the sea. Inside, the blue wooden house is very snug and the little snacks, such as the fresh bread or the sweet waffles, are always tempting.

Seyðisfjörður

L 3

Region: East Iceland **Population:** 700

Visitors arriving by ship get their first impression of Iceland as they come into the Seyðisfjörður. They could not ask for a much more captivating introduction to the country, as the fjord presents itself in picture-book beauty with tiered layers of basalt and volcanic slag running up green slopes. Following a bend to the left, the town of Seyðisfjörður comes into view, with its colourful houses nestling beneath the peaks, which even in summer are still sprinkled with pockets of snow.

On the day before the departure of the ferry, Seyðisfjörður is completely booked up and full of activity for a few hours after the arrival of the ship. But soon enough calm returns until the arrival of the next ferry, as most new arrivals head straight out, curious to see the rest of Iceland. In a way this is a shame, as it's worth spending a bit more time in Seyðisfjörður; the little town with the colourfully painted houses has a lot of charm. Seyðisfjörður too owes its exis-

dalur to the Lagarfljót lake, was an important postal and trading route (approx. 20km/12 miles). For longer tours, pick up a detailed hiking map from the tourist office.

Siglufjörður

G 2

Region: Northwest Iceland   **Population:** 1,500

Siglufjörður was discovered by the Norwegians – twice in fact! Around the year 900, the Vikings first came and settled here, and 1,000 years later they returned to transform this small village into the most important herring town in the world. A reminder of this boom is the award-winning herring museum.

It seems unlikely that anyone would have thought of settling on this unforgiving coast in the north of Iceland if it hadn't been for the huge shoals of herring at the beginning of the last century. The area is rough and inaccessible, offering practically no opportunities for agriculture. Even larger herds of sheep can't get much out of the steep, sparsely covered slopes. The wind is icy when blowing from the north, there is a lot of snow in the winter and transport links are tenuous. Thus, the next settlement, **Ólafsfjörður**, might only be 15 kilometres/9 miles away as the crow flies, but on the road, which has to make a sweeping detour inland, this turns into 60 kilometres/37 miles!

The herring boom   When herring fishing started, the town was pervaded by a pioneering spirit, and Siglufjörður grew within 40 years from a small fishing village to the fifth-largest town in the country, with 3,000 inhabitants. Herring was salted and pickled in barrels at 23 catching stations, and whatever was not suitable for salting was turned into fish oil and flour in five boiling houses. Thus, **Siglufjörður** became one of the most important ports in the country, generating in its heyday around 20% of Icelandic exports. It must have been rather like the times of the great gold rush. The herring speculators came and went, some becoming rich, others losing everything. A few thousand seasonal workers ensured the town stayed lively. Good and bad herring summers alternated, with usually more good than bad. As the years went on, catching methods became more effective and yields higher and higher. Then all of a sudden, in 1969, the herring disappeared. The stocks had been overfished, with dramatic consequences. Many factories had to close and many people left – the population fell by about half. Today, the economic situation of the town seems to have stabilized. The largest fish boiling plant in the country produces fish flour and oil from capelin and herring, complemented by two shrimp cooperatives. The heydays of herring fishing are remembered

► **Budget**

Stykkishólmur:
Farfuglaheimili Stykkishólmur
Höfðagata 1
Tel. 438 10 95, fax 438 14 17
50 beds, mostly in shared rooms.
Guests can use the house's own boat
for birdwatching tours.

Grundarfjörður:
Farfuglaheimili Grundarfjörður
Hlíðarvegur 15
Tel. 562 65 33, fax 438 64 33

This old house right in the town
centre has 21 beds, mostly in shared
rooms.

Arnastapi: Ferðaþjónustan Snófell
Tel. 435 67 83
Fax 435 67 95
Rooms and sleeping-bag accommodation in an excellent spot between
sea and volcano. The campsite also
has a wonderful location, but is rather
expensive considering the pretty basic
facilities.

extinct. In 2001, 167 sq km/65 sq miles around the mountain were
placed under protection as the Snæfellsjökull National Park. Among
the highlights of the national park are the many fine lava formations
and the spectacular coast, which may be explored on numerous hiking trails. Hellissandur has an information centre on the national
park (Klettsbud 7, tel. 436 68 60, snaefellsjokull@ust.is).

On the [54] from Borgarnes, just before the road leads across the   **Eldborg**
Haffjarðará salmon river and turns off west to the Snæfellsnes peninsula, it runs through the lava field of **Eldborgarhraun**. Amidst the
lava, the 112m/367-ft red »Fire Castle« (Eldborg) catches the eye, a
classic lava ring which formed 5,000 to 8,000 years ago. The crater is
best climbed from the southern side from the Snorrastaðir farm, and
it is also possible to go around the crater rim.

At the fork of the [54] to Ólafsvík and the [574] to the Snæfellsjökull   **Búðir**
is another lava flow worth seeing, the **Búðahraun**, which formed
through the activities of the Búðaklettur crater. 88m/289ft high, the
crater can be climbed via the historic Klettsgata path starting at the
little church. The numerous lava cracks don't just host an unusual
number of ferns – 130 different species of plant have been identified
here. Under the lava flow lies the **Búðahellir** cave, 400m/1,300ft long.
The historic trading post of Búðir, inhabited since the time of the
Settlement, is deserted today. The only remaining buildings are the
small, black wooden church dating from 1848 and the hotel, rebuilt
after a fire.

The small fishing village of Arnarstapi occupies an extremely scenic   **Arnarstapi**
position on a green plateau between Snæfellsjökull and the steep
coastline. To the east, the eye can see far across the sweeping bay of
Breiðavik with its pretty sandy beach, while inland the conical
432m/1,417-ft Stapafell mountain looms into view. The picturesque

harbour lies amidst a dramatic coast with imposing basalt cliffs, gnawed at by the waves for so long that now only stacks, arches and perforated rocks remain. This jagged coast extends west to the neighbouring village of Hellnar. In the summer, thousands of sea birds nest on the rocky ledges, easily observed from the harbour. Visible from afar, the main sight of Arnarstapi is the larger-than-life figure of Barður Snæfellsás made from lava rock.

Hellnar

A few kilometres further west a dead-end road leads to the neighbouring village of Hellnar, in a scenic seaside location. In the past, Hellnar was home to one of the largest fishing villages of the peninsula; today only a dozen people live in the tiny village, with its church in a picturesque cliff-top position. In recent times, Hellnar has turned into a **meeting place for mystics**, who use it as a base from which to search for the magic powers of the Snæfellsjökull.

Hikes between ocean and glacier

A 2.5km/1.5-mile waymarked trail leads from Arnarstapi along the coast to Hellnar. The reward at the end is the tiny **café in Fjöruhúsið**, awaiting its guests in a beautiful isolated position with a view of the cliffs. East of Arnarstapi, the [F 570] track branches off to the Snæfellsjökull and on to Ólafsvík. While the dirt road has steep gradients, in good conditions it is navigable by normal saloon car, while its spectacular views make it an outstanding hiking trail too. The highest point, the **Jökulháls Pass**, lies in the immediate vicinity of the glacier and is the starting point for two routes to the summit of the Snæfellsjökull.

The best church in town, yet nobody goes: Búðir was abandoned a long time ago

On the way west from Hellnar several dead-end roads branch off the [574] towards the sea. One of them leads to the most southerly point of the peninsula, the lighthouse of Malarrif. Nearby, look out for the two striking rock pinnacles of **Lóndrangar**, where many sea birds breed. **Hellissandur** and Rif on the northern coast were major settlements as far back as 1700. The maritime museum of Hellissandur exhibits the *Bliki*, the oldest rowing boat in Iceland, which was built in 1826. Two reconstructed old fishing huts are also on show (opening times: daily except Wed 9am – midday and 1 – 6pm).

The 412m/1,350-ft **transmitter mast**, jutting up into the skies outside Hellisandur, was erected in 1963 and is the tallest structure in Western Europe, even beating the mast at Donington in the UK.

From Hellnar to Hellisandur

The rich fishing grounds off Ólafsvík were behind the establishment of a trading post here in the 17th century, which was also used by Danish merchants. Today the fishing fleet in the harbour is still at the economic heart of village life. The **Pakkhús**, a listed warehouse on the harbour dating back to 1844, houses the tourist information and a maritime museum showing changing art exhibitions and fishing implements (opening times: in the summer daily 9am – 7pm). Another reason to stop at Ólafsvík is the **whale watching tours**, which run daily in the summer starting at 10am from the harbour. The waters around Ólafsvík are among the best in Iceland to see large whales. Alongside northern minke whales and orcas, there are regular sightings of humpbacks and blue whales. (Seatours, tel. 438 14 50).

Ólafsvík

Due to the good natural harbour, trade and fishing flourished early in Grundarfjörður. At the start of the 19th century, many French fishermen came to the village, but they only stayed 60 years and took everything that would fit on a boat back to France with them. The links with France have not been cut completely though: for the past few years Grundarfjörður has had a twinning arrangement with Paimpol in Britanny. The symbol of this small and fairly inconspicuous village is the 436m/1,430-ft local mountain of **Kirkjufell** on a peninsula in the fjord. Climbing the distinctive mountain is fairly difficult, but taking a stroll around its base is rewarding and much easier. Climbing **Klakkur** (380m/1,247ft) to the northeast is well worthwhile for the beautiful views from the summit onto the Grundarfjörður. Allow around three hours to get to the top and back, with the path starting at the Suður Bár farm on the [576].

Grundarfjörður

Stykkishólmur

The Þórsnes Peninsula juts far out into the Breiðafjörður's world of little islands and skerries. Stykkishólmur, at its furthest point, is the fishing and trading centre of the region. Protected by the island of **Súgandisey**, the harbour was a busy trading post as early as the 16th century, and has always been the nerve centre of the town.

Norska Húsið A good view over Stykkishólmur with its harbour and colourful houses can be had from the plateau on top of Súgandisey Island, easily accessible via a causeway. Thanks to a few old, lovingly restored houses, the appearance of the town is fairly harmonious by Icelandic standards. The oldest two-storey building in Iceland, the Norska Húsið (Norwegian House; Hafnargata 5), has been restored and is now used as a museum. It was built in 1832 by **Árni Thorlacius**, who in 1845 began making regular weather observations which were continued after his death. This made him the founder of the first weather station in Iceland. The Norwegian House hosts changing art exhibitions, the upper floor furnished as it would have been in Thorlacius' time, and the Galleri Lundi sells crafts. Opening times: June – Aug daily 11am – 5pm.

Church Stykkishólmur's modern church was consecrated in 1990. The striking white concrete building was designed by the architect **Jón Haraldsson** and is often used for concerts, taking advantage of its excellent acoustics.

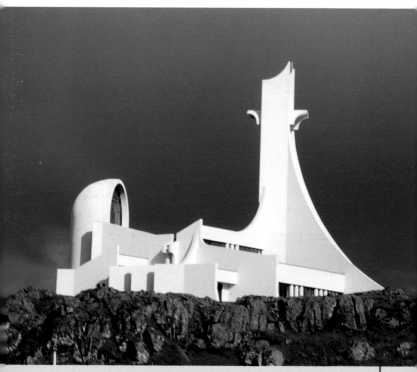

Striking Stykkishólmur: a white church against a blue background

Lying south of Stykkishólmur, the mountain of **Helgafell** has been a holy site since Saga times as the supposed burial place of the heroine of the Laxdalssaga, Guðrún Ósvifursdóttir. According to an old legend, anybody who climbs the mountain – only 70m/230ft high – for the first time is granted three wishes. However, this requires climbing the mountain without looking back or to either side, and also without talking. Once on the top of the hill, the wishes have to be spoken facing east. If the wishes are good ones and nobody over-hears them, they should be fulfilled. Those who don't believe in this tradition can at least enjoy the view. At the foot of the Helgafell lies the farm of the same name, inhabited at the time of the Settlement by the settler Þórólfur, as well as a small church.

Helgafell

Flatey, the largest of the roughly 3,000 islands in the Breiðafjörður, used to be a centre for the arts, mainly because of its **Augustine monastery**. Today, it is only inhabited in the summer. The quiet islet is well worth a visit for its pretty wooden houses and diverse bird life.

Flatey

★ Sprengisandur

Region: Highlands

Depending on the points of departure and arrival, the Sprengisan-dur [F 26] is between 200 and 250km/125 and 155 miles long, which makes it the longest of the Icelandic highland tracks. While used since the settlement of the island as a link between the north and the south of the country, it was always considered a difficult route due to its length and unpredictable weather.

In 1933, a car first passed the Sprengisandur Route, although it took an entire week to do so. Now the route can be done in a day, but it still counts among the most challenging highlands tracks and, due to unbridged rivers, should only be attempted in an off-road vehicle. In some places orientation can be a bit tricky, but the biggest problem is the rivers with their constantly changing fords, which may swell considerably after rains or hot periods.

Impressively desolate

The core of the Sprengisandur is the eponymous **highland desert be-tween Hofsjökull and Vatnajökull**, with an average altitude of 750m/2,460ft and a length of some 70km/43 miles. Due to its barrenness and bleak landscapes, this desolate grey and rocky highland plateau is an impressive experience, while in bad weather its relentless drea-riness can be downright depressing. There are different access roads from the north to the Sprengisandur proper, the most difficult being via the [F 910], coming from the ▶Askja and joining the Sprengisandur at the **Tungnafellsjökull**. There are additional northern access roads from the Skagafjörður via the [F 752], which branches off the ring road at Varmahlíð, or from Eyjafjörður at ▶Akureyri via Hrafnagil and the [F 821]. The simplest way to get to the Sprengisandur from the north starts at the Goðafoss on the ring road.

The route   Initially the [844], still well navigable here, follows the Bárðardalur, before the highlands begin at the Mýri farm and the road becomes the [F 26] dirt road. A short and worthwhile detour leads to the **Aldeyarfoss**, surrounded by pretty basalt columns. Before reaching the Sprengisandur proper, there is the opportunity for another detour west to the Laugafell. Warm water bubbles to the surface here, transforming the otherwise barren highland desert into a small green oasis, and a hot pot looks inviting. On the way back to the main route [F 26], and on the Sprengisandur that follows, time and again there are spectacular views of the nearby glaciers of ▶Vatnajökull, Hofsjökull and Tungnafellsjökull. **Nýidalur**, which lies near the geographical centre of Iceland, marks roughly the halfway point of the highland crossing. The valley, at an altitude of around 800m/just over 2,600 feet, surprises with its astonishingly varied vegetation. This is a good place to take a longer stop for hikes to hot springs or the glacier tongues of the Tungnafellsjökull. The dirt road, in pretty bad condition, leads on south between the big glaciers, past the large lakes of Kvíslavatn, Þórisvatn and Hrauneyalón to the **Hrauneyjar highland center** (▶ p. 318). Visitors with a bit more time on their hands should take advantage of the detour from here via the [F 208] to ▶Landmannalaugar.

 VISITING SPRENGISANDUR

INFORMATION
In Hrauneyjar
Tel. 487 77 82
Fax 487 77 81
www.hrauneyjar.is

TOURS

Visitors who don't have a suitable four-wheel drive can still cross the Sprengisandur from Mývatn via Goðafoss, Nýidalur to Hrauneyjar and on to Landmannalaugar on Mon, Wed and Fri on the high-clearance buses run by Austurleið (tel. 545 17 17, www.austurleid.is; departure 8.30am, arrival 6pm). For the return leg from Landmannalaugar to Mývatn, the buses run Tues, Thurs and Sun.

WHERE TO STAY

Nýidalur and Laugafell have simple sleeping-bag accommodation in the huts of the Icelandic Touring Association.
There is also the option of camping near the huts. Otherwise, all the places on the access roads have accommodation.

The beauty of solitude: the Sprengisandur leads right across the Icelandic highlands

★★ Vatnajökull · Skaftafell

Region: Southeast Iceland

Meet the giant amongst the glaciers of Europe. With a surface area of 8,300 sq km/3,200 sq miles it is 70 times bigger than the largest glacier in the Alps, the Aletsch Glacier, twice the size of the Malaspina Glacier in Alaska, and its ice is 1,000m/3,280-ft thick in places.

The Vatnajökull dominates and shapes the southeast of Iceland, in particular the stretch of coast between the Skeiðarársandur and the small town of ▶ Höfn, an area which is the subject of this chapter. The glacier's imposing ice caps, which even cover the **Hvannadals-hnúkur**, at 2,119m/6,952ft the highest mountain in Iceland, shape the landscape, and its lower reaches seem to creep scarily close to the settlements and ring road. The largest glacier in Europe dominates the region and its people through natural disasters too: glacier runs and volcanic eruptions underneath the ice cover have, in the past, regularly destroyed farms and arable land, roads and bridges.

Ice desert: by volume, the Vatnajökull is the largest glacier in Europe

The Skeiðarársandur Alluvial Plain

A land shaped by natural forces

Leaving the town of ▶ Kirkjubæjarklaustur (southwest of the Vatnajökull) on the ring road going northeast, after some 30km/19 miles drivers will pass the farmstead of **Núpsstaður** (▶p. 199), with its small 17th-century grass sod church, a listed monument. Núpsstaður is the last settlement before reaching the Skeiðarársandur alluvial plain, the piece of land which is most subjected to the elemental powers of the Vatnajökull: rivers of meltwater cross the sandur (glacial outwash plain) like countless veins, and glacier runs regularly flood the area. Today, the bridges across the occasionally raging rivers Núpsvötn, Gýgjukvísl and Skeiðará withstand the flooding, whereas in the past they were repeatedly destroyed and reconstructed again. Small wonder given the mighty masses of water of the big **glacier runs**: in 1996, run-off quantities of up to 50,000 cubic metres/13.2 million US gal per second were measured on their way to the sea. To put this into perspective, the mightiest waterfall in Europe, the Rheinfall near Schaffhausen in Switzerland, reaches maximum quantities of 1,100 cubic metres/290,000 US gal per second.

✳ ✳ Skaftafell National Park

At the northeastern edge of the Skeiðarársandur, a cul-de-sac branches off from the ring road to the campsite of the Skaftafell national park. The **visitor centre** at the campsite should be the first point of contact, both for visitors wanting to explore the national park on their own or those looking to join a guided hiking tour – this is the place to get hiking maps, tips and recommendations for hikes, and the meeting point for the two daily guided walks.

Looking at the full extent of the Skaftafell National Park (established in 1967 and expanded twice since, now covering a surface area of 4,800 sq km/1,850 sq miles), it immediately becomes apparent that only a fraction of the protected area, most of it covered by ice, can be explored on foot. This is the part between the glacier tongues of **Skeiðarárjökull and Skaftafellsjökull**, which offers good access to ice-free hiking trails. Solitude is a rare commodity here though, as the Skaftafell National Park is one of the most popular sights in Iceland. The rule here is the same as everywhere: the longer and more strenuous the hike, the smaller the crowds.

A fraction of the whole

 ## VISITING VATNAJÖKULL · SKAFTAFELL

INFORMATION

Skaftafell National Park Visitor Centre
Fagurholsmyri, 2km/1.2 miles north of the ring road
Tel. 478 16 27, fax 478 1627
The information centre houses an exhibition on the glacier, sells hiking maps and souvenirs, and has a small supermarket and café. There is a large campsite here and daily bus connections from the visitor centre into the highlands and to Reykjavík.

GLACIER TOURS

Jeep, ski and snowmobile tours from the Jöklasel lodge (▶p. 287).

WHERE TO STAY

▶ **Mid-range**
Hotel Skaftafell
Fagurholsmyri
Tel. 478 19 45, fax 478 18 46
Unpretentious hotel standing by itself on the ring road, in the immediate vicinity of the national park. Friendly service, in good weather views of the glacier. Sleeping-bag accommodation also available.

▶ **Budget**
Bölti
To the west, above the campsite
Tel. 478 16 26, fax 478 24 26
Guesthouse with cabins in beautiful location in national park territory. Doubles, sleeping-bag accommodation, cooking facilities.

Svinafell
Oræfi, tel. 478 17 65
Travellers finding the campsite at the visitor centre too full might prefer a quiet little meadow at Svinafell Farm a few kilometres further east. Another plus is the heated swimming pool right next door.

Skaftafell Map

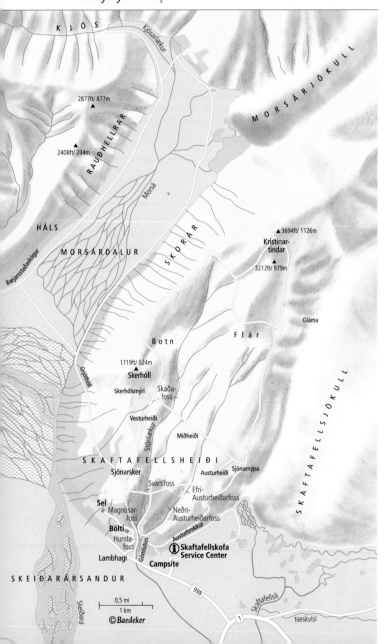

KJÓS

Kjósarlækur

MORSÁRJÖKULL

▲ 2877ft/ 877m

RAUÐHELLRAR

▲ 2408ft/ 734m

Morsá

HÁLS

Bæjarstaðaskógur

MORSÁRDALUR

SKORAR

▲3694ft/ 1126m
Kristinar-
tindar
▲3212ft/ 979m

Gláma

Botn   Flár

Gjáþófl

▲ 1719ft/ 524m
Skerhóll

Skerhólsmýri   Skaða-
foss

Vesturheiði

Miðheiði

SKAFTAFELLSJÖKULL

Stóralækur

S K A F T A F E L L S H E I Ð I

Sjónarsker   Austurheiði
                                    Sjónarnýpa
Svartifoss
            Efri-
            Austurheiðarfoss
Sel
    Magnúsar-   Neðri-
    foss   Austurheiðarfoss
Bölti   Austurbrekkur
Hunda-
foss   Gömlutún
Lambhagi   ⓘ Skaftafellskofa
            Campsite   Service Center

S K E I Ð A R Á R S A N D U R

Skeiðará

0,5 mi
1 km
©Baedeker

998

1

Skaftafellsá

Neskvísl

As there are no roads in the national park – apart from the access **Hikes** road to the farms of Bölti and Hæðir – there is no other choice but to explore the charming landscape on foot. Apart from the one leading directly to the glacier tongue of the Skaftafellsjökull, all way-marked trails lead uphill at first from the campsite, and through a small, **idyllic birch forest**. Following the path northwest, it doesn't take long (about 45 mins from the campsite) to reach the Svartifoss, whose water plunges down over black basalt columns, which look like organ pipes. The trail running northeast leads to the viewpoints of **Sjónarnýpa** (45 mins from the campsite) and **Gláma** (2 hrs) above the glacier tongue of the Skafta-fellsjökull, with views of the Öræfajökull volcano and the Hvan-nadalshnúkur on its northwestern rim. Continuing on this path, some 3.5 hours from the campsite hikers reach the **main summit of the Kristínartindar** (1,126m/3,694 ft). Although hard work, the ascent is manageable even for people with no great head for heights or experience in the high mountains. The tour, including an ascent of Kristí-nartindar and returning via the Skerhóll, the viewpoint of **Sjónarsker** and the Svartifoss (all in all 7 hrs walking time), is argu-ably the most beautiful in the na-tional park. Be sure to get an early start, otherwise the Svartifoss is only reached in late afternoon when the light is fading. The wonderfully photogenic waterfall is then difficult to capture in all its glory. Another very long but recommended hike leads to the source of the Skeiðará glacier river.

> **! Baedeker TIP**
>
> **An icy experience**
> Visitors not wanting to limit themselves to the ice-free zone of Skaftafell National Park should consider taking part in a glacier tour, in the most extreme case leading on to the summit of the Hvannadalshnúkur (information at the visitor centre and/or from: Icelandic Mountain Guides, tel. 587 99 99). However, there is an easier way: where the dead-end road branches off the [1] towards the national park, look for a small airfield where sightseeing flights take off across the endless expanse of ice – an unforgettable experience! For more information contact Jórvík Aviation, email: info@ats.is

Through the Öræfi to the Jökulsárlon

The year is 1362: the Hnappafellsjökull erupts, destroying at least 24 **»Wasteland«** farmsteads and the surrounding agricultural land between the **Skeiðará** river to the west and the **Breiðamerkursandur** to the east. The local farmers lose their livelihoods. Subsequently, new farm-steads are established, but these are destroyed again by a second eruption in 1727. From that time on, the benighted land is called Öræfi – meaning something like a barren area, wasteland, desert – while the name of the destructive glacier volcano is changed from Hnappafellsjökull to **Öræfajökull**, »wasteland glacier«. Today, the area southeast of Skaftafell serves as a nesting ground for numerous species of bird, among them skuas, a type of predatory Arctic gull.

Ingólfshöfði

Offshore from the sandar plains of the mainland, the island peninsula of Ingólfshöfði offers ideal breeding conditions for numerous species of bird. Being hardly separated from the mainland, Ingólfshöfði is more of a headland than an island proper and has only one building, a lighthouse. **Ingólfur Arnarson**, who began the permanent settlement of Iceland in the 9th century (►History p. 40), supposedly spent his first winter on the island that bears his name. A monument commemorates his stay here. Anyone wanting to take a trip to Ingólfshöfði should contact the farmer of the Fagurhólsmýri estate where the [988] turns off the ring road. Sigurður Bjarnason uses a tractor and hay wagon to lead visitors through the mud flats onto the island (tel. 899 64 88).

✳
Jökulsárlón

The ring road heads northeast from here across the gravel plain of **Breiðamerkursandur**. Emerging unexpectedly to the left are the icebergs of the Jökulsárlón, looming majestically out of the water. Even though there are two more iceberg lakes in the immediate vicinity, Breiðárlón and Stemmulón, it is only the Jökulsárlón that attracts tourists. This is probably due to its position – right on the ring road between the glacier tongue of the **Breiðamerkurjökull** and the sea – and the convenient access to the lake: simply pull in at the parking area near the water's edge and enjoy the breathtaking views of the bizarrely shaped blocks of ice on the water with the glacier in the background. The bewitching beauty of the **glacier lagoon** works its magic

Ice, water, fog …

whether on a clear day or in fog. Visitors wanting to get a close-up of the ice blocks can take part in a boat trip on the lake (information: tel. 478 21 22, email: info@jokulsarlon.is).

However, as well as the icebergs, **seals** are also often visible here, making the Jökulsárlón in high season anything but a quiet place.

30km/19 miles northeast of the Jökulsárlón, the [F 985] track turns off the ring road to lead uphill to the **Jöklasel** lodge at the edge of the Vatnajökull. This route requires an off-road vehicle. In 1991 the mountain lodge with facilities and overnight accommodation was built at an altitude of 840m/2,750ft right on the edge of the glacier. It is a base for **jeep, ski and snowmobile tours** onto the endless ice, which can be booked on-site or by contacting Glacier Jeeps (tel. 478 10 00, www.glacierjeeps.is).

Clients can be picked up on request at the junction of the [F 985] with the ring road and taken to the lodge. Otherwise it is possible to reach the lodge using the no. 15 and 17 buses of the Austurleið bus company from Skaftafell, Jökulsárlón, Smyrlabjörg or Höfn (www.austurleid.is; tel. 545 17 17).

> **? DID YOU KNOW …?**
>
> ■ …that Lee Tamahori was clearly also taken with the Jökulsárlon's natural beauty? The director shot a sequence of his film *James Bond 007 – Die Another Day* (2002) with Pierce Brosnan and Halle Berry on the frozen glacier lake.

… one element, three manifestations at the Jökulsárlon glacier lake ▸

Vestmannaeyjar

E 7

Region: South Iceland   **Population:** 4,400

Two events brought the Westman Islandsworldwide fame: the volcanic eruption of 1973, which nearly rendered the main island uninhabitable, and the 1998 arrival of the killer whale »Keiko«, protagonist of the _Free Willy_ film. Otherwise, life on the archipelago is rather quiet, apart from the screeching of millions of sea birds nesting on the rocks off the southern coast of Iceland each summer.

The Westman Islands consist of 30 rocky crags, skerries and islands, scattered across 1,000 sq km/386 sq miles off the southern coast of Iceland. Only the largest island, **Heimaey**, is inhabited. To be precise, the rocks plunging dramatically into the sea are not exactly uninhabited either, as in the summer **millions of seabirds** nest there, and Heimaey is also home to far more birds than people. From a geological point of view, the islands are all recent, as there has been underwater volcanic activity off the southern coast of Iceland for hundreds of thousands of years, while the first islets only started surfacing some 10,000 years ago. Most of them were only formed around 5,000 years ago, following eruptions of the volcanic fissure which runs 30km/19 miles from southwest to northeast along the ocean floor.

Following an underground volcanic eruption that started in 1963 at a depth of 130m/425ft and continued until 1967, a new island soon emerged southwest of Heimaey. This new island was named after the Nordic **fire giant Surtur**, which according to the Edda comes from the south to set fire to the world. The islet grew continuously and by the end of the eruptions had reached a size of 2.8 sq km/just over one square mile. However, as fast as it had emerged from the sea, so the sea reclaimed it piece by piece, so that today **Surtsey** is only about half its original size. The only people to be allowed onto the southernmost island of the archipelago are the scientists who have set up a research station here. Surtsey offers biologists the unique opportunity to research the establishment of plants on an entirely barren rock in the middle of the ocean.

Evacuating an entire island   At 2am on 23 January 1973, without any warning, a roughly 2km/1.2-mile long fissure opened at the **Helgafell**, sending enormous red fountains of lava into the night sky. Shortly afterwards a stream of incandescent lava began rolling inexorably towards the capital of the island. Luckily all the fishing boats had stayed in the harbour that night due to a storm, so evacuation could start immediately. Within a few hours, everybody had left the island. Over the following days, the whole of Heimaey was engulfed in black ash as the lava wall, up to 160m/525ft high, buried one house after another and threatened to make the entrance to the harbour impassable. As the **loss of the harbour** would have taken away the island's livelihood, there were frantic attempts to come up with plans to safeguard it. By using massive pumps, the hot lava flow was cooled down with cold seawater to the extent that it ground to a halt and the harbour was saved. When the eruptions came to an end in July, the island had grown by 2.2 sq km/over 0.8 sq miles, but some 400 houses, a third of the town, lay buried under the lava. Despite this, around 2,000 of the 5,300 evacuees returned to Heimaey that summer.

January 1973: a fountain of fire and lava threatens Heimaey

▶ VISITING VESTMANNAEYJAR

INFORMATION
At the harbour, Básaskersbryggja
Tel. 481 35 55, fax 481 29 91
www.vestmannaeyjar.is

GETTING THERE
The Herjólfur ferry – tel. 481 28 00,
www.herjolfur.is – runs daily between
Heimaey and Þorlákshöfn, taking 2 ¾
hrs. Íslandsflug (tel. 570 80 30,
www.islandsflug.is) run scheduled
flights between Reykjavík and Heimaey. Flugfélag Vestmannaeyja (tel.
481 32 55) fly to Selfoss, Bakki and
Reykjavík.

TOURS
Viking Tours offer sightseeing tours,
boat trips, bird and whale watching,
as well as deep-sea fishing. Suðurgerði
4, Vestmannaeyjar, tel. 488 48 84,
www.boattours.is.

EVENTS
On the first weekend of July, there is a
feast in memory of the end of the
volcanic eruptions. The biggest festival takes place in early August: the
Þjóðhátíð in the Herjólfsdalur com-
memorating the introduction of the
1874 constitution.

WHERE TO EAT
▶ Inexpensive to Moderate
Lanterna
Bárustigur 11

Tel. 481 33 93
Cosy restaurant with a maritime feel,
popular with the locals. Fish and meat
dishes served, including puffin (in
season).

Café Maria
Skólavegur 5
Tel. 481 31 52
Restaurant, café and pub. The menu
ranges from sandwiches via pizzas all
the way to fish and meat dishes,
including puffin.

WHERE TO STAY
▶ Mid-range
Hótel Eyjar
Bárustígur 2
Tel. 481 36 36
www.hoteleyjar.eyjar.is
Modern, comfortable and bright
apartment hotel.

▶ Budget
Gistiheimilið Árný
Illugagata 7
Tel. 481 20 82
Fax 481 20 82
Relatively large guesthouse with 30
beds, plus sleeping-bag accommoda-
tion. Modern and pleasant furnish-
ings, kitchen facilities, and generally a
welcoming atmosphere.

What to see on Heimaey

Kirkjubæjar-hraun On the largest (13.4 sq km/just over 5 sq miles) and only inhabited Westman island, traces of the 1973 eruption are everywhere still. The huge dark lava wall of the Kirkjubæjarhraun looms directly behind the colourful corrugated-iron houses. A view from above, the best being from the 221m/725-ft summit of the Eldfell, gives an idea of the extent of the 1973 eruption, which covered a sixth of the island with fresh lava. Right in the centre of the town, the **Landakirkja**, dating from 1778 and one of the three oldest stone churches in Iceland, catches the eye. Because of its compact size, Heimaey can be explored on foot in a day. For large stretches a path runs along the coast, giving excellent puffin watching opportunities. The southern cape of **Stórhöfði**, the most southerly inhabited point of Iceland, is occupied by a weather station and a lighthouse.

The documentary describes the eruption of 1973. Further films show the clean-up operation and the fresh start, as well as the **emergence of Surtsey Island**. Vestmannabraut/Heiðarvegur, tel. 481 10 45. Summer showings daily at 11am, 3.30 and 9pm.

Volcanic film show ⊙

The museum (Heiðarvegur 12) shows native fish, stuffed birds and a collection of rocks and minerals. Opening times: May to mid-Sept daily 11am – 5pm, otherwise Sat/Sun 3 – 5pm.

Natural history museum/ Aquarium

The museum centre (Byggðasafn, Ráðhúströð) consists of the heritage museum, showing many interesting exhibits on life on the Westman Islands, and the art gallery, which display works by Icelandic artists. The **Jóhannes Kjarval Collection** is particularly extensive. Opening times: May–mid-Sept daily 11am–5pm, otherwise Sat, Sun 3 – 5pm.

Regional museum ⊙

The »Sighvatur Bjarnason« in Heimaey harbour

Leap to freedom: but Hollywood is not reality. Keiko spent his life in captivity in order to entertain people

NO HAPPY ENDING FOR THE FILM STAR

The orca whale Keiko, protagonist of the film *Free Willy*, arrived on Heimaey in 1998 amidst the blaze of media attention reserved for a film star. At Klettsviks Bay harbour everything was prepared for him. Would he remember that as a youngster he had already swum in Icelandic waters?

Following his arrival, Keiko was cosseted and pampered, fed delicacies, and his every breath documented. The goal of a whole team of researchers was to get him used to **a life of freedom** – a venture that had never been attempted before. Keiko was not exactly young anymore; when he arrived in Iceland, he had spent 20 years in tiny concrete basins and performed all kinds of tricks for his audiences.

But Keiko found it hard to leave his full-board bay and to look after himself on the open seas. Endless training sessions and countless »Ocean Walks« finally convinced him of the attractions of a free life.

Without a chance

Eventually he swam to Norway, but didn't manage to live there without humans either; he died – far too early really – of a lung infection in December 2003. This marked the tragic failure of an experiment that had cost the **Free Willy foundation** many millions of dollars. This film star found no happy ending; for him a life of freedom was not to be.

To celebrate the thousandth anniversary of the Christianization of Iceland, in the summer of 2000 a stave church was given as a present by the Norwegian government. The simple building is the only stave church in Iceland and has been reconstructed following the example of the old church of Haltdalen in Norway. Visitors might be interested to see the remains of the 16th-century English fortification **Skansinn**, which represents the oldest part of town, and the oldest house in Heimaey, Landlyst. Opening times: daily 11am – 5pm.

Stave church

🕐

✷ Vík í Mýrdal

G 7

Region: South Iceland   **Population:** 300

Petrified trolls in the water, a church in a picturesque location on a hill in front of volcanic rocks covered with greenery, some colourful corrugated-iron houses and a great beach set against the backdrop of the Mýrdalsjökull – Vík í Mýrdal is a village with magnificent scenery.

The southernmost village in Iceland, Vík í Mýrdal is the only settlement on the coast without a harbour. This makes it one of the very few places in Iceland that doesn't rely on fishing for its livelihood; here, it is down to trade, services and tourism to fill the coffers. The best example is the Factory Shop on the main road where all buses pull over for a break. Inside, travellers will find everything that could broadly be termed a souvenir, plus of course a lot of wool, whether balls of the stuff or ready-knitted Icelandic jumpers. Another trump card for Vík is its location, with the striking **Reynisfjall** mountain in the immediate vicinity and its bizarrely eroded volcanic hills covered by lush green carpets. The 700 sq km/270 sq-mile Mýrdalsjökull with its glacier tongues and sandar is not far away either. Whilst the glacier is spectacular to look at, below the ice slumbers the **Katla**, a mighty caldera with a diameter of 10km/6 miles. In reality, the Katla has been quiet for far too long already, as the volcano becomes active every 40 to 80 years – and the last time was in 1918! Its eruptions are feared, as they melt massive amounts of glacier ice, causing vast quantities of water to pour across the entire coast south of the glacier.

What to see in Vík í Mýrdal

From the ring road, it is only a short distance by foot to the beach – whose fine black sand stretches for miles – with its raging surf and views of the dramatic coastline. In the summer, on the beach and in the meadows behind, one of the largest Icelandic colonies of breeding Arctic terns create an incredible racket and spectacle. According

✷
Beaches and trolls

to *Islands Magazine*, the beach at Vík ranks among the ten most beautiful in the world. Visible from the beach are the landmarks of the town, the **Reynisdrangar**. Protruding up to 66m/216ft from the water, the rock pinnacles at the foot of the Reynisfjall are unmistakable, even from afar. Supposedly these too are petrified trolls that tried to pull a three-masted ship onto land, but again didn't quite get the job done in time and were caught off guard by the sun. The Skessudrangur rock pinnacle is said to be the petrified troll woman, Langhamar, the pinnacle furthest away from the coast is the three-master, while the one nearest to the coast is Landdrangur, the giant accompanying the female troll.

The church of Vík   The old church of Vík used to stand in Höfðabrekka, east of the town centre. Having been destroyed in 1924 by a storm it was not rebuilt at the same site, even though there had been a church there since the 12th century. The modern 1934 church lies on a hill above the houses, giving good views over the town.

Trolls rock: the rocks of Reynisdrangar are said to be petrified mythical creatures

▶ VISITING VÍK Í MÝRDAL

INFORMATION
In the Museum Bryðebuð
Víkurbraut 28
Tel. 487 13 95, info@vik.is

WHERE TO EAT
► Inexpensive
Halldórskaffi
Bryðebúð
Víkurbraut 28
Tel. 487 13 95
Inside the museum there is a cosy
café, while outside a few tables stand
in the sunshine. The menu offers
snacks such as pizza, soup of the day,
burgers, coffee and cake.

WHERE TO STAY
► Mid-range to Luxury
Hótel Edda
Tel. 444 48 40
www.hoteledda.is
All 21 rooms en suite and with TV, in
a pretty hillside location. Those who
prefer something a bit different can
rent six small double cabins right on
the rock wall; the screeching of the
breeding birds comes free of charge.
Restaurant and golf course nearby.

► Mid-range
Hotel Lundi
Víkurbraut 26
Tel. 487 12 12, fax 487 14 04
This new hotel next to the museum
has ten comfortable doubles. The old
Hotel Lundi is now a guesthouse with
simple and good-value sleeping-bag
accommodation.

Hotel Dyrhólaey
Brekkur (9km/5.5 miles west of Vík)
Tel. 487 13 33, fax 487 15 07
dyrholaey@islandia.is
New guesthouse with 37 rooms, all en
suite. Nice location with views across
the bay; open all year round.

► Budget
Farfuglaheimili Vík í Mýrdal
Norður-Vík
Tel. 487 11 06, fax 487 13 03
300m/some 330 yds from the main
road, just above the town, with 36
beds.

Guesthouse Katrínar
Kirkjuvegur 4, tel. 487 11 86
Small older town house with good-
value sleeping-bag accommodation.

The Bryðebuð Museum (Víkurbraut 28) is housed in Vík's first trad-   **Bryðebuð**
ing house. Although it was built in 1831 on the Westman Islands,
Danish merchant Bryðe had it brought from the islands to Vík in
1895. The museum shows old photographs from the region and exhibitions on natural life. It also has information on the around 100
stranded ships that were shipwrecked off the coast over the course of
the last century. Opening times: daily 10am – 5pm.   ⊕

Around Vík í Mýrdal

A few kilometres west on the ring road lies the turn to Garðar. The   **Garðar**
tarmacked road goes around the **Reynisfjall** mountain and finally

ends at a seafront car park. The black sand and pebble beach here is definitely worth seeing: to the right the striking rock of Cape Dyrhólaey, to the left the Reynisfjall with numerous large caves and a frontage of vertical basalt pillars.

On its sea-facing side, the Reynisfjall is so steep and smooth that even the sea birds, content with tiny ledges, find very few places for nesting. From the beach, the Reynisdrangar can be seen again; from this perspective it looks like one of the trolls is sunk up to his empty eye sockets beneath the water, and that the other can only manage to poke its forefinger out of the waves.

Dyrhólaey

After circumnavigating the Dyrhólaós lagoon in a wide sweep on the ring road, the [218] turns off towards the most southerly point of Iceland, Cape Dyrhólaey. The 120m/394-ft Dyrhólaey rock owes its name (»Island with the Hill Door«) to a large archway on the southern point, tall enough for small boats to pass through. From the lighthouse on the cape the view reaches across the sea arch to the Reynisfjall and the Reynisdrangar. On the other side, the black **sandar of the Mýrdalsjökull** stretch to the horizon. Sea birds nest on the steep cliffs here, and it is particularly easy to see the dozens of puffins sitting on the ledges right underneath the cliff edge.

! **Baedeker TIP**

Tenting at the end of the world
One of the most beautiful campgrounds on Iceland is located at the end of the road to Þakgil. It may only be a grassy area on a valley floor but the green volcanic mountains around it are simply fantastic. A natural cave with candle lighting and a stove for heat serves as a commons room. A small waterfall nearby and, via steep meadows, the local mountain or Mýrdalsjökull are good hiking destinations. Tel. 8934889, www.thakgil.is

5km/3 miles east of Vík, the [214] turns off towards **Þakgil** and soon becomes a track, which is however passable by normal saloon car. The route leads through a **picture-book volcanic landscape** with bizarrely eroded volcanic rocks, often with a green cover, that could all be petrified trolls. The 14km/8.7-mile detour to the end of the road leads to a fairytale landscape at the foot of the Mýrdalsjökull.

Hjörleifshöfði

In its isolated position, the striking 221m/725-ft island of tuff rock on the southwesterly part of the **Mýrdalssandur** can be seen from the ring road. It was formed in an interglacial period during an underwater eruption. Up to the 14th century, it was still surrounded by the sea, but afterwards cut off by alluvial sands from the glacier runs of the Katla.

The rocky outcrop is named after Hjörleifur, the stepbrother of Ingólfur Arnarson, murdered by his slaves a year after arriving in Iceland. A track runs from the main road to the mountain, from where a hiking trail takes about an hour to reach the summit. It is also possible to circumnavigate the mountain on foot.

Vopnafjörður

K 3

Region: East Iceland   **Population:** 600

When the Danish king Haraldur Guttormsson was considering conquering Iceland, he sent north on a reconnaissance mission a sorcerer with the extraordinary gift of being able to turn himself into a whale. When the sorcerer wanted to land at Vopnafjörður, he was prevented from doing so by a dragon, thus thwarting the king of the Danes' plans for conquest. This is why Vopnafjörður's coat-of-arms bears a dragon.

Situated on the fjord of the same name, Vopnafjörður lies on the eastern bank of the Kolbeinstangi headland and served as an early trading post. A proper settlement was only established here in the late 19th century. The first settler was **Eyvindur Vopni**, who claimed the land here and built the Krossavík farm. To both sides of the rather sprawling town, with its conspicuously colourful, well-cared for houses, lie fine wide sandy beaches. Kaupvangur, the house where trading goods were once stored, has since its renovation been used as a café, for tourist information and exhibitions.

What to see around Vopnafjörður

The grass sod farm in the Hofsárdalur, southwest of Vopnafjörður, counts among the most beautiful and imposing in Iceland. For 500 years, up to 1966, the farmstead was inhabited by the same wealthy family. As early as 1943, **Methúsalem Methúsalemsson** bequeathed the old buildings, some of which date back to the year 1770, to the state, on the condition that the six-gabled farmstead with 27 rooms be kept as a museum for posterity. With his extensive collection of old artefacts, Methúsalemsson laid the foundation for today's museum. Opening times: mid-June – mid-Aug daily 10am – 6pm.

★
Bustarfell

⏱

 VISITING VOPNAFJÖRÐUR

INFORMATION
In the Kaupvangur
Tel. 473 13 31

WHERE TO STAY
► **Mid-range**
Syðri Vík
Tel./fax 473 11 99

On a farm 8km/5 miles south of Vopnafjörður, two red, stand-alone holiday cottages with veranda are available for rent, one sleeping 5 people, the other 9. Fine views across the wide valley with green meadows and the fjord.

Six gables and a set of antlers: the Bustafell farmstead in Hofsárdalur

Hellisheiði From Vopnafjörður, the [917] leads initially along the eastern banks of the fjord, then leaves it to wind in hairpin bends up onto the barren high plain of **Hellisheiði**, lying at an altitude of 700m/2,300ft. While the gravel track is quite drivable, it does have a gradient of up to 14% and no safety features. At the beginning it offers good views of the Vopnafjörður, and later onto the bay of Héraðsflói with the extensive river delta of the Jökulsá and the Lagarfljót, its large sedimentary tract visible far into the sea.

★ ★ Western Fjords

A-D 1-3

Region: Western Fjords

Dozens of mighty fjords, framed by dark basalt mountains and gouged deeply by the glaciers of the last Ice Age, make the Westfjords a natural spectacle without equal. Here the solitude is almost boundless, as over the centuries the barren land and harsh climate have driven many to despair. On this westerly corner of Europe lies the Látrabjarg, the largest bird rock in the North Atlantic.

Reaching out to sea like a many-fingered hand, the peninsula of the Western Fjords is only connected to the rest of Iceland by a narrow strip of land 10km/6 miles wide. Over 70 fjords, some large and wide, others narrow and long, pushing inland in a straight line or through tributaries, then again in a straight line, add up to a length

▶ VISITING WESTERN FJORDS

INFORMATION

Ísafjörður
Aðalstræti 7
Tel. 456 51 21, fax 456 51 22
info@vestfirdir.is

Hólmavík
In the community centre
Tel. 451 31 11, fax 451 34 03
info@holmavik.is

TOURS

The most comfortable way to experience the spectacular wilderness of
Hornstrandir is on one of the organized tours from Ísafjörður. In the
summer, a tour is available nearly
every day, ranging from a short trip to
Vigu Island to hikes lasting several
days (for more information contact
the Ísafjörður tourist office or check
www.vesturferdir.is).

WHERE TO EAT

▶ Moderate
Hólmavík: Café Riis
Hafnarbraut 39
Tel. 451 35 67

Built in 1897 by the Danish merchant
Richard Riis as a trading post, the
green corrugated-iron house is the

oldest in town. During the recent
renovation a lot of care was taken to
keep the original look. The use of
wood contributes to the cosy feel;
look out for the magic symbols
decorating all the beams – and the
good-value dish of the day.

▶ Inexpensive
Ísafjörður: Gamla Bakaríið
Aðalstræti 24
Tel. 456 32 26
Small café with just a few tables inside
and outside. Everything is homemade
here, including the large selection of
(cream) cakes and cookies.

Ísafjörður: Thai Koon
Hafnarstræti 9-13
Tel. 456 01 23
The small Thai restaurant, a welcome
respite from lamb and fish, closes at
9pm, the same time as the supermarket.

WHERE TO STAY

Baedeker recommendation

▶ Budget to mid-range
Reykjanes: Ferðaþjónustan Reykjanesi
Tel. 456 48 44
It takes some courage to want to convert a
former school building, 17km/10 miles
from the main road on a deserted peninsula, into a hotel that supports its owner.
The thermal spring bubbling out of the
ground in Reykjanes that warms not just the
hotel's hot pot, but also the seawater on the
shore, could be the trump card that makes
the project a success. Open all year round.
With sauna, sleeping-bag accommodation,
double rooms, petrol station, campsite and
restaurant.

Hótel Djúpavík

Modern 3-star hotel in the town centre. Fairly sober from the outside, but very comfortable inside.

► Mid-range
Djúpavík: Hótel Djúpavík
Tel. 451 40 37
www.djupavik.is
Arguably the most isolated hotel in Iceland. Nice furnishings and good food.

► Budget
Ísafjörður: Gamla Gistihúsið
Mánagata 5
Tel. 456 41 46
Small guesthouse with old-fashioned feel in a yellow corrugated-iron house with a red roof dating from 1897.

► Luxury
Ísafjörður: Hótel Ísafjörður
Silfurtorg 2
Tel. 456 41 11
info@hotelisafjordur.is

of coastline of 2,100km/1,300 miles. The largest fjord, the **Ísafjar -ðardjúp**, practically divides the peninsula into two halves. Sitting proudly in the eastern half of the peninsula, the plateau glacier of Drangajökull can be seen far across the more northerly Westfjords. Since the melting of the ice cap of the Gláma plateau this is the only remaining glacier in the region. The coast at the foot of the **Drangajökull** is called Snæfjallaströnd (»Snowy Mountain Coast«), as even in summer the snow fields here reach nearly down to the sea. Towering over the fjords are mighty table mountains with layers of basalt, ash and sediments, breaking off seawards with steep cliffs of up to 400m/over 1,300ft.

A hard life   Today, only about 8,000 people live in the Western Fjords, a good third of them in and around **Ísafjörður**, while the entire eastern part, the coast of Hornstrandir, is completely devoid of people. Many abandoned farms bear witness to the difficulty of making a living and defying the loneliness out here in the Westfjords. The climate is even harder than in the rest of Iceland, with the wind, rain and fog taking its toll on the spirits. In the winter, snow more often than not makes the high plains impassable, and even in summer transport links are limited. Endless **gravel tracks** winding around every fjord arm, while the destination is only a few kilometres away as the crow flies, are part and parcel of any trip into the Western Fjords. Travellers who come prepared to accept this and with plenty of time on their hands will be sure to succumb to the fascination of a magnificent and wild primeval landscape, unlike any other in Europe.

What to see in the Western Fjords

A circumnavigation of the western fjords from Brjánslækur ferry port on the southern coast via Látrabjarg, Ísafjörður and Hólmavik up to the Hrútafjörður, covers some 600km/375 miles – without any major detours – and takes a lot of time because of the often serpentine gravel tracks.

As soon as the few cars have rolled off the Stykkishólmur ferry in Brjánslækur, absolute silence reigns again over the few buildings here. After only a few kilometres the Western Fjords begin to show their typical face with mighty mountains and many-fingered fjords. Going east, the [60] leads for just under 180km/112 miles along twelve narrow fjords to the **Gilsfjörður**, the slenderest point of the peninsula. The only places worth mentioning along the road that have some basic infrastructure and shopping options are Reykhólar and Króksfjarðarnes. Going west from Brjánslækur, the southern coast is no more densely populated; the landscape however is even more imposing. Rugged mountains, lonely sandy beaches, gently curving bays running for miles, bright dune landscapes, sand banks reaching into the fjords and a turquoise sea escort drivers to the

Brjánslækur, Hnjótur

At the edge of the world: the lonely coast of Hornstrandir in the western fjords

westernmost point of Europe, the Látrabjarg. Along the way, at the **Patreksfjörður** near Hnjótur, is a privately operated aeronautical and folk museum. Up to his death, Egill Ólafsson collected all kinds of boats, aircraft parts and everyday items, including an old Russian Antonov biplane in good condition. The museum café is also well worth a visit. Opening times: in summer daily 10am – 6pm.

✷ ✷
Látrabjarg

The westernmost tip of Europe could not be more lonesome or spectacular. There is still a road up to the small lighthouse of Bjargtangi, and from the car park a path leads onto the cliffs and runs east along the edge for many miles. Látrabjarg is the largest bird rock in the North Atlantic, extending over 14km/nearly 9 miles, and reaching a height of up to 440m/1,440ft. On the rocky ledges of the vertical cliff nest an estimated **million seabirds**, creating an almighty racket. Arranged on different levels are kittiwakes, razorbills, guillemots, Arctic terns and of course puffins, which are particularly easy to watch, as their breeding caves are situated at the very top near the edge. Off the coast near Bjargtangi lie the waters of Látraröst, one of the most feared shipping passages in Icelandic waters, where many ships have sunk over the years. Even if somebody were to survive the ship going down, getting them to safety over the rock face would be practically impossible.

Breiðavík,
Látravik

With their wide, deserted sandy beaches and towering mountain backdrops, the two major bays of Breiðavík and Látravík, on the way to the Látrabjarg, are among the most beautiful in Iceland. Unfortunately, the water is so cold here that even in bright sunshine hardly anyone dares to dip more than their feet into the sea.

Patreksfjörður

Patreksfjörður, with its 700 inhabitants one of the largest settlements in the Western Fjords, owes its title to the Irish settlers naming it after Saint Patrick. Only with the construction of fishing huts in the late 19th century did the core of a town develop on two small peninsulas. While the high mountains in the background provide a **spectacular setting**, it stays pretty gloomy in winter, as the sun takes a long time to make it across the mountain range. Also, on several occasions avalanches have tumbled down above the town.

! *Baedeker* TIP

Hot pots off the beaten track

The tiny village of Tálknafjörður is not really enough to warrant the detour off the main road, but visitors looking for a soak in lonely hot pots should make the effort. After about 3km/1.9 miles' drive on the [617], look out for a path branching off to the right; just above the road await three hot pots of different temperatures.

With 200 inhabitants, **Bíldudalur** on the Arnarfjörður has been a fishing and trading post since the 16th century. Some old trading houses from that time are still standing today. A worthwhile detour from Bíldudalur runs along the western shores of the Arnar-

● VISITING ÞINGVELLIR

INFORMATION

Þingvellir service centre
Tel. 482 26 60, www.thingvellir.is

WHERE TO EAT/STAY

▶ Expensive/Luxury

Restaurant Hotel Valhöll
Tel. 486 17 77,
 fax 486 17 78
Fresh char from the neighbouring Þingvallavatn is the speciality in the restaurant of the traditional Valhöll hotel. It is served either exotically marinaded as a starter or roasted as a main course.

▶ Moderate/Mid-range

Hotel Nesbúð
Nesjavellir
Tel. 482 34 15

Fax 482 34 14
www.nesbud.is
Fairly spartan, as it was once the accommodation for workers during the construction of the power plant. However, the hot pots, friendly service and good restaurant make up for that, not to mention the spectacular location in the middle of the geothermal area.

WHERE TO STAY

▶ Budget

There are only two places where camping is allowed in the national park: at Leirar (4 campsites: Fagrabrekka, Syðri Leirar, Hvannabrekka and Nyrðri Leirar) and at Vatnskot near the lake.

future a place of extraordinary importance to the Icelandic people, but also to make it accessible. Thus, the park features a modern **Edutainment Center**, tarmacked roads, a dense network of hiking trails, large camping areas, a hotel, a cafeteria and a few summer houses.

The valley between the continents

Two plates and a valley The core of the national park is a depression above the tectonic fault, which marks the rift zone of the American and Eurasian continental plates. This depression is bounded to the west and east by large fault fissures. The **Almannagjá** (All Men's Gorge) on the American side, more famous due to its historical importance, is easily accessible, but the less-known **Hrafnagjá** (Ravens' Gorge) on the European side is also easily visible from the roads to the east of the national park. The Almannagjá stretches over 7km/4.3 miles from the slopes of the Ármannsfell to the north right up to the Þingvallavatn, and the Hrafnagjá is not much shorter. The continental drift is noticeable in two measurable movements: every year, the Almannagjá and Hrafnagjá drift apart by some 5 to 10mm/0.2 to 0.4 inches, while the bottom of the depression between them sinks on average half a centimetre/0.2 inches annually, and in extreme cases, such as during the **1789 earthquake**, by as much as half a metre/one and a half feet in ten days.

Today, this ground lies a good 40m/130ft below the surrounding land, having been level with it until round 9,000 years ago according to geologists.

Topped with thick vegetation, lava some 10,000 years old covers the low-lying terrain. In this protected location it is not only mosses – as well as the obligatory birch and willow shrubs – that thrive, but also a colourful spread of **wild flowers and berries**. And towards the end of the summer, the flora seems to want to show that North America is not only geologically close: this is the time when Þingvellir National-al Park seems to imitate the splendid colours of the fall foliage.

Protected plants flourish

Other than a national park manager, who doubles up as the pastor of Þingvellir church, nobody lives permanently in the park. It never gets too lonely though, as the holiday cottages around the Þingvalla-vatn lake are used in all seasons, and each year the national park sees around half a million visitors. It's a must-see for tourists from all over the world, an obligatory part of the protocol for guests of state, and the Icelanders love it too as one of the most popular destinations for a day trip in their own country.

Visitor magnet

Assembly of free men: the Alþing

Historic Þingvellir, the assembly field, lies in the west of the national park at the foot of the Almannagjá. It was here in 930 that the free men of Iceland first convened for the Alþing (▶ History p. 42), the national assembly, which Iceland's modern day parliament claims to be directly descended from. Until 1798, the Alþing convened once a year at midsummer for a 14-day session in Þingvellir. Rapidly, the Alþing developed into a complex system of legislative and judicial instruments for the young independent state. To be exact, Alþing stands for the full assembly of free men, a body that played a role in the original Icelandic Free State, but then gave up its authority, along with the country's independence, in 1262. In the long run, the **Lögrétta** law committee turned out to be the more important and lasting body. Even after the king in Copenhagen had become an absolutist ruler in 1622, it still convened for 176 years in Þingvellir as a **judicial organ**. Initially in the Lögrétta, the country's rich and powerful, the goðar and the bishops, were amongst their own. In the last years of the historical Alþing, the circle of members was reduced to a handful of legal men who were effectively only able to proclaim law following Danish royal laws that had been decreed in far away Copenhagen.

Early Þingvellir

Þingvellir is linked to many important dates in Icelandic history: this is where the decisions were taken to introduce Christianity in the year 1000, to establish a bishopric in Skálholt in 1056 and then a rival one in Hólar in 1109. It was here in 1097 that the young but al-

Hotbed of history

ready influential church succeeded in introducing, for its own benefit, a tithe as the first tax in the country. Here, the Icelanders pledged
allegiance to the Norwegian king in 1262, sealing the fate of their
own nation. It was also here in 1271 that for the first time a **code of
law**, no longer submitted by the Alþing but by a legal commission
under the aegis of the Norwegian king, was put to the vote. 1271 was
also the last time that the old laws of the land were recited orally in
front of the assembly.

**Public fair and
market place**
In the centuries under colonial rule the assemblies at Þingvellir
proved themselves to be a stronghold of the Icelanders' national
identity. Even when the nation no longer had any political clout, it
was at least still able to make **appeals to the king**. Moreover, the
Alþing as an assembly had developed an important social function,
becoming a mixture of public fair, market place, centre of trade, job
exchange, national marriage market and a place for families to meet
and catch up on news and gossip. According to Iceland's great cultural historian Sigurður Nordal, the assemblies in Þingvellir moulded
the people of the island into an Icelandic nation. Also the fact that

Þingvellir Map

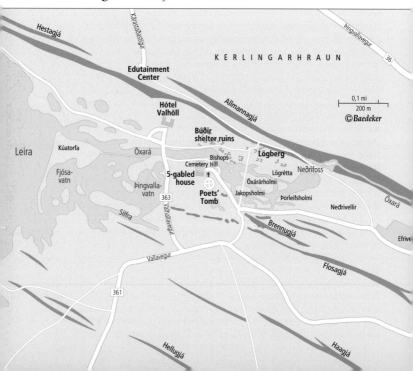

Þingvallavatn – clear, deep and full of fish

Iceland's largest natural lake, the Þingvallavatn, measures just under 84 sq km/32 sq miles, and at its deepest point of 114m/374ft even reaches below sea level. Sandey and the second island, Nesjaey, are easily recognizable as former **cone volcanoes**. Like the plain of Þingvellir the lake was formed by the area above the rift zone of the continental plates subsiding. Deep down, the Þingvallavatn must have abundant sources, as the inflows, of which the Öxará is the largest, are nowhere near enough to feed into the lake the 100 to 115 cubic metres/26–30,000 US gal of water per second that leave it at its southern point by way of the Sog river.

Iceland's largest natural lake

The water conditions in the Þingvallavatn are favourable to some species of fish. This is the only place in the world for instance where four varieties of the Arctic char coexist in one body of water. These trout-like relatives of the salmon love deep, rocky lakes and are coveted in turn by anglers, being considered a delicacy. One of them, the **murta**, has not been discovered anywhere else in the world outside the Þingvallavatn, which doesn't stop it from being tinned and sold as the lake speciality in the shop of Þingvellir's information centre, among other places.

? DID YOU KNOW ...?

■ ... that due to its steep gradient, the runoff of the Þingvallavatn, the Sog river, flows at high speed – making it look like some invisible force is sucking the water out of the lake. In fact, the name Sog can be derived from the Old West Nordic word for »suck«.

Fed by hot steam from numerous boreholes in the valley and on the mountain slopes, the geothermal energy plant in the Nesjavellir, southwest of the Þingvallavatn, produces hot water and electricity, and makes for a rather odd combination of fascinating **high-tech architecture** and spectacular panoramic views of nature. A visitor centre has information on the plant and its technology. Opening times: June – Aug Mon – Sat 9am – 5pm, Sun 1 – 6pm, Sept – May by appointment, tel. 480 24 08, www.or.is.

★ **Nesjavellir**

★ Þjórsárdalur

E/F 6

Region: South Iceland

The valley of the Þjórsá river has many aspects, with meadows and fields in the southwest giving way to a harsher, more barren landscape further northeast. While the Þjórsá west of the Búrfell is unspoilt, hydroelectric plants dominate the northeastern region.

The Þjórsárdalur proper is a tightly bounded valley north of the Þjórsá level with the Búrfell mountain. However, the name is also given to the landscape along the Þjórsá, accessible via the [32], the Þjórsárdalsvegur, and broadly covers the rural community of **Gnúp-verjahreppur** too. Approaching from the southwest and turning off the [30] into this area between the villages of Brautarholt and Fluðir, the first few kilometres travel through good agricultural land with lush hay meadows, greenhouses and cultivated fields. The more the journey continues northwest, the harsher, more barren and lonely the area becomes, with large parts of the soil covered in lava ash. Up to the level of the striking **Búrfell** mountain, the [32] more or less follows the northwestern banks of the Þjórsá. The course of the river, from its source at the watershed between northern and southern Iceland – in the middle of the ▶Spengisandur highlands route – to its mouth, at 230km/143 miles is longer than any other river in Iceland. The stream is visible everywhere from the road south of the Búrfell; it seems to be allowed to meander through the landscape unhindered, with many branches and offshoots. North of the Búrfell however, the Þjórsá and its tributaries show their other, more industrialized face.

▶ VISITING ÞJÓRSÁRDALUR

INFORMATION
Félagsheimilið Árnes
Árnes, 801 Selfoss
Tel. 486 60 44

Around the Árnes community centre, a few kilometres past the spot where the [32] turns off the [30], next to the tourist information visitors will find a restaurant, guesthouse, youth hostel, campsite and swimming pool. Further tourist information can be had from the Hrauneyjar Highlands Center (▶ Baedeker Tip p. 318).

WHERE TO EAT
▶ Inexpensive
Restaurant Árnes
Tel. 486 60 48
Large restaurant in the community centre with an attractive terrace. Good home-cooked food at relatively affordable prices.

WHERE TO STAY
▶ Mid-range
Steinsholt
801 Selfoss (on the [326], 4km/2.5 miles from the [32])
Tel. 486 60 69
Fax 486 60 29
gunnar@steinsholt.is
Cosy little guesthouse with five rooms. Hot pot for guests and many options for riding trips into the surrounding area.

▶ Budget
Farfuglaheimili Árnes
Gnúpverjahreppi, 801 Selfoss
Tel. 486 60 48
Fax 486 60 44
bergleif@centrum.is
Youth hostel with 26 beds, mainly in double rooms. Nearby there is a swimming pool with hot pots and a restaurant.

Energy Production on the Þjórsá

Over a distance of less than 50km/31 miles as the crow flies, tremendous volumes of water, with their source at the Hofsjökull and Vatnajökull, cascade downhill from a good 570 metres/1,870ft in height – the water level of the **Þórisvatn** – to a level barely above 120 metres/394ft on the Þjórsá south of Búrfell. At the time of the snow-melt, and when the early summer sun turns up the heat on the two glaciers to the right and left of the Sprengisandur, up to 42,000 cubic metres/over 11 million US gal of water per minute take this route. The latent **energy potential** here is consequently used for energy production, while the landscape is adapted to the requirements of technology: reservoirs, dams and interconnecting canals ensure that the water flows consistently all year round and is always able to provide sufficient power to the turbines of five power plants. All this was put into place from 1969 onwards, showing that even a highly prized green energy like hydroelectric power makes its demands on nature.

Lying at the foot of the Búrfell is the oldest and most southerly of the five power plants which currently make the river system of the Þjórsá Iceland's biggest source of power. The actual power plants are mainly built into the mountains and, compared to the dams and barriers, the artificial watercourses and lakes, the substations and power lines, are relatively inconspicuous. Still, humans have transformed a landscape previously untouched and practically uninhabited. Depending on the point of view, while critics would say the landscape has been ruined, others are fascinated by the particular **aesthetics of this combination of technology and nature**. The main consumers of the power are a few energy-intensive industrial companies, such as the aluminium factories of Straumsvík and on the Hvalfjörður.

A source of power

Striving for a positive image, the Landsvirkjun energy company regularly opens its power plants to visitors, puts a lot of money into reforestation projects around its facilities and has a tradition of commissioning contemporary artists to put »Construction Art« on its buildings. Thus, the 90m/295-ft long **Hávaðatröllið concrete relief** by Sigurjón Ólafsson adorns a façade of the Búrfellsvirkjun, and a few kilometres upriver, a sculpture made of 17 steel plates, completed in 2000, throws shadows that vary with the course of the sun onto the concrete walls of the Sultartangavirkjun power plant. Intended to symbolize energy waves, this work by the multimedia artist **Sigurdur Árni Sigurdsson** (* 1963) is called *Sun Wave*.

Art and power

The two main tributaries of the Þjórsá, the Tungnaá and the Kaldakvísl, have been altered perhaps even more. As a result the Þórisvatn – the most important reservoir of the whole system – has expanded from its original 70 sq km/27 sq miles to an artificial

**Tungn
Kal**

90 sq km/35 sq miles, making it Iceland's largest inland body of water. Three power plants – Hrauneyarfossvirkjun, Sigölduvirkjun and Vatnsfellsvirkjun – lie close to each other near the point where the two rivers flow into the Þjórsá, operating since 2001 as **peak load power plants** which always operate when demand for power is particularly high. The Hrauneyarfossvirkjun, with its control centre for all three facilities, also has a visitor and information centre which in the summer is often used for art exhibitions. Opening times in the summer: daily 1 – 5pm, with guided tours available.

What to see along the Þjórsá

The Hekla – volcano from a distance

On a clear day, the views across the Þjórsá of the 1,491m/4,892-ft ►Hekla volcano, shrouded in legends, turn the drive on the [32] into a truly spectacular sightseeing trip. As beautiful as the Hekla may appear in such conditions, it can also be very unfriendly; **Iceland's most active fire mountain** has repeatedly wreaked destruction on the Þjórsárdalur and indeed large parts of the whole country with ash rain and lava bombs, the worst example being in 1104.

Gaukshöfði

Where the mountains nearly push the road into the Þjórsá, the rocky ledge of Gaukshöfði juts out like a headland. While the main road below between its foot and the river was given a new route, the old road leads high up to a **viewpoint** – the steep detour is well marked, but not tarmacked. From the car park on the pass it's just a short scramble onto the summit of the Gaukshöfði. The reward for the effort is a wonderful view of the Hekla and the Búrfell, only half its height, as well as the Þjórsá way down below, which cannot be viewed anywhere else in its full expanse.

Soon afterwards the landscape opens up towards the north; this is where the real Þjórsárdalur begins. With its mountain backdrop, shaped by **vulcanism**, it is a beautiful if less well-known landscape, its charms attracting more Icelandic than foreign visitors. The two farms at the entrance are given over to tourism – horse riding tours, campsite, summer houses – and are the only ones in the whole valley to have continually defied the vagaries of the Hekla. Some

leep in any weather

accommodation compound left over from the
'ding of the power plant has been converted
the original but cosy Hrauneyjar Highland
nter. Visitors looking to fill their lungs with
hland air without forgoing all creature
forts, have come to the right place. Solid fare
the canteen fills hungry stomachs, while
bones can rest in small, cosily furnished
s on freshly-made beds or in sleeping bags.
f the 50 rooms has a name standing for a
weather condition, and the Icelandic
e still has enough alternatives in store
nexe. The travel centre awaits visitors in
f the Þjórsárdalur, where the Sprengi-
6] crosses the [F 208] to Landman-
r more information, call: tel.
ww.hrauneyjar.is

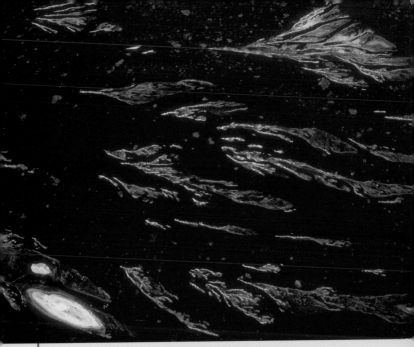

White on black: ice formations on the flowing Þjórsá

twenty others have been located by archaeologists further inland of the Þjórsárdalur since the late 1930s, many of them buried under ash. They were known about through medieval manuscripts telling of farms in the region which were still fertile at the time. Devastated by eruptions of the Hekla on a regular basis from 1104 onwards, the Þjórsárdalur was a **barren wasteland** for a long time, before massive reforestation in the 20th century once more gave it some touches of green.

Some 6km/3.7 miles north of the main road, amidst the mountain scenery at the edge of the Þjórsárdalur, look out for a well-equipped thermal spa. The Þjórsárdalslaug was built with excess concrete from the construction of the Búrfell power plant and to this day is funded by the Landsvirkjun energy company which runs the power plants on the Þjórsá. Opening times: June – Sept Wed – Fri 10am – 7pm, Sat/ Sun 11am – 7pm.

Þjórsárdalslaug

🕐

It only takes a minor detour off the [32] heading south to visit the Hjálparfoss in front of the backdrop of the Búrfell. Hundreds of **basalt columns** in interesting shapes form a cauldron into which the Fossá plunges through a crevice. Before the edge of the fall, a basalt island divides the river into two arms.

Hjálparfoss

PJÓÐVELDISBÆR

✱ ✱ In front of the farmsteads in Þjórsárdalur which were buried by the Hekla eruptions, the foundations of the Stöng farm, a little way off the [32], have been uncovered. Stöng is a defining moment in the architectural development from the simple nave of Viking times with only one hall, called »skáli«, towards a complex with several rooms serving different functions. A few kilometres from Stöng, the original has been reconstructed as a museum, the Þjórsárdalur farmstead, which gives insights into the daily life of 11th-century Iceland.

🕐 Opening times:
June–Sept 10am to midday and 1 to 6pm

① Entrance
Through the low entrance step into an anteroom with a closed storeroom in the opposite corner.

② Toilets
By today's standards, the toilet room is quite large for its purpose. However, at the time of the sagas, it was anything but a quiet retreat, as people were doing their business collectively.

③ Hall
A wooden wall separated the anteroom from the »skáli« hall. Here a good deal of daily life took place. In the centre a long fire was always burning, which would also be used for cooking. On the sidewalls, clad with wooden panels, broad earthen benches would serve as seats by day and for sleeping at night.

④ Living area
The room to the west in Stöng is the first proven example of its kind. In later centuries, this became the most important room on Icelandic farms, the »stofa«, used in daily life by women for spinning and weaving.

⑤ Dairy kitchen
The dairy kitchen was used to prepare skyr and to keep milk. The space where some barrels were set into the floor is still visible.

Þjóðveldisbær historic farmstead Plan

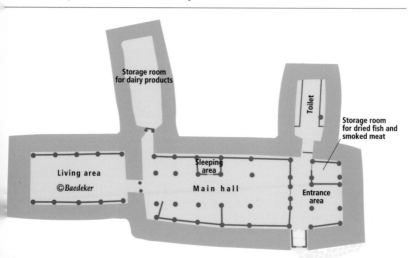

Storage room for dairy products

Toilet

Storage room for dried fish and smoked meat

Living area
© Baedeker

Sleeping area

Main hall

Entrance area

Hikes in Þórsmörk

The area from Þórsmörk up to the surrounding glaciers is crossed by paths of varying degrees of difficulty. The paths on both sides of the Krossá to its source at the **Krossárjökull**, a valley glacier of the Mýrdalsjökull, are popular because they are long but have few climbs. Don't be shocked on reaching it: as with so many glacier tongues in southern Iceland, it is more reminiscent of a slag heap than a mountain made of ice. While the ice melts, the ash and other deposits brought onto the glacier by volcanic eruptions or storms do not.

The hill of Valahnúkur due west of the FÍ mountain hut in the Langidalur can be managed even by less experienced hikers in just under an hour. They are rewarded by one of the most spectacular vistas in the whole country: the **green of the forests and meadows**, the ancient gravel beds of the glacier rivers – with the mountain hut and the cars parked there appearing as spots of colour – and the majestic glaciers as backdrop, provide a five-star photo opportunity.

Valahnúkur

Insights instead of views can be had at the southern bank of the Krossá, with a walk into the Stakkholtsgjá Gorge. With its steep walls, a good 100m/330 ft high, and a small waterfall at the end of a side gully, this is another popular destination for a short hike. However, visitors should take the precaution of checking locally for options of how to traverse the **Krossá**, as every spring, when the snows melt, it makes a new bed for itself.

Stakkholtsgjá

Þórsmörk is also the start and end point of the Laugavegur trek from ►Landmannalaugar, as well as of the challenging mountain tour via the **Fimmvörðuháls** to Skógar. The latter route leads near the Básar hut some 900m/2,950ft up the 1,116m/3,661ft pass between Eyjafjallajökull and Mýrdalsjökull. Up here extreme weather conditions such as ice and snow can occur even in summer.

Trekking via Þórsmörk

INDEX

LIST OF MAPS AND ILLUSTRATIONS

PHOTO CREDITS

PUBLISHER'S INFORMATION

Illustrations etc: 195 illustrations, 20 maps and diagrams, one large map
Text: Dr. Christian Nowak, Hans Klüche, Odin Hug with contribution by Werner Eckert (Special: Energy for Free)
Editing: Baedeker editorial team (Kathleen Becker)
Translation: Kathleen Becker
Cartography: Christoph Gallus, Hohberg; MAIRDUMONT/Falk Verlag, Ostfildern (map)
3D illustrations: jangled nerves, Stuttgart
Design: independent Medien-Design, Munich; Kathrin Schemel

Editor-in-chief: Rainer Eisenschmid, Baedeker Ostfildern

1st edition 2009

Based on Baedeker Allianz Reiseführer »Island«, 3. Auflage 2008

Copyright: Karl Baedeker Verlag, Ostfildern
Publication rights: MAIRDUMONT GmbH & Co; Ostfildern

Printed in China

BAEDEKER GUIDE BOOKS AT A GLANCE
Guiding the World since 1827

DEAR READER,

We would like to thank you for choosing this Baedeker travel guide. It will be a reliable companion on your travels and will not disappoint you.
This book describes the major sights, of course, but it also recommends interesting events, as well as hotels in the luxury and budget categories, and includes tips about where to eat or go shopping and much more, helping to make your trip an enjoyable experience. Our authors ensure the quality of the information by making regular journeys to Iceland and putting all their know-how into this book.

Nevertheless, experience shows us that it is impossible to rule out errors and changes made after the book goes to press, for which Baedeker accepts no liability. Please send us your criticisms, corrections and suggestions for improvement: we appreciate your contribution. Contact us by post or e-mail, or phone us:

▶ **Verlag Karl Baedeker GmbH**
Editorial department
Postfach 3162
73751 Ostfildern
Germany
Tel. 49-711-4502-262, fax -343
www.baedeker.com
www.baedeker.co.uk
E-Mail: baedeker@mairdumont.com